MODERN LEGAL STUDIES

DEVELOPMENT CONTROL

AUSTRALIA AND NEW ZEALAND
The Law Book Company Ltd.
Sydney : Melbourne : Perth

CANADA AND U.S.A.
The Carswell Company Ltd.
Agincourt, Ontario

INDIA
N. M. Tripathi Private Ltd.
Bombay
and
Eastern Law House Private Ltd.
Calcutta and Delhi
M.P.P. House
Bangalore

ISRAEL
Steimatzky's Agency Ltd.
Jerusalem : Tel Aviv : Haifa

PAKISTAN
Pakistan Law House,
Karachi

MODERN LEGAL STUDIES

DEVELOPMENT CONTROL

SECOND EDITION

by

JOHN ALDER, LL.B., B.C.L.
Senior Lecturer in Law, University of Exeter

LONDON
SWEET & MAXWELL
1989

Published in 1989 by
Sweet & Maxwell Limited of
11 New Fetter Lane, London
Laserset by P.B. Computer Typesetting
of Pickering, N. Yorks
Printed in Scotland

British Library Cataloguing in Publication Data

Alder, John.
Development control.—2nd ed.
1. England. Real Property. Development.
Control. Law.
I. Title.
342.064'4

ISBN 0–421–37170–6

Preface

The last few years have seen large advances both in the quantity and quality of development control law. Against a political background of disenchantment with strategic planning and conflict between local and central government, the ad hoc decision-making techniques embodied by the development control system have come to the forefront of political and legal concern. At last the courts are grappling with basic issues and lawyers are appreciating that planning law is a central aspect of public law rather than an appendage of conveyancing. The introduction of the application for judicial review procedure in the late 1970's has helped to raise the profile of public law in general but most planning decisions are still challenged as they always have been under special statutory procedures which now appear increasingly antiquated.

The main theme of this book in an attempt to place development control in its public law context and in particular to examine the contribution made by the courts to the town and country planning process. I make no apology for concentrating on the courts even though the current academic fashion is to emphasise non judicial techniques such as internal structuring and grievance resolution for making government accountable. Political and "participatory" methods of dispute resolution appear more than a little hollow within the authoritarian and secretive political culture of the British system of government. In this connection Farwell L.J. once remarked that "if ministerial responsibility were more than the mere shadow of a name the matter would be less important, but as it is, the Courts are the only defence of the liberty of the subject against departmental aggression." (*Dyson* v. *A.G.* [1911] 1 K.B. 411 at 424.) This is if anything even more apposite today. Whether the tools available to the courts for the purpose are adequate is a different question. The courts have in general kept to their traditional constitutional role and avoided imposing limits on the

v

political purposes for which planning powers can be used. They have left controversial issues such as that of "planning gain" substantially to the political forum. On the other hand the courts have perhaps been insufficiently willing to scrutinise the factual findings of government agencies or to impose external standards in relation to fact finding techniques. The idea that government must show that it has carried out a cost benefit analysis or canvassed alternative solutions to a problem has hardly begun to surface in English law. However the recent decision of Judge Marder Q.C. in *Wyre Forest D.C.* v. *Secretary of State* [1989] J.P.L. 270 gives a hint of a bolder judicial approach.

Publication of this edition was delayed because it was hoped to include references to the expected, and long overdue, consolidation of the planning legislation. Unfortunately this will not become law in time and citations are therefore to the Town and Country Planning Act 1971. Other reform proposals in the pipeline include, (i) the abolition of structure plans in favour of much shorter general statements of county policy with regional policies being determined by central government, (ii) some pragmatic reforms in the enforcement system with a view to making enforcement more effective and (iii) the introduction of a standard form of application for planning permission.

I should like to thank the students, colleagues and reviewers whose comments and ideas have directly or indirectly helped shape this edition and especially to thank Anne Waters and Tricia Day who typed the manuscript and made sense of my abnormally illegible handwriting. I am also grateful to the Law Department and Law Library at Exeter University for managing to conserve in a hostile climate sufficient resources to enable research and writing to continue. I have tried to state the law as it stood on the basis of material available to me on May 8th, 1989.

John Alder,
Exeter.
May, 1989.

Contents

Other Books in the Series

Table of Cases

xi

Table of Statutes

xxiv

Table of Statutory Instruments

Table of Abbreviations

Legislation

H. and P.A. 1986	Housing and Planning Act 1986.
L.G.A. 1972	Local Government Act 1972.
L.G.P. and L.A. 1980	Local Government, Planning and Land Act 1980.
L.G. and P.(A.)A. 1981	Local Government and Planning (Amendment) Act 1981.
The Act	Town and Country Planning Act 1971 (as amended).
T. and C.P.(M.)A. 1981	Town and Country Planning (Minerals) Act 1981.
G.D.O.	General Development Order 1988.
U.C.O.	Use Classes Order 1977.

Other Abbreviations

DoE	Department of the Environment.
E.G.	*Estates Gazette.*
Encyclopaedia	*Encyclopaedia of Planning Law and Practice*; 4 volumes.
E.S.R.C.	Economic and Social Research Council.
G.L.C.	Greater London Council.
Grant	Malcolm Grant, *Urban Planning Law* (Sweet & Maxwell Ltd. 1982).
J.P.L.	*Journal of Planning and Environment Law.*
L.P.A.	Local Planning Authority.
N.I.L.Q.	*Northern Ireland Law Quarterly.*
P.A.	*Public Administration.*
P.L.	*Public Law.*

Other Abbreviations—*cont.*

P.P.G.N.	*Planning Policy Guidance Notes.*
R.T.P.I.	Royal Town Planning Institute.
S.P.Z.	Special Planning Zone.
U.D.C.	Urban Development Corporation.

Abbreviations

Cullingworth — *Town and Country Planning in Britain.* J. B. Cullingworth (6th ed. 1976)

De Smith — *Judicial Review of Administrative Action.* S. A. de Smith (3rd ed. 1973)

Dobry — *Review of the Development Control System* (HMSO 1975, George Dobry, Q.C.

Encyclopaedia — *Encyclopaedia of Planning Law and Practice.* 4 volumes

Hamilton — *Development and Planning.* R. N. D. Hamilton (6th ed. 1975)

Heap — *An Outline of Planning Law.* Sir Desmond Heap (7th ed. 1978)

J.P.L. — *Journal of Planning and Environment Law*

McAuslan — *Land, Law and Planning.* Patrick McAuslan (1975)

Purdue — *Cases and Materials on Planning Law.* Michael Purdue (1977)

Telling — *Planning Law and Procedure.* A. E. Telling (5th ed. 1977)

Wade — *Administrative Law.* H. W. R. Wade (4th ed. 1977)

Wraith and Lamb — *Public Inquiries as an Instrument of Government.* R. E. Wraith and G. B. Lamb (1971)

1. General Background

An outline of the development control system

Development control law empowers local authorities to prohibit physical alterations to or changes in the use of land.

The development control system was created by the Town and Country Planning Act 1947 and is now embodied in the Town and Country Planning Act 1971 as modified by subsequent legislation.[1]

The core of the development control system is a discretionary power vested in local planning authorities, usually district councils (but see below, pp. 100–103), to prohibit "development" without "planning permission." This power is exercised by issuing an "enforcement notice" disobedience to which is a criminal offence (section 87). Development without planning permission, although unlawful in the sense of contrary to statute, is not usually itself an offence (but see Agricultural Land (Removal of Surface Soil) Act 1953) section 1. "Development" consists of "building engineering mining or other operations in on over or under land" or the making of a "material change of use" of land (section 22. See below, Chap. 4).

Planning permission can be obtained in several ways, (below, pp. 92–99), but principally by making an application for planning permission to the local planning authority. The authority has a broad discretion whether or not to grant permission and an equally broad power to attach conditions to a grant of permission (section 29). Planning conditions are a means of imposing a code of land use law upon development within a locality.

---

[1] Noteably Local Government Planning and Land Act 1980, Local Government and Planning (Amendment) Act 1981, Town and Country Planning (Minerals) Act 1981, Housing and Planning Act 1986, Local Government Act 1985 and Town and Country Planning Act 1984. All references are to the Town and Country Planning Act 1971 ("the Act") unless otherwise stated.

There are provisions permitting local planning authorities to enter into agreements with landowners relating to the use of their land, and the relationship between these agreements and the statutory powers is controversial (below, Chap. 7).

Development control powers are exercised within the broad framework of general policies approved by the central government and formulated in published "development plans" (see Circular 22/84). Developments Plans are prepared by local authorities after a certain amount of public consultation and after considering objections from the public (sections 8, 9, 12, 13). Development plans are not strictly binding upon development control decisions, but must be taken into account (section 29(1)). There are two complementary kinds of development plan.[2] "Structure plans" are broad statements of policy objectives in narrative form and without a map. They are made by county councils for the whole county and are confirmed by the Secretary of State (sections 7 and 9). Local plans are more detailed and include a map. They apply to specific areas or subjects within a country and are usually made by district councils, although county councils may also make them (section 11, 11A). Local plans do not have to be confirmed by the Secretary of State although he can "call in" a plan to approve alter or reject (section 14(3)) and can also regulate the plan making procedure (sections 11(3), 11B, 12(B)). A local plan must conform generally to the structure plan in force in the area (section 14(5). Unless the Secretary of State directs otherwise there is no obligation to make a local plan.

These arrangements create the potential for conflict between central and local government, between different levels of local government and between ideas of long term planning and the immediate pressures of individualised decision making. It must be remembered, however, that the majority of development control decisions concern local environmental issues, *e.g.* traffic, amenity, infrastructure, which may not have any particular impact upon the development plan, which is primarily concerned with choices between alternative uses.

Development control involves a combination of central and local government powers, but the balance of power is firmly tipped in favour of the central government. The powers of central government go well beyond the purely supervisory. For example,

_____

[2] In the case of metropolitan districts "unitary development plans" are made because there are no county councils in these areas (L.G.A. 1985, Sched. 1). Unitary development plans are in two parts corresponding to structure and local plans. See below p. 10.

the Secretary of State is empowered to make regulations that remove whole areas of discretion from local planning authorities (below, pp. 87, 93) and also to decide appeals against the refusal or conditional grant of planning permission (section 36) and against an enforcement notice (section 88). On appeal he can consider the whole matter afresh and substitute his discretion for that of the local planning authority. The Secretary of State can also "call in," without giving reasons, any application for planning permission to decide himself (section 35), although for political and practical reasons this power is sparingly exercised (below, p. 102). He can also issue an enforcement notice (section 276(5)(A)). Finally, the Secretary of State can issue directions to a local planning authority restricting any grant of planning permission (section 31(1)(a)). Again, this power is sparingly exercised. It is used mainly to require the Department of the Environment to be notified of certain kinds of application with a view to exercising its calling in power (below, p. 116).

The relationship between local and central government is impossible to state in general terms within the framework of the British Constitution. Barker and Couper ((1984) 6 *Urban Law and Policy* at 460) speak of "a general balance of central–local powers and accepted bonds of mutual trust" but everything depends upon the particular political and statutory context. In the context of development control the central government undoubtedly has the legal power to reduce the local role to that of an agent of central policy. In practise the position is more complex and governments generally use their powers with restraint in order to preserve a degree of local autonomy and because of manpower considerations.

In recent years the central government has increasingly used statutory and administrative powers to limit local discretion. These include removing areas of land and kinds of development wholly or partly from local jurisdiction and using appellate powers, including the power to award costs to impose central policies (see below, p. 204).

The courts have reinforced central powers of intervention by refusing to require the Secretary of State to justify a decision to exercise calling-in powers and by denying that local autonomy is of itself a sufficiently strong principle to attract a right to a hearing (*R. v. Secretary of State ex p. Southwark L.B.C.* [1987] J.P.L. 587; *R. v. Secretary of State G.L.C.* [1985] J.P.L. 543; *R. v. Secretary of State ex p. Newprop.* [1983] J.P.L. 386). Litigation between central and local government has increased markedly during the last decade, but the absence of clear constitutional principles governing the relationship between local and central government means that the courts have in the main deferred to central government initiatives. However, procedural protection in the name of a right to a hearing has occasionally been given to local authorities in cases where their financial interests have been directly involved.[2a]

The Act includes powers of compulsory acquisition, thus incorporating an element of "positive" planning into the process. However, market value compensation is payable and the conditions for the exercise of compulsory acquisition powers are restrictive, requiring the authority to show either that the land is suitable for and is required for development, re-development or improvement (section 112(1), (a)) or that acquisition is necessary in the interests of the proper planning of the area (section 112(1)(b)). In addition the Local Government and Planning Act 1980, Part X confers wide powers on the Secretary of State to require public bodies including local authorites to dispose of land holdings which in his opinion are not being used or not being sufficiently used (sections 97–99).

The Act provides additional controls in special cases. These include trees, historic buildings, mining activities, areas of special historic or architectural interest, waste land and hazardous substances. There are also land use controls created by other legislation which are interrelated with the development control system in the sense that planning permission is a prerequisite for another consent.[3]

Methods of land use control

From a broader perspective development control is only one of many instruments that governments use to implement land use policies. These can be classified in several ways depending upon the observers' perspective. For example, from the legal perspective there are important distinctions between public and private law methods of control and between discretionary powers and fixed rules. Distinctions can also usefully be made between regulation by means of incentives—tax concessions, grants etc., and by means of

[2a] e.g. R. v. Secretary of State ex p. Brent L.B.C. [1982] Q.B. 593. See Loughlin in Law, Legitimacy and The Constitution (McAuslan and McEldowney (eds.) (1985) Chap. 4; Loughlin, Local Government in the Modern State (1986) Chap. 9; Grant, Urban Planning Law (1983) pp. 58–61; Elliot, The Role of Law in Central Local Relations ES RC (1981).
[3] e.g. Caravan Sites and Control of Development Act 1960. See Esdell Caravan Parks v. Hemel Hempstead D.C. [1965] 3 All E.R. 737; Hartnell v. M.O.H. [1965] A.C. 1134.

deterrents such as the criminal law.[4] Less usefully perhaps, positive and negative controls can be distinguished. In theory development control is negative and is not designed to encourage growth. In practise the distinction is blurred. For example, knowledge of the development control policies of a local planning authority may act as a positive incentive to a developer and the granting of planning permission is a lever through which an authority can obtain "planning gain" in the form for example of public amenities (below, Chap. 6).

PUBLIC AND PRIVATE LAW

Development control depends upon statutory powers wielded by elected governmental bodies and is therefore a public law power *par excellence*. This has important implications for the method of challenging decisions in the courts (below, pp. 45–47) and also affects the way in which the courts interpret the Act. However, private law notions cannot be ignored. Local planning authorities often enter into agreements with landowners and developers for purposes related to their statutory powers, for example, to secure the provision of adequate drainage, roads, or parking facilities in connection with a proposed development. It is a vexed question whether these planning agreements should be governed by private law notions such as consideration or estoppel or should be seen as entirely public law concepts to be governed by broader notions of fairness and reasonableness and conformity to statute (below, Chap. 7).

Private law land use controls are typified by the common law of nuisance and by the law relating to covenants restricting the use of land. There is considerable debate, particularly in the U.S.A., as to whether private law controls are to be preferred to public law controls.[5] This debate presupposes that we can agree as to what are the proper purposes of land use control. There is, of course, no such agreement since the matter is one of political ideology. Planning is an instrument for achieving in the land use context whatever happen to be the political goals of the government of the day.

If we believe that the main purpose of development control should be the narrow one of remedying defects in the private

---

[4] See generally. Pearce *Urban Law and Policy 3* (1980) 115; Harte, *Landscape Land Use and the Law* (1985) pp. 88–105.
[5] See Elickson and Tarlock, *Land Use Control: Cases and Materials* (1981) Chap. 6; Pearce (1981) Town Planning Review 47; Grant, *Urban Planning Law* (1982) pp. 3–4; Denman, *The Place of Property* (1978).

market and resolving conflicts according to market principles (*e.g.* a developer should pay for the long term environmental costs imposed by his development on the community) then there is an argument for preferring private law devices since these centre upon the self interest of individual property owners, are primarily "rule" based, and are administered by courts who are relatively apolitical.[6] If, on the other hand, other political ideologies are pursued, for example wealth redistribution or citizen participation, then private law devices are inadequate, partly because they reinforce the status quo—what would be a nuisance in Belgrave Square would not necessarily be so in Bermondsey (*Sturges* v. *Bridgeman* (1879) 11 Ch.D. 852 at 865)—and partly because of the relative lack of information available to the courts. Private law centres upon relatively concrete claims by individuals. It is less comfortable with claims found on "community rights" and with nebulous rights such as a right to privacy or to a view. (See *Re Ellenborough Park* [1956] Ch. 131.) Other objections to private law devices include the famous "freeloader" problem (others benefit from litigation pursued by one person) and the element of bargaining and collusion.

Restrictive covenant law similarly reinforces the status quo—positive covenants do not bind successors in title although planning schemes depending on covenants or the landlord and tenant relationship (where positive covenants are enforceable) have been successful.[7] The "public interest" element in covenant law has been recognised by empowering the Lands Tribunal to discharge or modify restrictive covenants that are "obsolete" or which "would impede some reasonable user of the land for public or private purposes" (L.P.A. 1925, s.84(1)). However, compensation must be paid and the "reasonable user" ground applies only where the covenant no longer receives any practical benefits of substantial value or advantage to its owner.

Planning law is of course concerned with protecting the interests of individuals but it is not concerned with any private law rights that might be enforceable between landowners.

DISCRETION AND RULES

The development control system is discretionary and involves

[6] For discussion of these issues in the U.S.A. see Hagman, *Urban Planning* (1971) Chaps. 1, 4, 17; Elickson and Tarlock, *Land Use Controls: Cases and Materials* (1981) Chap. 6; McDougal and McDougal, *Property Wealth Land: Allocation Planning and Development*, (2nd ed., 1981) Chaps. 1, 2, 5, 6, 7.
[7] See McAuslan, *Land, Law and Planning* (1975) Chaps. 1 and 4.

tailoring decisions to individual cases. However, it is doubtful whether the term discretion is in itself particularly useful except as a loose description. Some writers define discretion as "choice" but this seems unacceptably wide.[8] The most famous analysis of discretion is that of Ronald Dworkin (*Taking Rights Seriously*, pp. 31–39). On this view discretion can be "strong" or "weak." Strong discretion exists where the decision maker makes up his or her own standards to apply. Weak discretion exists where the decision maker operates within a framework of rules, principles, standards or policies but has some area of choice relating to interpretation and application—"the hole in the doughnut." The notion of discretion is therefore essentially negative and is a matter of degree—a spectrum based upon the extent to which fixed guiding rules apply.[9]

For present purposes a discretionary power can be regarded as a power where the decision maker can determine the *weight* to be given to competing considerations in the light of a political or social objective, although operating within broad principles determined, in this case, by the Act, the courts and the central government. It is a cardinal principle of administrative law that a discretionary power cannot be fettered by applying a fixed rule. The decision maker must always be prepared to consider the merits of individual cases (below, p. 139). Thus, the development control system is not a hierarchy in which general principles can be rigidly applied. For example, a local planning authority can pre-empt the making or altering of a development plan by granting planning permission for development which is inconsistent with the proposed plan (below, p. 143). The court's role in this context is limited to securing a degree of rationality and consistency by requiring, for example, that departures from existing policies be identified and explained and that legitimate expectations be taken into account.

Discretion has obvious advantages—flexibility, detail, responsiveness to the justice of individual cases, personal responsibility. Rules also have obvious advantages—certainty, predictability, legitimacy, accountability. The precise mix to be applied in any given context depends upon practical convenience and political ideology. For example, in the U.S.A. the ideal of legality in the administrative sphere is highly valued. Land use controls are based upon zoning ordinances which set out in advance and in detail what

---

[8] See Davis, *Discretionary Justice* (2nd ed., 1971) p. 4; Jowell [1973] P.L. 178.
[9] See also, Harlow and Rawlings, *Law and Administration* (1984) pp. 130, *et seq.*; Galligan, *Discretionary Powers* (1987) Chap. 1; Schwartz and Wade, *Legal Control of Government: Administrative Law in Britain and the United States* (1972).

activities are permissible in each area, separating incompatible activities and providing for public services and amenities (see *Village of Euclid* v. *Amber Realty Co.* 272 U.S. 365 (1926)). This tends to produce uniformity and creates problems when unforeseen circumstances arise. Therefore, it is increasingly common for "flexibility" devices to be superimposed upon the traditional zoning ordinance permitting discretion to be exercised in individual cases. Legal control is secured by broad constitutional standards of "equal protection" and "due process" (fairness). Thus administrative formalism is combined with judicial discretion.[10]

In British culture administrative discretion is less objectionable but we rely to a greater extent on judicial formalism. We also place more faith in political and parliamentary controls over government than in the law. In practice, however, English v. American tradition meets in the middle. With us discretionary powers are structured or confined by various means.[11] For example, the 1971 Act confines discretion by requiring that statutory "development plans" be taken into account and backs this up by special procedural arrangements, contained in delegated legislation where a local authority wishes to depart from the plan (below, p. 119).

Central government regulates local discretion in several ways. These include regulations which grant automatic planning permission for prescribed activities (below, pp. 93–94), or which exclude classes of use of land from the need for planning permission (below, pp. 87–89).

Special zones may be designated—"enterprise zones" and "simplified planning zones"—within which normal controls are relaxed, a device broadly similar to the American zoning ordinance (above), but with the opposite purpose (below, pp. 96–99).

Central government also issues circulars, planning policy guidance notes, and other informal policy documents which purport to instruct or advise local authorities how to exercise their powers. The "green belt" policy is an example (below, p. 21). These documents are not usually binding as law[12] but must be taken into account, correctly interpreted in the eyes of the court, and

---

[10] See Purdue [1986] J.P.L. 84. See also, Atiyah and Summers, *Form and Substance in Anglo-American Law* (1987); Freilich and Stuhler, *The Land Use Awakening* (1981). Zoning is the basis of land use control in many other countries, *e.g.* Australia, Canada, New Zealand.

[11] See Davies *op. cit.* above, n. 8; Harlow and Rawlings, p. 134.

[12] The matter depends on the terms of the governing statute. Delegated legislation under the Act is usually required to be made by statutory instrument but "directions" which are legally binding can be made by the Secretary of State under s.31, and are promulgated by circular (see Encyclopaedia 4–009).

departures from them explained. They therefore blur the distinction between rule and discretion. Central policy may also be expressed through white papers statements in Parliament, letters, published reports, patterns of decision making and even speeches. See [1988] J.P.L. 538. Other policy documents relate to the European Directive on Environmental Impact Assessment which requires the making of environmental impact statement in relation to large projects (see Wood [1988] J.P.L. 310).

Finally, local authorities are guided by rules and policies which they formulate themselves outside the statutory development plan. These informal planning instruments are many and various. They include development control "notes," "briefs," "design guides," informal local plans, or "policy frameworks" and may relate to general subjects, particular problems, or specific pieces of land. They are used to formulate new policies and also to implement policies contained in statutory plans. Their use is defended by familiar arguments in favour of flexibility and responsiveness, and attacked because of their secretiveness.[13] However, their legality has been partly denied by Lord Scarman in *Great Portland Estates* v. *Westminster City Council* ([1984] 3 All E.R. 744 at 752–753). The Council's development plan reserved policy creation relating to office development to informal plans to be made later. His Lordship thought this improper and stated that all substantive policies should be included in the formal published statutory plan. However, statutory plans are intended only as general guides and his Lordship did not condemn informal plans concerning detailed implementation of or exceptions to policies promulgated in the statutory plan.

There is, therefore, a hierarchy of limits on discretion which in descending order is as follows (i) the Act (ii) the supervisory powers of the court, (iii) delegated legislation, (iv) the statutory development plan, (v) central government policy statements (vi) informal local policy documents.

Limits (i) (ii) and (iii) are absolutely binding as law. Limits (iv) (v) and (vi) fall within the fettering discretion principle and cannot do more than create presumptions and indicate the relative *weight* which must be attached to them. These matters will be discussed later in particular contexts.

Government policy is currently to reduce the importance of long term planning and to rely upon the ad hoc, market responsive aspect of the development control system, thus emphasising discretion rather than rules. In particular, the hierarchical

---

[13] See generally Bruton and Nicholson [1984] J.P.L. 552, 563 *cf*. Department of Environment Circular 4/79.

10 GENERAL BACKGROUND

relationship between structure and local plans and between plans and development control has been weakened in four ways: (i) District planning authorities are empowered to adopt local plans in advance of proposed changes to the Structure Plan[14]; (ii) The Secretary of State has excluded wide social and economic objectives from individual structure plans[15]; (iii) Applications for planning permission which conflict with development plans are no longer "county matters" (below, p. 101); (iv) The government has generally discouraged local authorities from preparing local plans (Circular 22/84, para. 3).

Government proposals currently under consideration include abolishing structure plans altogether, replacing them by simpler and shorter general statements of county objectives within a policy framework laid down by the central government. This has been justified mainly on the basis that structure plans are slow and expensive to produce and are soon overtaken by events. It has also been said that planning authorities should concentrate on specific local land use problems rather than upon broader social and economic issues.[16]

Regulation and ownership—property values

Development control concerns regulation of the use of land and falls short of empowering authorities to confiscate the entire beneficial interest in the land.[17] For example, a landowner is entitled to serve a "purchase notice" requiring the local planning authority to purchase his land from him in cases where planning permission is refused or granted subject to conditions so that the

---

[14] ss.15A, 15B. See Loughlin, *Local Government in the Modern State* (1986) pp. 137–143.
[15] See Jowell and Noble [1981] J.P.L. 466; (1980) 3 *Urban Law and Policy* 293; Healy (1986) 8 *Urban Law and Policy* 1; Boynton. Development Control—Thirty Years On [1979] J.P.L. p. 2. Social and economic matters as such have been relegated to supporting "reasons" for the land use policies in the plan and are no longer part of the plan itself (s.7(6A)). Similarly, the procedures for making structure plans have been simplifed and focused on land use matters and the importance of public participation has been reduced. See Circular 22/84; Town and Country Planning (Structure and Local Plans) Regulations 1982 (S.I. 1982 No. 555). See also Nott and Morgan [1986] J.P.L. 875; Rider [1988] *Town Planning Review* 57; Bruton and Nicholson. [1985] *Town Planning Review* 21. See also [1986] J.P.L. 717.
[16] See Bruton and Nicholson [1987] J.P.L. 687. White Paper. *The Future of Development Plans* (Cmnd. 569 (1989)).
[17] See, *e.g. Hall v. Shoreham U.D.C.* [1964] 1 All E.R. 1.

land has become "incapable of reasonably beneficial use in its existing state."[18] It is often said the "use rights" have therefore been "nationalised." This seems somewhat simplistic. The Act contains numerous concessions to individual property rights and in any event falls far short of applying the logic of nationalisation. Planning permission "restores" the use right to the landowner and, because planning permissions may be rationed, windfall profits can accrue to successful landowners. On the other hand, except in special cases, no compensation is payable to persons refused planning permission.[19]

What should happen to this windfall profit? A logical application of the principle that ownership does not carry development rights (which is expressed by the absence of compensation) would dictate that all development value should be appropriated by the state. This principle was adopted by the 1947 Act which provided that a development charge be paid to a public authority by those who realised the fruits of planning permission, normally on a sale of land. However, such a concept is prey to clashes of political ideology and also to practical and economic difficulties. The original scheme was abandoned in 1954, partly because of political pressures and partly because it was alleged to have an adverse effect upon the supply of land available for development, and to inflate land prices. Vendors were accused of adding on the development charge to what would otherwise have been the market price (*cf. Earl Fitzwilliam's Wentworth Estates* v. *Minister of Housing and Local Government* [1952] A.C. 362).

Since then the treatment of development value has fluctuated according to the political complexion of the government in office (see Cullingworth, *Town and County Planning in Britain*, (6th ed., 1976) Chap. 7). The most comprehensive recent attempt to secure development value for the community was the Community Land Act 1975. This conferred powers upon local authorities to acquire land suitable for development, ultimately at existing use value and then to develop it themselves or to sell it to the private sector at full market value (see Land. Cmnd. 5730 (1974)).

---

[18] ss.180–191. See Moore, *A Practical Approach to Planning Law* (1987) p. 251 *et seq.* See further, Grant, pp. 16 *et seq.*

[19] (i) Restriction of existing rights (ss.45, 51, 164, 170) but see below, p. 147 for an example of judicial willingness to override vested rights. (ii) Unexpended balance of development value (s.134) refers to pre-1947 claims. (iii) Restriction of Development within existing use of land (s.169). (iv) Stop Notices, s.177 (below, p. 185) Town and County Planning (Compensation) Act 1985.

The Community Land Act 1975 was not seriously implemented (except in Wales) and was repealed by the Conservative Administration of 1979–1983. Since then a *laissez faire* ideology has prevailed.[20]

It is theoretically possible to achieve justice by transferring some of the profits made by the person granted planning permission to the landowner who is refused permission. This is based upon the assumption that development value, like energy is never created anew but shifts from one piece of land to another so that A's gain is B's loss. Such a principle appears to be unworkable because there is no direct correspondence between development value and the amount of money required for compensation. Development value can only be confiscated when actually realised by a sale of the land. Moreover, because of the vagaries of human behaviour it is reasonably certain that less land will actually be developed than could in theory be developed. Development value is therefore said to be "floating" value. For example, if 10,000 acres are capable of development for housing, perhaps houses will actually be built on half that much. Nevertheless if the 10,000 acres is refused permission for development each landowner can equally claim that the floating value could settle on his land. The position is like that of a lottery. Thus, the total compensation bill, adding together each separate claim, will always exceed the money actually available when development takes place.

It was this consideration which *inter alia* persuaded the promoters of the 1947 Act to abandon a general right to compensation (see Report of the Uthwatt Committee on Compensation and Betterment, Cmnd. 6386 (1942)).

The purposes of development control

The 1971 Act does not state the purposes for which development control powers may be used. Indeed, in a sense the development control system is the antithesis of "planning," relying as it does upon uncoordinated initiatives

---

[20] A fee is payable for applications for planning permission and appeals, but this is essentially an administrative change (L.G. and P.A. 1980, s.80. See S.I 1983 No. 1674). The windfall element also encourages the negotiation of agreements between local authorities and developers for the purpose of persuading developers to provide public benefits—planning gain—in return for planning permission (below, Chap. 6). See Grant.

from individual developers both public and private, not all of whom are subject to control.[21]

Academic and practicing planners sometimes discuss their goals in general terms through such nebulous notions as "managing change," "redistributing resources," etc. The following are examples:

(i) "A principle or style informing the management or governing process whereby the process will have certain characteristics. That is to say it will be anticipatory, analytical, purposeful, evaluative, innovatory, apparent, responsive, corrective, effective and adaptive."[22]

(ii) (a) "To enhance and develop the beauty and true usefulness of land and buildings, town and countryside, (b) to reconcile competing needs and to see that any change ... is for the common good. (Royal Institute of Chartered Surveyors, *Caring for Town and Country* (1979) p. 1.)

(iii) "enhancer of the quality of life," "provider," "instrument of social justice," "steward and manager," "controller," "source of information." (Royal Town Planning Institute, *Planning in the Future* (1976)).

(iv) "The deliberate social or organisational activity of developing an optional strategy of future action to achieve a desired set of goals for solving novel problems in complex contexts, and attended by the power and intention to commit resources and to act as necessary to implement the chosen strategy" (Alexander, *Town Planning Review* 52(2), April 1984 at p. 137).

If these statements mean anything at all they indicate that planning has no particular purposes of its own but is a microcosm of government or society as a whole. They also show that in a market economy development control is not the same as planning if only because the "controllers" lack the power and resources to implement any chosen plan (see Allison, *Town Planning Review* 51(1) January 1986 at p.5).

Planners have sometimes adopted what Professor McAuslan (above, n. 22) has described as a "megalomaniac vision" of planning, *i.e.* that the scope of planning includes broad matters of

---

[21] Switzer. (June, 1978) Chartered Surveyor p. 344 described development control as "bluff, bargain, blackmail and buy."

[22] Centre for Environmental Studies Working Group Report, (Vol. 1.) *Progress in Planning* (Pergamon, 1973). Quoted by McAuslan (1974) 37 M.L.R. 134 at 140.

social engineering, that planners are entitled to use their powers to achieve their own vision of a just society and that scientific techniques, based in the case of planning upon "systems" theory can predict and order human behaviour.[23]

These notions overlook the most fundamental feature of the Act, which is that planning powers are placed in the hands of politicians and can be used for a range of purposes which ultimately depend on political value judgments (see *Cardiff Corporation* v. *Secretary of State for Wales* (1971) 22 P. & C.R. 718 at 722–723). Some may be relatively uncontroversial, concerned with physical questions of amenity or efficiency, while others require a choice to be made between conflicting values, *e.g.* conservation and housing. At the most general level there is a debate about whether government power should be used for the purpose of achieving distributive justice or whether it should be confined to corrective justice in the sense of remedying market distortions.

Subject to an important qualification (below, p. 19) the Act permits any political ideology to be adopted so that debates about which of these is the "proper" goal of planning seem fruitless. Indeed much of the academic debate about the purposes of planning law has really been about the general policies of successive governments.[24] As we shall see, the courts have recognised the political basis of the Act and have rarely excluded any social, political or economic consideration as irrelevant to planning. They have usually deferred in this respect (as opposed to procedural matters) to the government of the day (below, pp. 129–132).

Generalisations about the ideologies or goals of planning are therefore of limited value. It is true that broad political "conflicts" can be discovered within the planning system, as indeed within any area of government. These have often been analysed in terms of conflict between "private property" and "public interest" to which Professor Patrick McAuslan has added the ideology of "public participation."[25]

Public interest in this context does not refer to any particular social, economic or political goal but to the claim that officials should be free to determine the use of land in their discretion

---

[23] See, *e.g.* McLoughlin, *Urban and Regional Planning—A Systems Approach* (1969). Eversley, *The Planner in Society* (1973), Chap. 5.

[24] See, *e.g.* Jowell (1977) 30 C.L.P. 63; Hall (1983) 6 *Urban Law and Policy* 75; Reade [1982] J.P.L. 8; McAuslan (1981) 4 *Urban Law and Policy* 215.

[25] The Ideologies of Planning Law (1980); see also, Eversley, *The Planner in Society* (1973) Chaps. 7–9.

without being required to justify themselves or to defer to any other "rights." Legitimacy is conferred by the electoral process. However, the concepts of public interest, private property, and participation are not simple. Each can be subdivided to reveal internal tensions and potential conflicts. For example, "government" is not a single entity but comprises different groups of people who may have competing interests claims and goals and different political and cultural perspectives. They include, for example, ministers, civil servants, professional advisors such as lawyers, strategic planners employed by County Councils, elected local councillors, political parties and officials charged with enforcing development control powers on a day to day basis.

Each group may be further sub-divided. In particular, local councillors who are ultimately responsible for initiating the development control process may be indifferent to planning theory, and concerned with immediate social and political pressures. On a broader level the incidence of litigation between central and local government over the extent of central government powers over local government has increased markedly since the mid 1970's.[26]

Administrative structures are also important, including the level within the central or local hierarchy at which any given decision is taken. (See Barker and Couper, 6 *Urban Law and Policy* (1984) 363 at 432 *et seq.*) Despite the introduction of corporate management techniques into local governments, interdepartmental rivalries still exist, particularly at a time of competition for limited resources. Perspectives on the goals of planning may differ depending upon whether there is a separate planning department or whether development control falls within the empire of the District Engineer or Architect or, at central level, whether a decision is taken by an Inspector, or within the department.

Nor is "private property" a monolithic concept. Different kinds of private property interests may conflict with each other and a legitimate purpose of planning is to mediate such conflicts. For present purposes we should distinguish between two kinds of private property ideology. The first which can be called the "commercial ethos" is the notion of individual freedom and the seeking of profit through the market. The second is associated with the network of people who comprised, at least in 1947, the traditional ruling elite, *i.e..* the affluent professional and land owning classes. This has been categorised as "the rural myth" and

---

[26] See Loughlin, *op. cit.* above, n. 14 at 193–198; *R. v. Secretary of State ex p. London Borough of Southwark* [1987] J.P.L. 587—denying legal protection to local autonomy as such.

embodies a notion of country life from the perspective of the
affluent town dweller or worker, *i.e.* as park, dormitory, museum
and playground. On this view property is a means of conserving rather than increasing wealth and is allegedly a source of
social stability and moral uplift. Respect for tradition and
continuity, a liking for small communities and contempt for
commercial and urban values are its mainsprings.[27] Its effect
is to preserve existing privileges and to exclude the dis-
advantaged.

Participation is also a complex notion. There are many kinds
and levels of "participation," ranging from a right to inform
decision makers of the impact of proposals upon the "participants" interests to decision making by popular referendum.
(See Harlow and Rawlings, *Law and Administration* (1984),
pp. 437–448). The notion of direct participation does not fit
in easily with principles of representative democracy and also
presuppose that all "participants" have equal opportunity to
participate. Furthermore the relationship between "participation" and the power of decision is unclear. Advocates of
participation appear to assume that participation is capable
of producing consensus, although evidence for this is not
available.

Professor McAuslan adds a further dimension by linking
"participation" first to the notion of "opposition to the status
quo" and secondly to hostility to economic and technological
growth (*op. cit.*, n. 25 above at p. 6). However, it is difficult
to reconcile the latter concern with democratic theory and there
seems to be no inherent connection between opposition to the
status quo and anti-technology values. Participation in this
sense seems to overlap with the "rural myth" property ideology
discussed above. Indeed, several influential pressure groups
such as the Council for the Protection of Rural England are
dominated by "rural myth" interests.[28] Furthermore, the
participatory ideology relies upon *a priori* theory and has no
significant roots in public opinion nor in existing governmental institutions. It appears to envisage an idealised and closely
regulated future society where resources are equally shared
and people are "educated" and leisured enough to be interested

---

[27] See Eversley, *op. cit.* above, n. 24 at 74–77; see also, McAuslan, *op. cit.* n. 26
above, Chap. 4; Glass, Anti-Urbanism in Stewart (ed.) *The City* (1972); Williams,
The Country and the City (1973).
[28] Harlow and Rawlings *op. cit.*, above, 449–452; Eversley, op. cit. above note 25 at
pp. 180–188.

in the business of government.[29] The idea that "ordinary people" are affluent and conservation minded, bizarre though it may be, is frequently expressed by commentators. For example, Roots (*Planning for Growth or Decline* (1987) J.P.E.L. Occasional Papers No. 13, p. 70) said to a conference of planning practitioners "While you search for a means to plan for growth, the man in the street is filling in his deed of covenant for his local preservation society."

The Act permits local and central government considerable discretion to invite public participation in development control decisions but confers virtually no legal rights to participate upon anyone other than persons with interests in the land itself or public authorities.[30] The only case where such rights are conferred by the Act itself and are not contingent upon either ministerial regulations or executive discretion concerns development affecting a conservation area (section 28, see below, p. 116). Even at appeal level there is no *duty* to hear anyone other than the applicant and the local planning authority. In practice public local inquiries are frequently held in relation to central government decisions, but there is no legal obligation to do so (sections 35(5), 36(4), 282). Even where a public inquiry is held full legal rights to participate are very limited (below, pp. 217–221).

We have said that the Act as interpreted by the Courts is flexible enough to enable development central powers to be used for virtually any political, social or economic purpose related to land use. On the other hand, the Act embodies certain biases so that some political objectives may run against its grain. The Act was shaped by a century of evolution originating in Victorian concerns about public health arising out of the rapid expansion of urban areas after the Industrial Revolution and the squalid conditions in which the mass of poorer people lived. (See Cullingworth *Town and Country Planning in Britain*, (6th ed., 1970) Chap. 1). These concerns were underpinned by certain general values which were advocated by powerful pressure groups. They include the following:

(1) Utilitarian philosophy. The belief developed particularly by

---

[29] See Prosser in *Law, Legitimacy and the Constitution* (eds. McAuslan and McEldowney) Chap. 8. Also Harlow *ibid.* Chap. 3. See, *e.g.* McAuslan, *The Ideologies of Planning Law* (1980), pp. 269–274, quoting Macpherson, *The Life and Times of Liberal Democracy*. See also Prosser (1982) 9 J. Law and Society 1. J. R. Lucas, *Democracy and Participation*.

[30] The courts have been more generous (below, p. 5). See *Turner* v. *Secretary of State* (1973) 28 P. & C.R. 123 at 138–139. McAuslan *op. cit.* above, p. 53. (But a rural myth, ratepayer case).

Jeremy Bentham that government should aim to achieve the greatest happiness of the greatest number by using legislation to balance conflicting interests.

(2) Paternalism. The notion that an elite is entitled to impose its values upon a passive majority and is responsible for "improving" not only the physical environment but also the moral standards of others. The notion that officials should be trusted and need not justify their actions is deeply embedded in English legal culture. It manifests itself in principles such as the presumption of validity which places the onus on those seeking to challenge government action to prove that a decision is defective. It also manifests itself in the absence of a general common law duty to give reasons.

Dicey's much vaunted "rule of law" has limited application outside the regulation of property and commercial relationships and little relevance to the dispensation of benefits and services by government. In this connection a feature of development control law is that it straddles the boundary between these ideas. In one sense it concerns the regulation of property rights, but in another sense planning permission is a discretionary benefit. The common law right of a landowner to develop his land has effectively been abolished by the planning legislation. This may be a reason for the conflicts and inconsistencies that pervade our subject.

(3) Utopian thinkers of the nineteenth century such as Ebenezer Howard and William Geddes who idealised rural values. Howard and his disciples advocated "planned" communities intended to combine the advantages of urban and rural life within small self-contained settlements of not more than 30,000.

(4) Experiments with private settlements designed and built on behalf of evangelical industrialists and businessmen for the purpose of housing their workforces. Developments such as Port Sunlight on Merseyside, Bournville in Birmingham, and Saltaire near Leeds are surviving examples and there are numerous smaller industrial villages. The "garden suburb" movement followed. This was not linked to a workplace but designed to be a self governing community with a mixed population (apart from the ruling elite itself). Such planned communities formed the model for more recent new towns and suburban developments.

(5) A strong tradition of protecting property rights and in particular of ensuring that land is freely available in the market. This factor is not in harmony with the others and represents the first of our two competing versions of private property. The nineteenth century reforms in private land law which culminated in the 1925 property legislation were designed first and foremost to free the market. According to Professor McAuslan this has inhibited

notions of public participation in planning decisions (see (1984) 37 M.L.R. 134).

The 1947 Act was a reaction to "problems" which were said to be created by suburban expansion. These included declining inner cities, loss of agricultural land, migration of population to the South East with resulting inefficiency in the provision of public services, and the deterioration of the traditional landscape.[31] The title of the Act enshrines the distinction between town and country and some of the ideas that underpin the Act find common ground in the notion of urban containment. Apart from its alleged environmental and economic benefits, urban containment has been described as a convenient instrument of social control arising out of fear of the "urban working class assembled en masse" (Hall, *op. cit.* n. 31, pp. 370–371).

The Act, although conferring wide discretionary powers, contains ingredients that support the values of private property in both senses but most strongly the "rural myth" version.[32] Political policies that deviate from this, whether in favour of centrally directed planning or the unleashing of market forces, run against the grain of the Act and generate conflict. This helps to explain the increased amount of central government intervention in the planning process that has been a feature of the last decade.

The "rural myth" concepts embodied in the Act include.

1. The central notion of development.[33] This means "change" of a positive kind either to the land itself or in the use of the land (below, Chap. 4). Activities which do not in themselves constitute change are not development even though they may raise social and economic problems (see, *e.g. Wealdon D.C.* v. *Secretary of State*

---

[31] See Report of the Royal Commission on the Distribution of the Industrial Population (Barlow Report) Cmnd. 6153 (1940); Report of the Committee on Land Utilization in Rural Areas (The Scott Report) Cmd. 6378 (1942); Hall, *The Containment of Urban England.* Vol. 2, Chap. 1. Grant (1977), Chap. 1.

[32] For dicta in favour of the "public interest" ideology see *Hall* v. *Shoreham R.D.C.* [1964] 1 All E.R. 1 at 7 (decided in favour of private property interests below, p. 145); *Fawcett Properties Ltd.* v. *Buckinghamshire C.C.* [1961] A.C. 631 at 679; *Britt* v. *Buckinghamshire C.C.* [1963] 2 All E.R. 175 at 179–180; *Kingston on Thames B.C.* v. *Secretary of State* [1973] 1 W.L.R. 525 (*cf. Esdell Caravan Parks* v. *Hemel Hempstead R.D.C.* [1966] 1 Q.B. 895, 923–924); *Westminster Bank* v. *M.o.H.* [1971] A.C. 508. Compare Lord Reid at 529, Viscount Dilhome at 535; *Mixnams Properties* v. *Chertsey U.D.C.* [1965] A.C. 735, 754–755. See further Chaps. 2 and 6 below. For dicta in support of the "rural myth" see *Co-Operative Retail Society* v. *Taff Ely B.C.* (1980) 39 P. & C.R. 223 at 238–239, *per* Lord Denning M.R.; *Copeland B.C.* v. *Secretary of State* (1976) 31 P. & C.R. 403.

[33] This is perhaps the work of the courts rather than of the statute itself, which gives little guidance as to what "development" means. (See below, Chap. 4).

[1988] J.P.L. 268). This has raised difficulties where an activity
increases in intensity. The courts have concluded that "intensification" can be development but only in extreme cases where
the "character of the land" has entirely changed (below, p. 77).
Conceptually, intensification has to be regarded as the addition of a new element to an existing activity and the authority
is empowered only to prohibit this addition and must not prevent
the landowner from continuing the original level of activity.
Similarly, the demolition of a building is not apparently development in itself (below, p. 69). However, it is a criminal offence
to demolish a building which has been listed as a building of
special, architectural or historic interest by the Secretary
of State or which is the subject of a "building preservation
notice" issued by the local planning authority (sections 54,
55, 58). Thus the conservation of poor quality buildings capable of providing temporary accommodation for the homeless is given lower priority than the cultivation of aesthetic
sensibilities.

Planning permission for development is therefore for a specific
"operation" or "change" and not for the building or use so
produced. This raises major conceptual problems. On the one
hand, there is the advantage, from the point of view of the public
interest, that changes from use A to B and back to A *each* require
planning permission so that the authority can consider each change
in the light of circumstances existing at the time. The same applies
to buildings that are demolished and rebuilt. On the other hand, if a
planning permission relates only to a finite act or series of acts and
not to a continuing state of affairs it is difficult to see how conditions
attached to a planning permission other than those relating to the
act of change itself can be of continuing effect. Such a restriction
would be highly undesirable from the public interest perspective
(see *West Oxfordshire D.C.* v. *Secretary of State* [1988] J.P.L.
324). For example, in connection with mining development it
is desirable that conditions should outlast the mining itself and
deal with such matters as restoration and, given that mining
operations often last many years, should cater for unforeseeable
changes in circumstances. These considerations among others
led to the enactment of the Town and Country Planning (Minerals)
Act 1981 which confers special powers on local planning authorities (in this case County Councils) in relation to mining development. These include a power to impose "aftercare" conditions
(below, p. 152) and a power to revise existing planning permissions with a special compensation code (see Encyclopaedia Table
of abbreviations 2–1912).

2. Agriculture and forestry enjoy generous exemptions from planning controls. In 1947 these could be explained on economic as well as cultural grounds, but are more difficult to justify today given the large agricultural surpluses that are a feature of current policies and a result of technological advances.

Market oriented ingredients include the following:

1. The Act's enforcement machinery is weak. Development without planning permission is not an offence in itself and the elaborate and cumbersome enforcement machinery contains generous safeguards for the property owner (below, Chap. 9).

2. The Act confers few legal rights on persons other than those with property rights. Public rights to object, to be informed, to appear at inquiries, etc. where they exist at all, are subject to the considerable administrative discretion. In particular, a right of appeal against a refusal of planning permission is available to the applicant, but there is no right of appeal available to a third party and no right of appeal against an unconditional grant of permission. Central government can readily intervene for the purpose of restraining an interventionist local authority, but it is more difficult to override a laissez faire authority.

3. There is a presumption in favour of planning permission and reasons must be given for a refusal or a conditional permission.

4. The Act's financial provisions are ambivalent (above, p. 11).

A manifestation of the rural myth philosophy is the famous "green belt" policy which is often regarded as the epitome of British planning. Except in relation to London, green belt policy is not statutory but derives from central government circulars (see Circular 50/57, 14/84). Green belts are "cordons sanitaire" surrounding urban areas, which serve the purposes of conserving countryside, restraining urban sprawl, providing amenities for urban dwellers, and stimulating development in inner cities, albeit in the latter case without obvious success. Green belt policy rations development and raises land values within the designated belt, thus effectively preserving the existing privileges of the more affluent.

Green belt policy does not assume that green belts are worth protecting because of their intrinsic beauty. On the contrary, some green belt areas are desolate pieces of no-man's land on the urban fringe. This leads to a further problem in that pressures for development are increased in relation to land beyond the green belt which may be environmentally more attractive. There is a plethora of government circulars, particularly about housing policy, which has created a complex framework of presumptions based upon attempts to predict future demand for housing. (below, p. 140). Green belt policy is at the mercy of changing commercial and political pressures. These have been particularly acute in the present decade reflecting smaller family units, faster transport, increased demand for employment and housing in the south east, and an increasing desire by industrial and commercial concerns to locate in "greenfield" areas. Furthermore, because of advances in technology there is no longer a convincing economic case for increased agricultural production. Thus green belts and the rural areas beyond them have become a battleground for the opposing property ideologies of commerce and the rural myth. Participation as an expression of democracy and "public interest" in the sense of strategic planning have little part to play.

Conclusion

The Act embodies conflicting values and can lawfully be used to achieve whatever political purposes are favoured by the government of the day, albeit some purposes are more compatible than others with the Act's machinery. McAuslan argues that this "disarray" can be cured by an injection of "participation." (op. cit. above, n. 25 at p. 6). However, the idea that participation is capable of producing consensus seems implausible. Far from being undesirable, conflict and "disarray" are necessary features of a pluralist democracy and the complex network of conflicting interests that feature in the Act—between central and local government, between different levels of local government, between different kinds of property interest, between the long term and the short term, between different kinds of professional, between the haves and the have nots—add up to a loose system of checks and balances that is characteristic of the United Kingdom constitution. The Act attempts to provide a structure within which these conflicts can peacefully be resolved. Within this, the particular task of the law and the courts is to ensure that decisions and policies are made and applied according to generally accepted ideas of fairness, coherence and consistency. These matters will be taken up in the following chapters.

2. The Courts and Development Control

Development control is an activity where the courts have a relatively high profile. Development control involves restrictions upon the exercise of traditional property rights and therefore raises issues with which the common law tradition is at home. The grant or refusal of planning permission often has a substantial effect upon land values giving property owners an incentive to litigate. Moreover there are many opportunities for landowners to challenge development control decisions in the courts. The general judicial review machinery is available against local planning authorities, but most central government decisions are challengable only by way of special statutory procedures (below, Chap. 3).

The purpose of judicial review

Because the United Kingdom has no clear cut system of constitutional values the purpose and therefore the scope of judicial review is controversial. Broad assertions abound but are largely question-begging. Notions of "the rule of law," fairness, accountability and protection against abuse of power have been invoked together with the statement that "policy" is not for the courts and a supposed distinction between the decision making process and the merits of the decision itself.[1] A pervasive question is whether judicial review should be about policing government as an end in itself or whether it should focus more

---

[1] See e.g. *I.R.C.* v. *National Federation for the Self Employed* [1982] A.C. 617 at 644. *Preston* v. *I.R.C.* [1985] A.C. 835. *I.R.C.* v. *Rossminster Services Ltd.* [1980] A.C. 952 at 977. *Chief Constable of North Wales Police* v. *Evans* [1982] 3 All E.R. 141, at 144, 154. *O'Reilly* v. *Mackman* [1983] 2 A.C. 237 at 282. *Council of Civil Service Unions* v. *Minister for the Civil Service* [1985] 1 A.C. 374 at 415.

narrowly upon individual rights and expectations.[1a] The present law seems to be a muddled compromise characterised by broad discretionary powers.

Parliament can in theory do anything so that the ultra vires doctrine has traditionally been the conceptual basis of judicial review.[1b] In *R.* v. *Boundary Commission for England ex p. Foot* [1983] 7 Q.B. 600 at 615 Sir John Donaldson M.R. said:

> "It is of the essence of parliamentary democracy that those to whom powers are given by Parliament shall be free to exercise those powers subject to constitutional protest and criticism and parliamentary or other democratic control. But any attempt by ministers or local authorities to usurp powers which they have not got or to exercise their powers in a way which is unauthorised by Parliament is quite a different matter. As Sir Winston Churchill was want to say 'that is something up with which we will not put.' If asked to do so, it is then the role of the courts to prevent this happening."

However in *R.* v. *Lancashire C.C. ex p. Huddleston* [1986] 2 All E.R. 941 and 945 the same judge offered a significantly broader approach emphasing a "partnership" between courts and government for the purpose of achieving high standards of public administration.

As Eric Barendt has pointed out ((1987) 7 O.J.L.S. 125) judicial review is not well suited to securing the redress of individual grievances. There is no general right to damages or compensation in respect of invalid governmental decisions (above). Nor is there any guarantee that the citizen will receive a favourable decision in the end. After losing a judicial review case on the ground, say, of improper procedure, the government can put its procedure right and make exactly the same decision again. On the other hand the courts, steeped as they are in private law tradition are reluctant to set aside government action unless the applicant has suffered substantial injury. Legality as an end in itself does not seem to be highly valued.

There are special features of judicial review, some of which are

---

[1a] On which judicial attitudes are ambivalent. See *e.g. I.R.C.* v. *National Federation for the Self Employed* (above n. 1) at 644. *Nottinghamshire C.C.* v. *Secretary of State* [1986] 1 All E.R. 199 at 204.

[1b] Except for the anomalous but important case of error of law on the face of the record. But even this may have been absorbed within the extended notion of ultra vires as error of law adopted from *Anisminic* v. *Foreign Compensation Commission* [1967] 2 A.C. 147. See Beatson (1984) 4 O.J.L.S. 22; see n. 3 below.

less favourable to the individual than ordinary private law litigation. The main features are as follows:

1. The locus standi requirement is broader than for private law purposes (below, p. 51).

2. The court has wide discretionary powers, relating to procedure including the power to control the use of oral evidence and witnesses. Proceedings are normally based on affidavits and factual disputes are rarely entertained. See *O'Reilly* v. *Mackman* [1983] 2 A.C. 237.

3. The applicant must satisfy a judge that he has an arguable case before he can commence proceedings, and questions of public interest may also be raised at that stage. (See Sunkin (1988) 138 N.L.J. 257). Ordinary civil actions do not normally involve leave to apply, nor do the statutory procedures for challenging central government decisions.

4. Judicial Review proceedings are not "civil proceedings" and are therefore not subject to the various restrictions upon suing Crown Servants contained in the Crown Proceedings Act 1947. (See *R.* v. *Governor of Pentonville Prison ex p. Herbage* [1986] 3 W.L.R. 504. See also *Waldron Re* [1984] 1 W.L.R. 392).

5. Judicial Review proceedings do not create *res judicata* between the parties, at least in prerogative order cases (*R.* v. *Secretary of State for the Environment ex p. Hackney L.B.C.* [1983] 1 W.L.R. 524, affirmed [1984] 1 W.L.R. 592).

6. There is a three month time limit for applications for leave to apply for judicial review. This is strictly applied and even within three months an application must be made promptly (see *R.* v. *Friends of the Earth* [1988] J.P.L. 93).

It is sometimes suggested that judicial review is marginal and even unnecessary.[2] Arguments focus upon the randomness of litigation, and upon the alleged political bias of judges pointing out that non-interference is just as "political" as interference. They also emphasise that judicial review is "after-the-event" and remark upon the relatively small number of judicial review cases.

The question of judicial bias will be discussed later. Suffice it to say here that judges are necessarily required to make political value judgments so that the important question is not whether or not they are "biased" but whether their biases are acceptable to the community at large. Judicial review, in other words, is concerned with basic standards of constitutional morality.

---

[2] *e.g.* Hutchinson [1985] 48 M.L.R. 302. See also Harlow and Rawlings, *Law and Administration* Chap. 9; Sunkin [1987] 50 M.L.R. 432.

As regards the *ex post facto* nature of judicial review, this seems largely irrelevant. *Ex post facto* remedies are a necessary aspect of any system of accountable government. "Control" has the dual function of prescribing rules in advance in order to structure or confine administrative action, and of ensuring that these rules are obeyed. The latter must necessarily be *ex post facto*, this being the specialised function of the courts. The Franks Committee on Tribunals and Inquiries (1957) dealt with both aspects of control over government and provided the ground rules for the modern system of planning appeals (below, Chap. 10). Indeed so far as the courts are concerned the two aspects are inseparable. A decision by a court that a government decision is invalid operates as an instruction to the government to take the decision again in the light of the guidelines laid down by the court. It also operates more broadly, as does the common law generally, to guide future government decision making. (See Kerry (1986) 64 P.A. 163).

Finally, arguments about the "small" number of judicial review cases make little sense, unless either there are judges with time on their hands, or we have some *a priori* notion of what is the "right" number of cases. There are between 1000 and 1300 judicial review applications per year, of which about 30 per cent. are successful (see annual judicial statistics). This figure is meaningless in terms of whether judicial review is of value, even if we compare the figure with the several million government decisions taken annually. We might as well compare the total volume of contract litigation in any one year with an estimate of all contracts made in that year. However, in as much as judicial review concerns the redress of individual grievances, it is worth remarking that the Parliamentary Commissioner and the Local Government Commissioners deal with a substantial number of planning cases on grounds which overlap with the work of the courts. These officials have the advantage over the courts of informality, relative cheapness and wide ranging process of investigation. On the other hand, they have no power to make binding orders.

The ultra vires doctrine as the theoretical basis of judicial review

It is frequently argued that the *ultra vires* doctrine is no longer adequate as a guide to judicial behaviour.[3] There are three main reasons for this. First, governmental powers are sometimes exercised through mechanisms such as contract or property law, which derive from economic power rather than statute. These private law concepts are laden with values that assume equality between the parties to a transaction and do not therefore cater for the political and economic inequalities inherent in, for example, contracts between local authorities and developers. Secondly, statutory powers, notably so in the context of development control, are often conferred in wide discretionary terms without specifying the purposes for which the power can be exercised or the factors that can be taken into account. Thus the *ultra vires* doctrine becomes merely a formal framework within which the courts are forced to make up principles of their own. Thirdly, the powers of a reviewing court are highly discretionary.

The concepts created by the courts for the purpose of judicial review have become increasingly broad and nebulous and difficult to relate to notions of ultra vires. They include, for example, "fairness," "rationality," legitimate expectation" and "reasonableness." (See *Council of Civil Service Unions* v. *Minister for the Civil Service* [1985] 1 A.C. 374). Crucial distinctions such as that between law and fact (below, Chap. 3) and between mandatory and directory procedural requirements (below, pp. 123–125) are also vague. The remedies available in judicial review cases are almost all discretionary and in recent years this has been heavily relied upon in order to avoid conceptual problems (*e.g. Leech* v. *Deputy Governor of Parkhurst Prison* [1988] 1 All E.R.). If the courts choose to apply political policies of their own there is little to prevent them doing so.

It has become fashionable for commentators to advocate replacing the ultra vires doctrine by broad concepts derived partly from *a priori* theories about "democracy" and partly

---

[3] See Oliver [1987] P.L. 543. The conceptual problems associated with the ultra vires doctrine, particularly the distinction between void and voidable decisions have in the past caused serious problems. See Rubinstein, *Jurisdiction and Illegality* (1965); Wade (1967) 83 L.Q.R. 499, (1968) 84 L.Q.R. 95; Craig, *Administrative Law* (1983) p. 368. The courts seem to adopt a pragmatic—even an unprincipled—approach today. See, *e.g. Hoffman-La-Roche* v. *Secretary of State for Trade and Industry* [1975] A.C. 295; *London and Clydeside Estates* v. *Aberdeen D.C.* [1979] 3 All E.R. 876 at 833, but *cf. Anisminic* v. *Foreign Compensation Commission* [1969] 2 A.C. 147; *Ridge* v. *Baldwin* [1964] A.C. 40. The issue is important mainly in relation to invalid or void enforcement notices in which the technical logic of ultra vires is still dominant (below, pp. 197–200).

from the United States. These include "process," "rationality," "participation," "purpose" and "accountability."[4] Apart from the major differences in political culture and ideology between British and American society, it is difficult to see how these notions are in themselves sufficiently meaningful to do more than restate the problem. For example, the notion of "rationality" seems to be question begging. What are the goals against which "rationality" is measured? What standard of rationality is appropriate? Is it the American "hard look" standard by which a government decision must be justified as "better" than all alternative solutions,[5] or is it merely the "rational relationship with the objects of the Act" test embodied in English law? Whose view of "rationality" is decisive? Is it the decision maker's own opinion formed in good faith, that of the court, or that of some other political body? None of these propositions seem to grapple with the central issue of what standards the courts should apply.

The same applies to the notion of "irrelevant considerations." Following dicta in the House of Lords in *Anisminic* v. *Foreign Compensation Commission* [1969] 2 A.C. 147 it is superficially plausible to subsume all the detailed heads of judicial review under the broad notion of taking irrelevant considerations into account or failing to take relevant considerations into account, or—to include the principles of natural justice—to incur a risk of so doing. This merely restates the problem without giving a hint of what is to be regarded as "relevant."

Given the prevailing constitutional framework of English government it seems futile to attempt to discard the ultra vires doctrine since in every case the statutory framework is decisive. On the other hand, the ultra vires doctrine cannot be discussed in a vacuum. We must therefore attempt to outline our own theoretical assumptions such as they are.

I shall adopt a positivist position. This is not the version of positivism described by Harlow and Rawlings and labelled by

---

[4] See, *e.g.* Prosser (1982) 9 *Journal of Law and Society*, 1–19; Prosser in *Law, Legitimacy and the Constitution* (McAuslan and McEldowney eds.) (1985), Hutchinson above, n. 2. Stewart (1975) 88 Harv. L.Rev. 1669. See also Galligan [1982] 2 O.J.L.S. 257; Galligan, *Discretionary Powers* (1987); Loughlin (1983) 46 M.L.R. 66; Richardson (1986) P.L. 437. These theories owe much to the radical traditions expressed by Thomas Paine and which have been submerged in British political culture throughout the twentieth century. The dominant culture is authoritarian, and subservient to charismatic leadership.

[5] Richardson, *loc cit*. above, p. 439.

them "red light" theory[6] (*Law and Administration* (1984), Chap. 1). I do not believe, therefore, that law is "objective" or distinct from politics and morality. I believe that law as a specialised branch of politics contains certain distinctive values and methodologies but do not believe that the main function of the courts is to "control" government, conceived of as primarily malevolent. An important task of the courts is to place limits upon governmental activity, but this serves to legitimate government as well as to control it. The concept of demarcation, or the drawing of boundaries seems to be a more appropriate metaphor than that of red lights, reminding us that boundaries keep outsiders away as well as restrain those inside. Finally, I do not suppose that legal rules are always logical and coherent and capable of supplying "right" answers to problems.

The positivist position means only that we must attempt to assess the performance of the courts in terms of concepts and values that are actually embodied in our existing governmental arrangements and not against *a priori* moral and political values of our own. These are not objective but are explicit or implicit methods of justifying the exercise of governmental powers. In the absence of a written constitution these principles form the ground rules which are applied by the courts through their judicial review powers. They are used by the judges as aids to interpreting statutes and evaluating official behaviour. I shall call them "non-controversial values." They can be discovered only by empirical investigation and reflect the judges own beliefs as to their role.

Ultimately all legitimate political values derive from public consent or acquiescence, not necessarily in the sense of a positive consensus but in the negative sense of the absence of substantial dissent. Non-controversial values may therefore be the values of an elite imposed upon a passive majority. Non-controversial values are likely to embody widely shared but not necessarily consistent notions of justice, logic, and coherence, to reflect the status quo

---

[6] Since no-one could seriously adopt in their pure forms either the "red" or "green light" standpoints, in reality we are all "amber light" theorists. (Harlow and Rawings, p. 47). Thus this terminology does not seem illuminating. On the contrary it seems to be essentially an expression of the familiar right wing/left wing spectrum or a restatement of the belief that the law is biased towards individualistic values in general and property rights in particular. See also the Laski/Jennings challenges to Dicey, and McAuslans public interest/private property dichotomy (above, p. 14). See Jennings, *Law and the Constitution* (5th ed., 1959) Chap. 2, Appendix 2, Jennings (1935) 49 Harv.L.Rev. 429; Jones (1958) 58 Col.L.R. 143; Laski, "Appendix to Report of Committee on Ministers Powers" Cmnd. 4070 (1932); Arthurs (1979) Osgoode Hall L.J. 1.

and to be grounded in tradition. (See Rawlings (1987) 7 O.J.L.S. 1; Jowell & Lester [1987] P.L. 368).

The judges' special function is to attempt to identify and apply non-controversial values. This is no easy task and is complicated in the case of the English judiciary by an apparent lack of internal agreement about their rôle, and by the rigid procedural and evidentiary constraints operating in British courts.

Non-controversial values may be vague and conflicting. The judges are therefore compelled to make their own value judgments but are constrained by deference to established conventions of legal reasoning and by self-awareness of their delicate constitutional role. A judicial decision must not be manifestly out of line with popular opinion or established practices, but this leaves a range of legitimate solutions that are necessarily "political" and subjective. Just as judges must permit the executive considerable freedom of action, so must we allow the judges freedom including the possibility that they may disagree among themselves. They are appointed to make value judgments and if the kind of value judgments they make are widely disliked the solution lies with the electorate.

The notion of non-controversial values is the closest approximation offered by English law to a constitutional framework. Appeals to "the rule of law" are essentially appeals to non-controversial values. For example, the principle of judicial independence of the executive is a non-controversial value. This value helps to explain why judges are normally required to interpret statutes on the basis of the statutory language, unaided by extrinsic materials indicating the intention of the government in promoting the bill. This restriction is often criticised in its application to judicial review cases, but has two "non-controversial" advantages. First, it makes it more likely that those who have to rely on the statute, and who may not have access to specialist materials, for example, local officials and ordinary citizens will be able to predict how a court might interpret the statute. Secondly, it sets up a barrier between the court and the government of the day. It requires whose who draft legislation to make their intention particularly clear if radical changes in the status quo are to be made, but does not prevent them from making such radical changes.

Non-controversial values are not all of the same status. Some are purely procedural, *e.g.* the right to a fair hearing. Others bring in substantive matters. These include the obligation to give adequate reasons for decision; to take all relevant factors into account; and to avoid "unreasonableness". In most cases the court can ensure that officials take non-controversial values into account but cannot require that any particular weight be given to them. An example of this is arguably the protection of private property rights. This example also illustrates how the importance of a value may change as public opinion changes. Thus the traditional common law presumption that private property rights should not be restricted without clear and specific legislative language seems in the context of planning law to be of less significance today.

Two cases illustrate how non-controversial values are applied by the courts. In *Hall* v. *Shoreham U.D.C.* [1964] 1 W.L.R. 240 the Court of Appeal held that a planning condition was invalid because it required the developer to dedicate a piece of land as a public highway without compensation. Controversial issues arise from this about the extent to which local authorities can exact "gain" from the pockets of aspiring developers (below, Chap. 7). Nevertheless the decision is well within the limits of the non-controversial value concept. Planning is about regulating the use of land and not about the "confiscation" of the landowner's entire beneficial interest in the land. In the U.S.A. this is a major constitutional issue known as the "taking" problem. There is plenty of room for disagreement about what counts as a "taking,"[7] but the judges must be permitted to make their own value judgments.

In *Bushell* v. *Secretary of State* [1981] A.C. 75 the House of Lords (Lord Edmund-Davies dissenting) held that an objector at a highway inquiry was not entitled to cross-examine a civil servant on the methods by which the department predicted traffic needs. We can criticise this by reference to our own political beliefs, but the decision is well within the bounds of non-controversial values. Our system of government is a representative and not a participatory one. Why should those who are sufficiently wealthy and leisured to attend a public inquiry be especially favoured? One justification for our non-participatory system of government is that it lessens the risk of discrimination in favour of vested interests and articulate well-heeled pressure groups such as the environmental lobby, which in Britain as in the U.S.A. can be a vehicle for the protection of privilege.

Judicial bias

A common belief is that judges are influenced by a political bias in favour of individualistic values—in particular, private property

---

[7] See Sax (1974) 74 Yale L.J. 36; *Pennsylvania Coal Co.* v. *Mahan* 260 U.S. 393 (1922); *Penn Central Transportation Co.* v. *City of New York* 438 U.S. 104 (1978).

rights—and against what Professor McAuslan has described as "collective consumption." (see (1983) 46 M.L.R. 1). The strength of this bias may ebb and flow at particular times and may vary with individual judges but it has been said to be the "only coherent jurisprudence" of administrative law during the period of the evolution of the welfare state (*ibid*.).[8] There is no doubt that the law is sufficiently flexible to give the judges the opportunity to apply bias of this kind. Nor is there much doubt that the common law, influenced as it was by the political ideologies of the mid-nineteenth century, embodies a strongly individualistic philosophy. The same kind of bias has also been postulated on the basis of welfare economic analysis. (See Stevens and Young (1985) 1 U.L. and P. 133, below, p. 135).

Given the intellectual, social and economic background of the English judiciary, the hypothesis of a pro-property bias deserves to be taken seriously. We have already said that private property is a non-controversial value, but that it is not an overriding one. The courts can require that government takes individualistic values into account (*e.g. Stringer* v. *M.o.H.* [1970] 1 W.L.R. 1281) but they should not prefer private property values except where the legitimate concerns of government could be equally well achieved without infringement of private property rights. Professor McAuslan argues that the judges do more than this, and that they go out of their way to protect private property rights.

In later chapters we shall suggest that there is no coherent judicial bias of this kind but, at most, isolated examples. There are, however, coherent judicial biases, first towards deference to the executive and secondly towards values associated with certainty.

First, however, we must discuss the problems inherent in making any kind of analysis of judicial bias. Once we accept, as we surely must, that private property rights are a legitimate concern of the courts, we are forced to explain what counts as *improper* bias. Existing analyses are anecdotal and construct an edifice of general principle upon a narrow base. They concentrate upon the effect of a decision on the parties, ignoring the wider context. They select isolated cases from which they attempt to induce patterns or inconsistencies. They do not explain why these particular cases are selected nor do they attempt a broad analysis either of streams of cases or of general doctrines. Nor do they place their analysis in its full *legal* context by identifying contingent or random factors, for

---

[8] See also McAuslan, *The Ideologies of Planning Law* (1980); Brownsword and Hardin (1981) 1 *Legal Studies* 94; Stevens and Young (*op. cit.* below, p. 135) and refs. n. 6 above.

example, counsel's argument, procedural and evidentiary matters, and pre-trial negotiations, that influence the judge's decision. Nor do proponents of the bias thesis explain what is to count as bias in terms of how much weight should be given to individualistic values as against other values. Perception of bias is necessarily influenced by the observer's own biases. Finally, bias cannot be properly evaluated without recognising the importance of internal legal "process" values, for example, confirmity to precedent, linguistic and logical consistency. It is question begging to dismiss these on the basis that "a statute has not been drawn that could not be interpreted in exactly the way Lord Denning wanted to interpret it." (McAuslan, *op. cit.* above at p. 15).

We can recognise bias only after constructing a theory about the limits of acceptable judicial reasoning. A judge can be accused of bias only if, taking account of all the ingredients of the case, his reasoning exceeds those limits. In particular it is difficult to see any theoretical justification for attributing to the judges some unstated ideological position, inconsistent with what they actually say, even when what they say is mystifying or ambiguous. Judicial language can be given a range of meanings as a tool of argument and has no objectively correct meaning. (See Hoffman (1989) 105 L.Q.R. 140.)

Another problem lies in identifying what sort of interests actually count as individualistic or private property interests. McAuslan contrasts individualistic interests with the notion of "collective consumption," by which he means services that "have to be organised, planned and managed on a collective or public basis as they are consumed collectively" ((1983) 46 M.L.R. 1 at 2–3). However, because our society is structured upon the basis of specialisation of function, it is difficult to imagine any service or process that could not at least partly fall within this definition. Furthermore the question of what services can best be provided collectively is a matter of fundamental political controversy. It is by no means settled that land use is best regulated collectively and some people argue that market forces can do the job better than governmental regulation. Thus the boundaries between individualism and collective consumption are ill-defined, constantly changing, and leave plenty of room for the commentator's own biases.

We can illustrate these difficulties by discussing some cases particularly favoured by those who believe in judicial bias in favour of individualism.

First, there is a group of cases concerning local authority powers. In *Secretary of State for Education* v. *Tameside M.B.C.* [1977] A.C. 1014 the House of Lords held that the Secretary of State had exceeded his powers by attempting to restrain a local authority from implementing a scheme to restore selective education in some of its schools. The council had been elected with a mandate to do so but the proposal was opposed by many teachers and was to be implemented in a matter of months without the normal process of selection. Under the governing statute the Secretary of State could intervene only if he believed the scheme to be "unreasonable." The House of Lords held that "unreasonableness" in this context meant the same as in the general law, thus entitling the Secretary of State to intervene only if he believed the scheme was completely arbitrary or improper and not merely because it was undesirable, risky, or inefficient. He had therefore misdirected himself since he had not applied the proper test, and indeed had not taken into account relevant information which was available to him and which affected the operation of the scheme.

According to Professor McAuslan the individualistic bias lay in the approval expressed by their Lordships of the council's political duty to carry out an electoral mandate. He contrasts this with *Norwich Corporation* v. *Secretary of State for the Environment* [1982] Q.B. 808 where the Court of Appeal permitted the Secretary of State to interfere with the Corporation's activities in connection with the sale of council homes, so as to speed up the process on behalf of would-be purchasers. This was contrary to the Corporation's policy and the Corporation had shown itself unsympathetic to the statutory "right to buy" conferred upon many public sector tenants by the Housing Act 1980. However, the language of the Housing Act 1980 bore no relationship to the language applied in *Tameside*. In particular there was no threshold requirement of "unreasonableness." The Secretary of State could intervene "where it appears to [him] that tenants have or may have difficulty in exercising the right to buy effectively and expeditiously" (section 23). Thus, the reasonableness of the local authorities' policy was irrelevant. Moreover the council had a statutory duty to sell, so that no question of mandate arose.

Comparison between these cases seems unhelpful. They have virtually nothing in common except that both concerned central/local relations. Although they do not exclude the possibility of judicial bias they can be explained perfectly well independently of the bias hypothesis. Indeed, on the face of it *Tameside* shows the courts supporting the value of local autonomy, and there seems no reason to impute more sinister motives. It is also helpful to compare *Tameside* with *Smith* v. *I.L.E.A.* [1978] 1 All E.R. 411, where a local authority proposal of the opposite kind was upheld by the court. *Smith* is of interest because the Court of Appeal's decision seems to have been at odds with the expressed personal preferences of at least one of its members (Lord Denning M.R. at pp. 415, 418). In *Smith* the Court of Appeal refused to grant even an interim injunction to parents who objected to a proposal to turn a long established grammar school into a comprehensive school on the ground, (consistent with *Tameside*), that there was no arguable case that the authority had acted unreasonably.

The final case in this group—*Manchester City Council* v. *Greater Manchester County Council* (1980) 78 L.G.R. 560 described by Professor McAuslan as an "extraordinary decision" concerned a resolution of the Greater Manchester Council under section 137 of the Local Government Act 1972 to transfer ratepayers funds to a trust for the purpose of financing places at independent schools for local children. Professor McAuslan compares this with *Bromley L.B.C.* v. *G.L.C.* [1983] 1 A.C. 768 in which subsidies to London Transport (as it was then) by the left wing G.L.C. were held invalid. There is little in common between the statutory provisions involved, and in the Manchester case the crucial point—could the Council lawfully use the money for this purpose?—was conceded by both sides. The only matters argued before their Lordships related to the particular machinery chosen for the purpose. It is therefore impossible to draw any conclusion about judicial bias.

Secondly, Professor McAuslan discusses four development control cases as examples of a pro-property bias. ("Ideologies" n. 8 above, pp. 162–171). In *Fawcett Properties* v. *Buckinghamshire County Council* [1961] A.C. 636 the House of Lords held that a condition attached to a planning permission limited the occupancy of a cottage in the green belt to persons employed or whose last employment was in agriculture. Their Lordships held that the condition was sufficiently certain and rationally related to generally accepted policy objectives of the planning system, notably the protection of the countryside against urban sprawl, and providing housing for agricultural workers. Their Lordships therefore upheld the wide discretion conferred by the Act upon local planning authorities despite the infringement of the common law liberties of private property owners. On its face *Fawcett* does not seem to be an example of private property bias. Indeed Lord Denning said (at 679)

> "The courts . . . must remember that (the conditions) are made by a public representative body in the public interest. When planning conditions are made, as here, so as to maintain the green belt against those who would invade it they ought to be supported if possible. And credit ought to be given to those

who have to administer them, that they will be reasonably administered."

By contrast, in *R.* v. *Hillingdon London Borough Council ex p. Royco Homes Ltd.* [1974] Q.B. 720 the Queens Bench Division held that a condition requiring that an urban developer offer homes to persons on the council's waiting list on terms similar to council house terms was *ultra vires*. The distinction between the cases is not that housing considerations or even the need for public housing are outside the objectives of the planning system (below, pp. 133–134). In *Royco* the authority had gone further. The condition was held to be unreasonable because in effect it required a transfer of the local authority statutory housing duties to the private developer. Whether this reveals an undue individualistic bias depends entirely on the observer's political perspective and attitude to the controversial issue of planning gain.

Thirdly, in *Esdell Caravan Parks Ltd.* v. *Hemel Hempstead Rural District Council* [1966] 1 Q.B. 895 a caravan site licence condition was in principle upheld limiting the maximum number of caravans on an existing site to 24. The effect was to deprive the site owner of existing rights conferred by the main planning legislation. The condition was upheld on the basis that severe social problems could arise in the district if there were to be a major increase in the number of caravans on the site—including overcrowding in the schools, shopping and transport problems. The Court of Appeal held that there was an overlap between planning considerations and site considerations, but that from a planning point of view a wide range of social and economic considerations could be taken into account. Again, deference to local discretion was stressed. (at pp. 748, 851, 752). Finally, in *Chertsey Urban District Council* v. *Mixnams Properties Ltd.* [1965] A.C. 735 the House of Lords set aside a caravan site condition that empowered the Authority to control the rents charged by the owner of the site to its licensees.

Of the four cases *Royco* is the easiest to identify with a private property bias. In *Mixnams* Lord Upjohn and Lord Reid emphasised the value of freedom of contract but a majority based their reasoning primarily upon the more limited basis that the conditions did not relate to the physical use of the site, bearing in mind that caravan site legislation is narrower than is the general planning legislation. Lord Radcliffe pointed to the futility of deferring to common law property rights, because after all it is the purpose of the legislation to restrict them (at pp. 754, 755).

In *Mixnams* and in *Royco* the result favoured private property rights. On the other hand, even in *Mixnams* the actual reasoning of the court emphasised the values of fidelity to local land-use policies and deference to executive discretion.

Professor McAuslan's analysis is more subtle. He suggests that the private property ideology espoused by the courts is not necessarily synonymous with the freedom of a landowner to use his land as he likes, but includes the values of an "enlightened" or "responsible" landowner. Thus, where the landowner loses (*Fawcett, Esdell*) the local authority is upholding traditional rural values—preservation of the countryside, etc.—which are actually the values of responsible landowners, in other words the "rural myth" concerns outlined in Chapter 1. On this reasoning there is a distinction between "rural" and "urban" cases. In urban areas the responsible landowner need not be concerned with traditional values, but supported by the court can pursue profit. This may be plausible but is not actually expressed by the judges. The only way to test such a hypothesis is inductive by showing that most of the cases fit into this pattern. This requires an examination of a representative number of cases, not merely a small sample. It also requires (on the principle of Occam's razor) that the hypothesis must be the simplest and most natural explanation of the cases.

We are not excluding the possibility of a pro-individualistic judicial bias, but claim only that the anecdotal methods used by commentators to test the hypothesis are insufficient. Even if these four cases can be interpreted to fit Professor McAuslan's hypothesis, there are other cases that are ambivalent or contradictory. For example, *Westminster Bank* v. *Beverley Borough Council* [1971] A.C. 508 was an "urban" case. The bank was refused planning permission to extend its premises on the ground that its proposals might prejudice the possible future widening of the road. The bank asserted the familiar "private property" argument that statutory powers should not be exercised so as to interfere with property rights without compensation. It relied upon the Highways Act 1959, which provided an alternative method of protecting road widening schemes but which required the payment of compensation. The House of Lords held that the powers conferred by the Planning Acts to restrict development without compensation were, on a natural reading, broad enough to justify the authority's decision and that the authority was not obliged to choose the method that attracted compensation. Lord Reid said that if there is "reasonable doubt" as to the meaning of an Act the subject should be given the benefit of it (at p. 529), but regarded this as overridden by the general principle, that the planning legislation does not confer a right to compensation. Moreover, the local authority when exercising a discretion is entitled to make a choice as to who should bear the financial burden, in this case between the landowner and the general body of ratepayers.[8a] See also *Clyde and Co.* v. *Secretary of State* (below, p. 133).

It is perhaps more helpful to identify broad doctrines than to single out individual cases. On this basis the general doctrines of development control law do not seem to support an individualistic bias theory either in its crude form or in Professor McAuslan's more sophisticated version. For example, (i) the courts have been critical of attempts to import private law notions into planning law. In particular, neither contract nor estoppel can be used to restrict the statutory powers of planning authorities except in special and limited circumstances.[9] (ii) Documents such as planning permissions, decision letters and enforcement notices must be construed in a liberal spirit with a general presumption in favour of the authority. (iii) A planning permission is binding only when formally notified (below, p. 176). (iv) By contrast time limits for challenging a ministerial decision run, not from the notification of that decision, but from the date of the decision itself.[10] (v) Planning conditions can remove or restrict vested rights previously granted under the planning legislation (below, p. 147). (vi) The meaning of "development"—the key to the development control system—is not a question of pure law for the courts but a question of "fact and degree" thus requiring the court to defer to the opinion of the local planning authority. (below, Chap. 4). (vii) Questions of policy and related value judgments are left alone by the courts. In each of these contexts a genuine choice was open to the judges, but each time they rejected private property notions, in favour of other non-controversial values, notably deference to the executive and the advantages of certainty.

In general, the courts fulfill their traditional constitutional function of deference to the executive, subject to limitations based upon non-controversial values. They are particularly reluctant to interfere with policy and value judgments and with judgments based upon specialist expertise. They uphold notions of representative democracy but have an ambivalent attitude to direct participatory democracy. They are concerned with basic levels of

---

[8a] Again showing that individualism is not monolithic. The court is required to choose between conflicting individual interests, here between ratepayers and the bank's shareholders and customers. See also *Bromley L.B.C.* v. *G.L.C.* [1983] 1 A.C. 768.

[9] *Pioneers Aggregates* v. *Secretary of State* [1984] 2 All E.R. 258 (below, p. 172).

[10] *Griffiths* v. *Secretary of State* [1983] 2 A.C. 51. Other time limits are also strictly applied against the individual (below, pp. 198).

relevance and procedural fairness but are not prepared to impose high standards of evidence, and investigatory stringency upon government. They often express distaste for challenges to government action based upon legalistic technicality particularly in the context of enforcement notices and emphasise the need to make the planning system work smoothly. They have even spoken of the exclusion of judicial review as a desirable aim.[10a]

[10a] See *R.* v. *Westminster City Council ex p. Monahan* [1989] J.P.L. 107 at 113. See also *West Oxfordshire D.C.* v. *Secretary of State* [1988] J.P.L. 324 at 325, *Nelsovil* v. *Minister of Housing* [1962] 1 W.L.R. 404, *R.* v. *Secretary of State ex p. Ahern* T.L.R. March 29, 1989.

3. The Powers of the Court

There are a bewildering variety of procedures for challenging planning decisions in the courts. They all result in a hearing before the Queen's Bench Division on similar grounds, but there are differences in the powers of the court and in the procedures involved.

Only one kind of decision is completely excluded by statute from judicial review and even this exclusion has been interpreted restrictively.[1] Decisions by local authorities as to whether planning permission is required, as to the grant or refusal of planning permission, and in certain cases against the issuing of an enforcement notice can be challenged in the High Court by means of an application for judicial review under section 31 of the Supreme Court Act 1981. Alternatively, there is often a statutory right of appeal to the Secretary of State with a statutory procedure for challenging his decision in the courts.

Appeal and review

Judicial review is the only legal remedy open to a third party such as a neighbour who seeks to challenge a grant or refusal of planning permission by the local planning authority. There is no right of appeal open to a third party, a fact that goes to the heart of the planning system. The applicant for planning permission or a person affected by an enforcement notice may either appeal to the Secretary of State or seek judicial review although in enforcement cases the choice is severely restricted by statute (below p. 196). Whether an appeal to the Secretary of State is preferable to judicial review depends on the particular circumstances. The court may in

---

[1] A challenge on the ground that a decision has been taken by the wrong local authority. See L.G.A. 1972, Sched. 16, para. 51; *Co-operative Retail Services* v. *Secretary of State* [1980] 1 W.L.R. 271.

its discretion refuse to entertain an application for judicial review if it considers that a statutory appeal is an equally appropriate and advantageous remedy. This may be the case, for example, where legal issues are intermingled with questions of fact as is usually the case when the definition of development is involved. If, on the other hand, questions of procedure or abuse of discretion are involved, judicial review may be more appropriate.[2]

Where there is a choice between appealing to the Secretary of State and challenge in the courts it is important to realise the range of remedies available in each case. In the case of a planning permission appeal the Secretary of State has full power to make a new decision or to alter the decision of the local planning authority in any way he chooses (below, Chap. 10). Thus the appeal can reconsider any matter and not merely questions of law. The court, on the other hand, can only declare the law, quash the decision or remit the matter to the planning authority with directions (see below, p. 49).

In the case of an enforcement appeal the Secretary of State's powers are almost as wide. He can quash, correct or vary the enforcement notice, discharge or alter conditions or grant planning permission for the development or part of it which is the subject of the notice (below, p. 204).

In judicial review proceedings the court may sever the invalid from the valid part of a decision. This power is particularly important where it is alleged that a planning condition is ultra vires, but where the landowner seeks to retain the permission itself. Until recently the courts were reluctant to sever a decision so that if part was invalid the whole would normally fall, unless the invalid part consisted of a condition that was merely trivial or incidental.[3] The modern cases embody a more sophisticated approach. First, if the matter reaches the court in the form of a challenge to the Secretary of State's decision on appeal, the court will defer to whatever the Secretary of State has decided and will interfere only if he has acted grossly unreasonably (*Newbury D.C.* v. *S.O.S.* [1981] A.C. 578). In cases where the decision of a local planning authority is challenged directly, the court has to wield the axe itself. The prevailing approach seems to be to avoid private law analyses which rely purely on grammatical and semantic considerations and to look at the matter broadly in the light of all the circumstances. Moreover,

---

[2] *Square Meals Frozen Foods Ltd.* v. *Dunstable B.C.* [1974] 1 W.L.R. 59 at 65; *R.* v. *Hillingdon D.C. ex p. Royco Homes Ltd.* [1974] Q.B. 720.

[3] e.g. *Hall* v. *Shoreham R.D.C.* [1964] 1 W.L.R. 240; *R.* v. *Hillington B.C.* (above); *Kent C.C.* v. *Kingsway Investments Ltd.* [1971] A.C. 72.

there is a presumption in favour of upholding the validity of government action. In *Thames Water Authority* v. *Elmbridge B.C.* [1983] Q.B. 570 it was said that if the valid part can conveniently be separated from the invalid part without altering or rewriting the valid element the court will allow severance. The question is whether the decision looked at without the defective part is

> "clearly valid in the sense that there is nothing inherently unenforceable about it and all the surrounding circumstances indicate that commonsense and the intention of the maker of any document which includes both good and bad parts would give effect to it" (at 585).[4]

This general approach is not altogether easy to apply to the case of a planning condition. In the *Elmbridge* case severance was straightforward since the order complained of covered an excessive geographical area. In the case of a planning permission severance may result in a perfectly workable planning permission but one which the local planning authority would not have granted had they known that the condition was beyond their powers.

In *Kent C.C.* v. *Kingsway Investments Ltd.* [1971] A.C. 72 their Lordships expressed a variety of views on the question of severance. A majority held that the matter depended upon the importance of the conditions (Lords Morris, Upjohn and Donovan), but a different majority (Lords Morris, Guest, and Donovan) decided that the condition was valid anyway. No precise guidelines were laid down as to how to identify severable conditions. Their Lordships employed such phrases as "affect the character of permission," and being "part of the structure of the permission" which do not take the matter much further. Lord Upjohn suggested that the correct approach was to ask whether the authority would have granted permission had they been aware that their condition would be illegal. This leans rather too much in favour of the authority. Indeed, the majority who supported the "importance" test failed to agree upon its application to the particular circumstances. Lord Upjohn favoured severance, but Lords Morris and Donovan would not have done.

Lord Reid attempted to supply a more specific test (at pp. 90–91). He distinguished three classes of invalid condition. First, those imposed for reasons entirely unrelated to planning. These should always be severable; secondly, those imposed for

---

[4] See also *Potato Marketing Board* v. *Merricks* [1958] 2 Q.B. 316 at 33; *Dunkley* v. *Evans* [1981] 1 W.L.R. 522; *R.* v. *Secretary of State for Transport ex p. G.L.C.* [1985] 3 All E.R. 300.

proper planning reasons but invalid on the ground of unreasonableness—for example an excessively harsh condition. These should not be severable if they relate to the way in which the development is carried out since unlike the first case the authority might have been able to refuse permission for the same reasons. They should not therefore be required to tolerate an activity which they did not intend to permit. The third category consists of conditions which are unreasonable but which do not affect the way in which the development is carried out. Severance of these depends upon whether the condition can be severed without affecting the character of the planning permission itself. In the light of the recent cases it is suggested that Lord Reid's approach is to be preferred. Lord Reid's approach is also consistent with the result (but not the dicta) in the planning cases, in some of which severance was allowed without discussion (*e.g. Mixnams Properties* v. *Chertney U.D.C.* [1965] A.C. 735).

Questions of fact. Another limitation of judicial review is that the court is reluctant to investigate factual issues by means of oral evidence or cross examination. It will normally confine itself to looking at the material that was before the decision-maker and fresh factual evidence is only admissible in limited circumstances.[5] The onus of proof is on the applicant and there is a strong presumption in favour of the facts as presented by the planning authority. However, the court will intervene where a finding is entirely without factual foundation (below, p. 62) and also where there is a serious factual misconception continued in a statement of reasons (*Hollis* v. *S.o.S.* [1983] J.P.L. 164). In the case of policy or value judgments there is no "factual foundation" requirement (below, pp. 211–212). Distinctions between fact and policy or value judgments pervade the subject of development control.

Damages. The court may award damages in judicial review proceedings but only where another remedy is also sought and

---

[5] To establish jurisdictional defects or fraud or to determine what material was before the decision maker; *East Hampshire D.C.* v. *Secretary of State* [1979] J.P.L. 533; *R.* v. *Secretary of State ex p. Powis* [1981] 1 W.L.R. 584; *cf. O'Reilly* v. *Mackman* [1983] 2 A.C. 237 at 280. In the case of jurisdictional facts, the courts may examine the facts *de novo; White and Collins* v. *Minister of Health* [1939] 2 K.B. 838. However, in development control many crucial factual findings are expressly made subjective, *e.g.* section 87(1). In the case of a statutory right of appeal on a point of law the court is even less willing to admit factual evidence (see below, pp. 50 *et seq.*, 57. An authority is taken to know whatever any of its staff knows, see *R.* v. *Basildon D.C.* [1987] J.P.L. 863.

where damages would have been awarded in an ordinary action. In other words there is no special provision for public law damages (Supreme Court Act 1981, s.31(4)). This raises no particular problem where damages are sought against an individual officer in respect of false or misleading advice or information. The ordinary law of negligent misstatement is applicable and damages can also be obtained in the ordinary courts (*Davey* v. *Spelthorne B.C.* [1984] A.C. 262).

It is more difficult to obtain damages against a planning authority in respect of an improper planning decision. First, an ultra vires decision may be invalid, but it is not unlawful as such and cannot in itself constitute a cause of action. (*Dunlop* v. *Woolahra M.C.* [1982] A.C. 158). Furthermore, the refusal of planning permission is not a violation of any existing common law rights. It does not therefore fit easily into ordinary notions of tort liability in the same way as, say, trespass on land. On the other hand, it is arguable that a landowner who is refused planning permission could base an action for negligence upon economic loss, or could sue for breach of statutory duty. A problem in both cases is that it is doubtful whether the duties of a local planning authority are owed to any specific individual. They are general public duties owed to the community at large and not therefore actionable in private law. The existence of statutory methods of challenging planning decisions reinforces this.[6]

---

[6] *Peabody Donation Fund* v. *Sir Lindsay Parkinson and Co. Ltd.* [1985] A.C. 210; *Buxton* v. *M.o.H.* [1961] 1 Q.B. 278; *Evans* v. *L.C.C.* (1960) 12 P. & C.R. 172; *Ryford Homes Ltd.* v. *Sevenoaks D.C.*, *The Times*, 15th February 1989. The policy/operational distinction applied by Lord Wilberforce in *Anns* v. *Merton L.B.C.* [1978] A.C. 728 at 751–752 may also be relevant. It is not clear whether this distinction was intended to create a "threshold requirement" that a policy decision must be ultra vires before any duty of care is broken or, as suggested by Lord Keith in *Rowling* v. *Takaro Properties Ltd.* [1988] 1 All E.R. 163 at 171–172, is intended to determine whether liability is excluded altogether. On the latter view a planning decision will never be actionable in negligence. In *Takaro* the Privy Council criticised the policy/operational distinction and preferred to rely on such pragmatic considerations as the availability of a judicial review remedy, the danger of imposing excessively severe restrictions on public authorities, and the fact that public duties are owed to the community as a whole. These considerations apply particularly strongly in planning cases. (*Takaro* concerned ministerial controls over the sale of Crown land). The court was also concerned with the practical difficulties involved in deciding when a minister should seek legal advice concerning the exercise of statutory powers. It was held on the facts that the Minister was not negligent. In *Jones* v. *Department of Employment* [1988] 1 All E.R. 725 (C.A.) it was held that the whole statutory framework must be taken into account, including other remedies with a view to seeing whether it was "just and reasonable" to impose a common law duty of care. On the basis of this case, planning officers are unlikely to be liable for negligence in respect of invalid decisions.

There remains the possibility of seeking damages for the special tort of malicious abuse of public office. Here the gist of the action *is* that the decision is ultra vires. However, an authority is liable only if it knows that its actions are ultra vires or if it acts maliciously. (*Bourgoin SA* v. *Minister of Agriculture* [1986] Q.B. 716).

Choice of remedy

LOCAL PLANNING AUTHORITY DECISIONS

In the case of decisions by local planning authorities the applicant has a choice between (i) appealing to the Secretary of State, or (ii) applying for judicial review in the Queen's Bench Division or (iii) doing nothing and raising a defence if the local planning authority eventually takes enforcement proceedings. In the case of an enforcement notice special grounds of appeal to the Secretary of State are provided and an enforcement notice cannot be challenged *on these grounds* by any other means (below, p. 196). In a few cases, for example applications for costs, there is no statutory right of appeal and judicial review is the only remedy. Challenging a decision of a local planning authority to refuse planning permission or to impose a condition is undoubtedly a "public law" matter. The judicial review procedure is therefore appropriate. The House of Lords has held that, public law "litigation" must normally be pursued only by means of an application for judicial review.[7] As we have seen this involves several restrictions (above, p. 25). Where private rights are involved the judicial review process is not exclusive even if there is also a public law element in the case (*Davey* v. *Spelthorne R.D.C.* [1984] A.C. 262—negligent advice). The citizen can either institute judicial review proceedings, pursue an ordinary action, or raise a defence.[8] The validity of a decision to grant or refuse planning permission is a matter purely of public law because there is no private right to develop land, such rights having

---

[7] *O'Reilly* v. *Mackman* [1983] 2 A.C. 237; *Cocks* v. *Thanet D.C.* [1983] 2 A.C. 286; Quaere whether planning agreements are public law matters.

[8] *Gillick* v. *West Norfolk Health Authority* [1986] A.C. 112; *Cocks* v. *Thanet D.C.* (above); *Wandsworth B.C.* v. *Winder* [1984] 3 W.L.R. 1254; The question of asserting a private right in a civil action as opposed to raising a defence has not been authoritatively litigated. It is suggested that it is implicit in the reasoning in *O'Reilly* and *Cocks* (above) that such an action could be instituted by writ unless in the particular circumstances there is an abuse of process. See, *e.g.* the discussion of *Pyx Granite Co.* v. *M.o.H.* [1960] A.C. 260 in *O'Reilly* v. *Mackman* [1983] 2 A.C. 237. See also *R.* v. *Jenner* [1983] 1 W.L.R. 873— stop notice could be challenged by defence.

been removed wholesale by the planning legislation. Planning permission is required for the development of land and permission is entirely discretionary.

On the other hand, if a landowner argues that he has not disobeyed an enforcement notice or that an enforcement notice is invalid (except on matters within the statutory appeal grounds (above)) or that he is not subject to planning control he is relying upon existing private rights of ownership. The same applies where the landowner is seeking to rely on the validity of an existing planning permission, and there is a dispute involving questions of construction (see *Wivenhoe Port* v. *Colchester B.C.* [1985] J.P.L. 396). In all these cases he can arguably seek a remedy without resorting to the special application for judicial review procedure.

The distinction between public and private law seems to break down where the landowner is arguing that his proposed activities are not development within the meaning of the Act. Here he seems to be asserting a private right. On the other hand, the courts have consistently held that the meaning of "development" is a mixed question of fact, degree and law, to be decided primarily by the local planning authority but subject to review on legal grounds (below, pp. 60–63). There is much to be said for the dissenting view of Ackner L.J. (as he was then) in *Wandsworth B.C.* v. *Winder* [1984] 3 W.L.R. 563). His Lordship would apparently regard every matter involving a discretionary governmental decision as one of public law and thus subject to the exclusive judicial review regime whether or not private rights are in issue.[9]

In *Waverley B.C.* v. *Hilden* [1988] 1 W.L.R. 246, Scott J. introduced a further refinement of the public law/private rights distinction. The local planning authority decided to apply for an injunction in respect of the defendant's gypsy caravan site. It was held that the decision to institute proceedings was a matter purely of public law and could be challenged only by judicial review. A defence in civil proceedings was therefore struck out, although the court might have adjourned the proceedings had there been a significant chance of success in judicial review proceedings (see also *Avon C.C.* v. *Buscott* [1988] 1 All E.R. 801). The distinction drawn by his Lordship was that, unlike the *Winder* case, the defendant had no substantive defence to the merits based on private rights, but was relying solely on the public law argument that the decision to take enforcement action was unreasonable. His Lordship stressed the advantages of the judicial review procedure from the point of view

---

[9] Compare *Plymouth City Council* v. *Quietlynn* [1987] 3 W.L.R. 1096 with *R.* v. *Reading Crown Court ex p. Hutchinson* [1988] 1 All E.R. 333.

of safeguarding governmental interests. It seems therefore that neither the public law/private rights, nor the defence/action distinction is conclusive, but the substance of the allegation must be looked at. This seems to be a move in the right direction.

CENTRAL GOVERNMENT DECISIONS

Where the applicant appeals to the Secretary of State there are statutory provisions for further challenge in the courts. In most cases this procedure excludes all other methods of challenge. There are two main statutory procedures. They are more advantageous to the citizen than the ordinary judicial review procedure in the sense that application does not require leave of the court. However, as in the case of judicial review, discovery of documents and the bringing of oral evidence are matters for the discretion of the court. In all cases the court can give interim relief.

Planning permission appeals. These are governed by sections 242 and 245. The majority of final decisions taken by the Secretary of State fall within these provisions except those involving enforcement notices and decisions under section 53 as to whether planning permission is required.[10]

The main feature of the section 245 procedure is that by virtue of section 242 the decision of the Secretary of State must be challenged within a period of six weeks from the date on which the letter recording the Secretary of State's decision is signed and dated (*Griffiths* v. *Secretary of State* [1983] 2 A.C. 51). All other methods of challenge are excluded with the possible exception of an action for damages in tort (above, p. 44). Within six weeks, challenge is possible on all the normal grounds of judicial review. The extent to which extrinsic evidence is admissable seems to be similar to the position in judicial review proceedings (above).

The question whether a statutory ouster clause is effective to exclude judicial review has been muddled because of the speeches

---

[10] Incidental matters such as challenges to the appointment of the inspector, decisions about adjournment of the inquiry and about costs are not subject to section 245. In these cases judicial review is appropriate. Decisions for the approval of reserved matters on "called in" applications are also excluded. *Turner* v. *Secretary of State* (1973) 72 L.G.R. 380. See also *Co-operative Retail Services Ltd.* v. *Secretary of State* [1980] 1 W.L.R. 217, *cf. Chalgray* v. *Secretary of State* [1977] 33 P. & C.R. 10. See also *R.* v. *Secretary of State ex p. Kensington and Chelsea L.B.C.* [1987] J.P.L. 567. For the purpose of s.245 the applicant must be aggrieved by the decision itself and not merely by some aspect of its reasoning. *G.L.C.* v. *Secretary of State* [1985] J.P.L. 868.

of the House of Lords in *Anisminic* v. *Foreign Compensation Commission* [1969] 2 A.C. 147. Their Lordships held that a statutory provision that "a determination" of the Foreign Compensation Commission shall not be questioned in the courts did not prevent the court declaring that a decision of the Commission was a nullity. The earlier decision of the House of Lords in *Smith* v. *East Elloe R.D.C.* [1956] A.C. 736 which concerned the six weeks time limit clause was criticised in *Anisminic* but not overruled. The scope of an ouster clause is a matter of construction of the particular legislation and the notion that an ultra vires decision is a nullity provides at most a presumption of statutory interpretation.[11]

Although the House of Lords has not decided whether the *Anisminic* principle applies to the six weeks time limit clause, the argument that the clause precludes all judicial review after six weeks seems overwhelming. First, and as a matter of literal language, the clause refers to "action" (by the Secretary of State) which is "not within the powers of this Act" (section 245(1)(*b*)). This necessarily includes action which is a nullity. Secondly, policy considerations favour a literal application of the six weeks time limit in order to minimise uncertainty. Thirdly, the cases consistently support the proposition that there should be no review after six weeks (see *R.* v. *Secretary of State ex p. Kent* [1988] J.P.L. 706).

The grounds of challenge under section 245 are divided into two; (i) that the order or action taken is "not within the powers of the Act" and (ii) that any if the relevant requirements have not been complied with. After initial doubt it has been generally accepted that the first ground includes natural justice or "fairness," and misuse of discretionary power as well as ultra vires in the narrow sense.[12] The second ground includes procedural defects and errors of law, not only in relation to the Act itself but also in relation to subordinate legislation such as the Inquiries Procedure Rules (below, Chap. 10) or indeed any other relevant requirement.

There is an overlap between the two grounds in that an ultra vires decision *ipso facto* constitutes a failure to comply with a "requirement," and, a breach of the Inquiries Procedure Rules will often constitute a breach of natural justice (below, p. 215). However, it seems that disregard of the Inquiries Procedure Rules as such does not make the decision *ultra vires* (*Reading B.C.* v. *Secretary of State* [1986] J.P.L. 115), nor does a failure to give

---

[11] See Alder (1975) 38 M.L.R. 274; Gravells (1978) 41 M.L.R. 383; Alder (1980) 43 M.L.R. 670; Harlow and Rawlings, *Law and Administration* (1984), pp. 98–118.
[12] *Webb* v. *M.o.H.* [1965] 2 All E.R. 193, doubting *Smith* v. *East Elloe R.D.C.* (above) on this point.

adequate reasons (below p. 55). The status of a decision vitiated by lack of evidence is also uncertain (*Coleen Properties* v. *M.o.H.* [1971] 1 W.L.R. 433).

The difference between the two grounds is that under the second head the court may quash the decision only if the interests of the applicant have been "substantially prejudiced." In cases of ultra vires it may always quash.[13] However, even where a decision is ultra vires the court still has a discretion whether or not to quash. In *Miller* v. *Weymouth and Melcombe Regis Corp* (1974) 27 P. & C.R. 468, Kerr J. refused to quash a local authority order upon the grounds that the appellant had suffered no prejudice (the defect was an error concerning dates). His Lordship held that the notice was not ultra vires but thought that the same discretion would exist even in the case of an ultra vires order (see also *Richmond B.C.* v. *Secretary of State* (1984) J.P.L. 24).

The two ground formula seem to serve no useful purpose. It originated in the 1930s at a time when the notion of ultra vires was narrowly conceived. Now that virtually any defect can be squeezed into the ultra vires doctrine there seems to be little to be said for preserving the distinction.

The court's only power under section 245 is to quash the offending order or action, although it can give interim relief. Moreover, the court cannot apparently sever the invalid from any valid parts of the decision (above).

The whole decision is quashed, thus leaving the appeal outstanding. In *Kingswood D.C.* v. *Secretary of State* [1988] J.P. 249 it was held that the Secretary of State must take the decision again, since the effect of quashing is to leave him with a clean sheet. Whether this requires the whole procedure to be repeated including any public inquiry depends upon the nature of the particular defect. If, for example, the defect consists solely of a failure to give adequate reasons and there is no change in circumstances, another decision letter could be issued (*Price Bros. (Rode Heath) Ltd.* v. *Department of Environment* (1979) 38 P. and C.R. 579). However, the Secretary of State is obliged to take into account new circumstance arising between the date of the quashed decision and that of its replacement. The Inquiries Procedure rules reflect this by requiring the Secretary of State to give the parties an opportunity to make further representations.[13a]

---

[13] In natural justice cases prejudice may also be required as part of the substantive law. See below, p. 216.

[13a] See Town and Country Planning (Inquiries Procedure) Rules 1988 (S.I. 1988 No. 944) R. 18; Town and Country Planning Appeals (Determinations by Inspectors) (Inquiries Procedure) Rules 1988 (S.I. 1988 No. 945) R. 9.

Enforcement appeals. Enforcement appeals are governed by different provisions. There is a right of appeal or to a case stated to the High Court upon a point of law (section 246(1)). This must be exercised within 28 days. The court's powers are confined to remitting the matter to the Secretary of State with directions (R.S.C. Ord. 94 R. 12(5)). It cannot therefore quash or vary the notice. However, the difference between this power and the section 245 power to quash is largely technical. In both cases the appeal remains in being and the Secretary of State must reconsider the whole matter if new circumstances arise (see *Newbury D.C.* v. *Secretary of State* [1988] J.P.L. 185). The main significance of the courts power to remit is that the enforcement notice (although its operation is suspended (below)) remains in existence and the authority is not required to issue it again. The section 246 appeal, unlike the six weeks time limit machinery, does not exclude the ordinary judicial review procedure. However, as a matter of discretion an application for judicial review is not likely to be granted where there is an appropriate statutory appeal.[14]

Decisions taken by the Secretary of State on appeal against a "section 53 determination" whether planning permission is required can be challenged by means of an appeal on a point of law to the High Court under section 247. Only the applicant and the local planning authority may appeal. As with section 246 this is not an exclusive remedy. Its scope appears to be similar to that of section 246.

There is an overlap between the six weeks time limit procedure and the section 246 enforcement appeal. The Secretary of State in an enforcement appeal may grant planning permission for the development to which the enforcement notice relates or discharge a condition or limitation (section 88B(1)). This can be challenged either under section 246 or under section 245 (see section 242(3)F) and *Gill* v. *Secretary of State* [1985] J.P.L. 710).

The court's powers to examine factual evidence are apparently narrower in the case of a section 246 appeal than in relation to judicial review or a section 245 challenge (above, p. 43). It seems that under section 246 the court can look only at the inspectors report and the decision letter to see whether there was an error of law and cannot consider other evidence. In *London Parachuting* v. *Secretary of State* [1986] J.P.L. 428 Mann J. held that

---

[14] See *R.* v. *Huntingdon D.C. ex p. Cowen* [1984] 1 W.L.R. 501; *R.* v. *Epping and Harlow General Commissioners* [1983] 3 All E.R. 257; *R.* v. *Ipswich Crown Court* [1981] 1 All E.R. 596; *Bone* v. *Mental Health Review Tribunal* [1985] 3 All E.R. 330 at 334 (see below).

the court had no power in section 246 proceedings to decide questions of fact even in relation to matters of procedure or to settle disputes concerning the material that was before the inspector.[15] Therefore, it was not open to the court to decide whether the appellants had been improperly prevented from calling witnesses. In such a case there must be an application for judicial review. In the particular circumstances such an application was too late. However, in *Rhymney Valley D.C.* v. *Secretary of State* [1985] J.P.L. 27 Nolan J. was prepared to treat section 246 proceedings as if they were an application for judicial review, despite the absence of any statutory authority for this. It is also arguable that the section 246 procedure is not available where the enforcement notice is a nullity (below, p. 199).

The procedures for challenging planning decisions in the courts seem excessively complex and pointlessly technical. They date from a time when the law of judicial review was even more technical. Now that the general law relating to judicial review remedies has been improved, there seems little justification for retaining special statutory machinery for challenge and in particular for providing different procedures for planning permission appeals and enforcement notices. In particular, leave is not required to exercise the statutory remedies so that there is no filter to exclude hopeless challenges intended as delaying tactics. This problem is particularly acute in enforcement notice cases because an enforcement notice is suspended until all rights of appeal exercisable under the Act have been exhausted (below p. 198. See *R.* v. *Kuxhaus* [1988] J.P.L. 545). In judicial review proceedings the court has a discretion (R.S.C. Ord. 53 R. 10(3)).

Locus standi

A special feature of the judicial review procedure is that the applicant must show that he or she has "sufficient interest" in the subject matter of the application (Supreme Court Act 1981, s.31(3). The *locus standi* question must be decided at the full trial since it is closely bound up with the substantive issues. However, the

---

[15] Compare *R.* v. *Secretary of State ex p. Newprop* [1983] J.P.L. 386 (judicial review); *East Hampshire D.C.* v. *Secretary of State* [1978] J.P.L. 182 (s.245). *George* v. *Secretary of State* (1979) 77 L.G.R. 689 (s.245) and *cf.* R.S.C. Ord. 55 r. 7. See also *Gwillim* v. *Secretary of State* [1988] J.P.L. 213. In *Kingswood* v. *Secretary of State* [1988] J.P.L. 248 Mr. Graham Eyre Q.C. deputy judge thought that outside evidence could be looked at to establish what material was before the decision maker. See also *Forkhurst* v. *Secretary of State* [1982] J.P.L. 448.

preliminary "leave to apply stage" can filter out obviously hopeless cases.

"Sufficient interest" is not confined to cases involving the infringement of private rights. The application for judicial review is a special legal procedure and is not an adjudication between competing rights. Whether an applicant has sufficient interest depends upon the scope of the governing legislation. Is the applicant within the range of persons for whose benefit the legislation was enacted? (*I.R.C.* v. *National Federation for the Self Employed* [1982] A.C. 617). For example, a conservation society could well have standing to challenge a planning decision affecting the society's concerns. Indeed, if a decision has widespread national implications it may be that any member of the public would have standing (see *R.* v. *Hammersmith L.B.C. ex p. People Before Profit* [1981] J.P.L. 869). Earlier cases which appear to place ratepayers in a specially favourable position are thus of little relevance in the planning context unless some special charge upon the rates is involved. If an ordinary civil action is pursued, that plaintiff must have a proprietory interest. (*Steeples* v. *Derbyshire C.C.* [1984] 3 All E.R. 468) at 499–500.[16]

A second factor is the nature and gravity of the allegations made. The more serious they are from the point of view of the public interest, the wider the range of persons permitted to apply for judicial review. For example, it is unlikely that a local resident as such could complain that *someone else* has not been given a fair hearing, but could have standing as regards allegations of bias. The strength of the applicants case on its merits is also relevant.

Thirdly, the particular remedy sought may be important. For example, it may be easier to establish sufficient interest to obtain a declaration than to obtain an enforceable order of mandamus.

The *locus standi* rules are therefore essentially a matter of the courts discretion. The law has recently become liberal in this respect, and the courts have openly recognised the concerns of neighbourhood and other pressure groups.

In the case of the statutory remedies, the phrase used in section 245 is "person aggrieved." *Buxton* v. *M.o.H.* [1961] 1 Q.B. 278 suggests that only a person whose legal rights are affected is a person aggrieved. Because the statutory procedure has no filter to exclude frivolous or malicious challenges (apart from the court's

---

[16] However, Webster J.'s view in *Steeples* that *locus* is the same for a civil action as in judicial review proceedings is difficult to support. See *Gouriet* v. *U.P.O.W.* [1978] A.C. 435; *Barrs* v. *Bethel* [1981] 3 W.L.R. 874. Compare *R.* v. *Bradford-upon-Avon U.D.C.* [1964] 1 W.L.R. 1136; *R.* v. *Hendon R.D.C. ex p. Chorley* [1933] 2 K.B. 696.

general power to prevent an abuse of process). A stricter approach to *locus standi* has much to be said for it (see *Covent Garden Community Association* v. *G.L.C.* [1981] J.P.L. 183). However, later first instance cases have been generous, conferring standing upon neighbourhood pressure groups and neighbours who actually appeared at the inquiry (*Turner* v. *Secretary of State* (1974) 28 P. and C.R. 123; *Bizony* v. *Secretary of State* [1976] J.P.L. 306—point reserved). The matter is therefore open. See also *Wilson* v. *Secretary of State* [1988] J.P.L. 540.

In the case of appeals to the High Court under section 246 *locus standi* is expressly limited to the applicant, the local planning authority or any other person having an interest in the land to which the notice relates. Finally, section 247 appeals, (relating to decisions whether planning permission is required under section 53) are limited to the applicant and local planning authority. In both cases other persons could seek to apply for judicial review.

Reasons for decisions

The onus of proof in judicial review proceedings is normally on the applicant. It is therefore important that the authority should give reasons for its decision. Indeed, the giving of reasons could be regarded as a fundamental public law principle inherent in the notion of accountable and democratic government.[17] Nevertheless, there is no general common law duty to give reasons for decisions.

In the context of development control there are statutory duties to give reasons. These are as follows:

1. Local Planning authorities must give reasons in writing for the imposition of a condition upon a planning permission or for the refusal of permission but not for the unconditional grant of permission (G.D.O. 1988 Art. 25). As in the related context of rights of appeal the interests of neighbours and the local community generally are given no statutory protection except in special cases (below, p. 219).

---

[17] See Richardson [1986] P.L. 437. The arguments against giving reasons are based mainly on administrative convenience and the subjectivity of value judgments (see, *e.g. McInnes* v. *Onslow Fare* [1978] 1 W.L.R. 1520). They sometimes fail to distinguish between a duty to give reasons as such and a flexible approach to the content of the reasons. It can also be argued that a duty to give reasons has an effect on the substantive content of decisions and imposes "rationality" requirements. This kind of argument is popular in the U.S.A. See Reich (1985) 94 Yale L.J. 1617; Diver (1982) 95 H.L.R. 393; Richardson (above); Galligan, *Discretionary Powers* (1987) pp. 266–280.

2. An enforcement notice must specify the reasons why the local planning authority consider it expedient to issue the notice (below, p. 195).

3. The Secretary of State or the Inspector must give written reasons for any decision taken after the holding of a statutory inquiry or where a person could have required the holding of a statutory inquiry if requested to do so on or before the giving or notification of the decision (Tribunals and Inquiries Act 1971, s.12). This duty applies whether or not an inquiry is actually held, and the term statutory inquiry is wide enough to cover any statutory hearing (*ibid.* section 19). Where an inquiry is held, the various inquiries procedure rules impose an obligation to give reasons in writing whether or not requested to do so.[18] There is probably no duty on the Secretary of State to give reasons for "calling in" an application for planning permission (*R.* v. *Secretary of State ex p. Newprop.* [1983] J.P.L. 386).

There are indirect ways of securing the giving of reasons. An apparently arbitrary decision or a finding of fact unsupported by evidence may be quashed.[19] Natural justice in its modern form of "fairness" may require the reasons of a decision to be disclosed, particularly where there is a statutory right of appeal or where a decision must be taken on prescribed grounds.[20] In certain cases local planning authorities must invite consultation and this obligation carries with it a duty to provide sufficient information and reasons to make the consultation process effective. Furthermore, once a case has come to court and there are grounds for challenging a decision, there is then a duty to assist the court by giving adequate reasons (see *R.* v. *Lancashire C.C. ex p. Huddlestone* [1986] 2 All E.R. 941 at 946).

The existence of a duty to give reasons not only makes it easier to discover defects in the decision making process but also provides

---

[18] See note 13a (above). R. 17(1), R. 18(1). In the case of "written representation" decisions (below, p. 216) the duty to give reasons is on request and depends upon s.12 of the Tribunals and Inquiries Act 1971. But see *Grenfell-Bains* v. *Secretary of State* [1985] J.P.L. 256. That case seems explicable on the basis the S.o.S. actually gave reasons that were inadequate. See *Westminster City Council* v. *Secretary of State* [1984] J.P.L. 27). Compare *R.* v. *Secretary of State ex p. Newprop* [1983] J.P.L. 386.

[19] *Padfield* v. *Minister of Agriculture* [1968] A.C. 997 at 1661; *R.* v. *Secretary of State ex p. Haldon* (1984) 48 P. & C.R. 28. But there must be some independent factor raising an implication that the decision is improper. See generally Foulkes, *Administrative Law* 6th ed. Chap. 9; Craig, *Administrative Law* (1983), 182–183, 277–278.

[20] *Brown* v. *A.E.U.* [1971] 2 Q.B. 175; *R.* v. *Home Secretary ex p. Danneburg* [1984] 1 Q.B. 766; *R.* v. *Home Secretary ex p. Harrison* [1988] 3 All E.R. 86.

what is effectively an additional ground of judicial review enabling the court to intervene if the reasons are not adequate. The effect of a failure to give reasons depends upon whether the failure is that of the local planning authority and therefore challenged in ordinary judicial review proceedings (above) or that of the Secretary of State or Inspector on appeal and challenged under the statutory procedures. In both cases the giving of reasons is a mandatory (essential) requirement. However, a failure by a local authority to give adequate reasons does not invalidate the permission or condition itself but is an entirely separate requirement (*Brayhead (Ascot) Ltd.* v. *Berkshire C.C.* [1964] 2 Q.B. 303). The appropriate remedy is therefore mandamus to require a proper statement of reasons. The position is different if the statement of reasons discloses some other defect. Under the statutory procedures a failure to give reasons is in itself a ground for quashing.[21]

ADEQUACY OF REASONS

The court will ensure that the reasons given are "adequate." This means that even if a substantive defect is not disclosed, a decision could be set aside if the statement of reasons is obscure, or contains an omission or a manifest error of law or fact. How stringent is the duty to give reasons? On the one hand there is justification for requiring a statement of reasons to be as full and clear as possible in order to improve the quality of decision making and to legitimate the decision making process by increasing public confidence. On the other hand, a lower standard might be tolerable if the primary purpose of giving reason is to facilitate appeals or challenge in the courts. There are arguments against imposing unduly stringent standards. These include (i) administrative efficiency cost and speed, (ii) the aim of making decision letters comprehensible (iii) the difficulty of rationalising decisions that are ultimately based upon subjective value judgments and the balancing of competing policies and (iv) the risk of last resort tactical challenges in the courts in order to reopen the case. In general the courts impose basic requirements of coherence, comprehensiveness and clarity while leaving the authority free to make subjective valuations.

[21] As a "requirement" in the case of s.245. See *Givauden* v. *M.o.H.* [1967] 1 W.L.R. 250, and as a "point of law" under ss.246, 247. However, "defective reasons" is not in itself "substantial prejudice" (*Bell and Colvill* v. *Secretary of State* [1980] J.P.L. 823) so that the applicant must show that he has been placed at a disadvantage. Failing to take a relevant factor into account will normally suffice (see, *e.g.* *Rogelan Ltd.* v. *Secretary of State* [1981] J.P.L. 506; *Preston B.C.* v. *Secretary of State* [1978] J.P.L. 548 at 551). *Greenwich L.B.C.* v. *Secretary of State* [1981] J.P.L. 809.

A much quoted formulation of the duty to give reasons was provided by Megaw J. in *Re Poyser and Mills Arbitration* [1964] 2 Q.B. 467. This was adopted by the House of Lords in a planning context in *Great Portland Estates* v. *Westminster City Council* [1984] 3 W.L.R. 1035 at 1045 . . .

> "Parliament having provided that reasons shall be given, and in my view that must be read as meaning that proper, adequate reasons must be given. The reasons that are set out whether they are right or wrong must be reasons which will not only be intelligible but which deal with the substantial points that have been raised."

In *Bradley* v. *Secretary of State* [1982] J.P.L. 43, Glidewell J. added that reasons can be briefly stated.

The same general standards apply to all cases where reasons must be given, although where an inquiry has been held the Secretary of State can simply adopt the Inspectors report as his statement of reasons. In the case of "written representation" appeals where the facts are not in dispute, reasons can be particularly brief.[22] Shorter statements are also acceptable where the decision is made by the Inquiry inspector. Conversely the fullest statement is required when the Secretary of State disagrees with the inspector's report. (See *West Midlands Co-operative Society* v. *Secretary of State* [1988] J.P.L. 121 at 122; *French Kier Developments* v. *Secretary of State* [1977] 1 All E.R. 296.) In all cases, however, the reasons must be "site specific" (*Wycombe D.C.* v. *Secretary of State* [1988] J.P.L. 111).

In general, the courts adopt a liberal approach in favour of the authority. For example, reasons do not have to be couched in precise lawyers' or statutory language. Nor are decision letters subjected to rigorous semantic or philosophical analysis. The test is one of "real and substantial doubt" and the standard that of the informed reader with knowledge of the factual and policy background. Indeed, expertise and "intelligence" in construing a decision letter is apparently required (see *Godden* v. *Secretary of State* [1988] J.P.L. 99, *London Residuary Body* v.*Secretary of State* [1988] J.P.L. 637 at 647).

The statement of reasons must set out the relevant policies, findings of fact, the matters that are regarded as important and the weight given to competing factors. It must be specifically stated

---

[22] See *Grenfell-Baines* v. *Secretary of State* [1985] J.P.L. 256. Compare *Westminster City Council* v. *Secretary of State* [1984] J.P.L. 27. See also *London Welsh Association* v. *Secretary of State* [1980] J.P.L. 745.

whether the decision is based on the application of a policy or is an exception to the policy (*Wycombe D.C.* v. *Secretary of State* (above)).[23] Value judgments or judgments based upon the Inspectors own expertise must be identified as such, but need not be supported by evidence. Conversely, finding of *fact* must be supported by evidence and reasons given for rejecting contrary views.[24] On the other hand, the statement of reasons can be selective and need not state every fact or every point raised at the inquiry. It is presumed in the absence of evidence to the contrary that all relevant matters have been taken into account, the standard being one of balance of probabilities.[25] For this purpose evidence can be brought as to the material that was before the inspector at the inquiry (*East Hampshire D.C.* v. *Secretary of State* [1978] J.P.L. 182.

In general then, the court will look broadly at the statement of reasons and will interfere only if a substantive defect is disclosed or if the actual basis of the decision is incomplete, misleading or unintelligible. The court may look at evidence outside the decision letter but will do so only in exceptional cases.[26] Complaints from Whitehall that an undue burden is being placed upon those who draft decision letters would not appear to be justifiable. On the other hand, the court has considerable discretion. This creates the risk that the court may be tempted to intrude into the merits of a planning decision. This risk has occasionally materialised (*e.g.*

---

[23] This may be difficult in borderline cases since the line between interpreting or departing from a policy may be a fine one. See, *e.g. Surrey Heath D.C.* v. *Secretary of State* (1987) 53 P. & C.R. 428. See also *Thornville Properties* v. *Secretary of State* [1981] J.P.L. 116; *Reading B.C.* v. *Secretary of State* (1986) 52 P. & C.R. 385; *Volvex Establishment* v. *Secretary of State* [1988] J.P.L. 400.

[24] *Sainsbury* v. *Secretary of State* [1978] J.P.L. 379; *French Kier Developments* v. *Secretary of State* [1977] 1 All E.R. 296 at 303–4. See also *Mason* v. *Secretary of State* [1984] J.P.L. 332; *Westminster Renslade* v. *Secretary of State* [1983] J.P.L. 454. Material errors of fact may also invalidate. *Hope* v. *Secretary of State* [1979] J.P.L. (see *Elmbridge* (below n. 26). (See further Richardson [1986] P.L. at 458 *et seq.*)

[25] *Bradley* v. *Secretary of State* [1983] J.P.L. 44; *Bell and Colville* v. *Secretary of State* [1980] J.P.L. 823; *Myton* v. *M.o.H.* (1963) 16 P. & C.R. 240; *Preston B.C.* v. *Secretary of State* [1978] J.P.L. 547; *Hatfield Construction Ltd.* v. *Secretary of State* [1983] J.P.L. 605 (but see comment at 606). Evidence which was not available to the decision maker at the time of the inquiry cannot be raised to challenge the inquiry's findings. *Glover* v. *Secretary of State* [1981] J.P.L. 110.

[26] *West Midlands Co-operative Society* v. *Secretary of State* [1988] J.P.L. 121 at 123–124 (but see above p. 50). *Chichester D.C.* v. *Secretary of State* [1981] J.P.L. 591; *Elmbridge D.C.* v. *Secretary of State* [1980] J.P.L. 463; *Mason* v. *Secretary of State* [1984] J.P.L. 332; *Preston B.C.* v. *Secretary of State* (above, n. 25). See also n. 21 above.

Niarchos v. *Secretary of State* (below, p. 134)) but in general, the courts adopt a sympathetic approach to the draftsman. In *London Residuary Body* v. *Secretary of State* [1988] J.P.L. 637 at 646 Simon Brown J. remarked that this ground of challenge "should be advanced sparingly, scrutinized critically and not readily acceded to."[27]

The grounds of review

The role of the courts in relation to development control decisions depends upon the ultra vires doctrine filled out by values created by the judges, who have a constitutional mandate to make up their own values within the framework of the statutory language. In the following chapters we shall examine the law of development control in the light of this. The terminology used to describe the grounds of judicial review is inconsistent and sometimes incoherent. It is not profitable to reduce the grounds of review to general formulae such as "procedural propriety or irrelevant considerations". On the other hand the various grounds of review overlap and run into each other so that any general scheme provides only a convenient descriptive framework. We shall adopt the following scheme.[28] The various grounds of review are common to all planning decisions, but are particularly important in the following chapters.

1. Express ultra vires in the sense of exceeding substantive statutory limits, *e.g.* granting or refusing planning permission in respect of conduct that is not capable of constituting development of land (Chap. 4).

2. Violating statutory procedural requirements or the procedural notions of fairness implied by the common law (Chaps. 5 and 10).

3. Failing to exercise a discretion by *a priori* fetters on the decision making power, notably in the case of reliance upon

---

[27] For general statements see *Givauden* v. *M.o.H.* [1967] 1 W.L.R. 250 at 278. *Vale Estates (Acton)* v. *Secretary of State* (1971) 69 L.G.R. 543 at 557; *Myton* v. *M.o.H.* (above n. 25) at 250; *Iveagh* v. *M.o.H.* [1964] 1 Q.B. 395 at 410 and, for examples, *Comben House (Midlands) Ltd.* v. *Secretary of State* [1985] J.P.L. 321; *Arlington Securities* v. *Secretary of State* [1985] J.P.L. 550; *Rogelan Ltd.* v. *Secretary of State* [1981] J.P.L. 507—unclear whether planning history and personal hardship considered. *Worthy Fuel Ltd.* v. *Secretary of State* [1983] J.P.L. 173—letter did not make clear whether one or two operations involved. *London Residuary Body* v. *Secretary of State* (above)—misleading formulation of policy. *French Kier* (above n. 24)—inconsistent reasons. See also Richardson [1986] P.L. at 462 *et seq.* and below, p. 140.

[28] Forbes J. in *Seddon Properties* v. *Secretary of State* [1981] 47 P. & C.R. 26 is often treated as a locus classicus. See *Beydell and Lewis*, [1989] J.P.L. 156.

departmental circulars or planning agreements (Chaps. 6 and 7).

4. Abuse of discretion by taking irrelevant factors into account or failing to take relevant factors into account or acting unreasonably (Chap. 6).

5. Errors of law (Chaps. 4 and 9).

4. Development

Introduction

"Development" has been described as a key word in the planners' vocabulary. This is because with some exceptions (see below, Chap. 5), planning controls can be exercised only in respect of activities which fall within the definition of development contained in section 22 of the Act.

The definition of development is of interest both for its intrinsic importance and as an example of judicial creativity within a statutory régime. The Act itself provides little by way of definition and the judges have been required not only to explain what development means but also to produce supplementary concepts of their own in order to enable the concept of development to be used effectively. A clutch of novel jurisprudential entities has been introduced into our land law, which may partly compensate those who regret the demise of such playthings as the legal contingent remainder, or the use upon a use.

On the other hand, the House of Lords has issued a warning against letting the process of supplementing the statutes go too far. In *Pioneer Aggregates (U.K.) Ltd.* v. *Secretary of State* [1985] A.C. 132 at 140, 141, Lord Scarman emphasised that where a field of law is governed by a comprehensive legislative code, as is the case with development control, it is an improper exercise of the judicial function to introduce private law concepts merely because they appear to achieve a fairer solution. Only where the code is incomplete or ambiguous may the courts resolve difficulties by applying common law or equitable principles. This applies in particular to notions such as abandonment of rights or estoppel (see *Newbury D.C.* v. *Secretary of State* [1981] A.C. 574). However, the statutory provisions relating to development are extremely broad and contain many gaps. Thus, despite Lord Scarman's strictures the courts have considerable room for manoeuvre. For example, the notion of abandoning a use, the planning unit concept, and the ancillary use are primarily judicial creations. Each can be justified on the basis that they are necessary to make sense of the statutory concept of development.

This does not mean that the courts have a free hand to determine what development means. While the meaning of a statutory term and its application to the facts of a particular case (essentially the same thing) are prima facie questions of law, this is not always the case. English law does not categorise all inferences from primary facts as questions of law. Where a statutory term is broad and vague and embodies notions found in everyday language, the courts tend to treat questions of application as primarily questions of fact, on the basis that lawyers are not especially qualified to determine this kind of issue and that reasonable people can disagree. The same applies where statute uses terminology peculiar to specialist disciplines other than law such as engineering or architecture. Conversely, questions that can only be determined by a trained lawyer are treated as questions of pure law.[1] It is settled that most questions concerning the definition of development are "questions of fact and degree," and are therefore primarily matters of discretion for the local authority (see, *e.g. Bendles Motors* v. *Bristol Corporation* [1963] 1 W.L.R. 242). The court will interfere only if the authority has misused its discretion by applying inappropriate criteria or acting totally without evidence.

The initial question of what category a particular statutory word falls into—*i.e.* is it a legal term of art or does it have a broader meaning—is, of course, one of pure law, but subject to that the court's function is to lay down general guidelines prescribing what factors the planning authority must take into account. The question for the court is not "is this development?" but "could the authority reasonably take the view that this is development?" Occasionally the court will adopt a stricter approach, for example in connection with the definitions of "owner" and "agriculture" in the Town and Country Planning Act 1971. The first is a term of legal art, the second is defined in some detail leaving little room for a broader approach (see below).

The central government frequently issues circulars offering its opinions on matters of statutory interpretation. These are not legally binding, but must be taken into account and, according to Lord Wilberforce in *Coleshill Investments* v. *M.o.H.* [1969] 1 W.L.R. 746 at 765, could acquire "solidity and strength" when they

---

[1] See *Edwards* v. *Bairstow* [1956] A.C. 14; *Brutus* v. *Cozens* [1973] A.C. 454; *Emery and Smythe* (1984) 100 L.Q.R. 612; *Peiris* (1987) 103 L.Q.R. 66 at 88; *Beatson* (1984) 4 O.J.L.S. 22.

are acted upon and become part of established practice (see below). As far as local authorities are concerned, governmental circulars indicate how a case is likely to be treated on appeal and are sometimes slavishly followed.

The court will normally confront the question whether a given activity is development only by way of review of a decision taken by the local planning authority or Secretary of State. Indeed the court is likely, as a matter of its inherent discretion, to reject an application for a declaration in the abstract, that a proposed activity is or is not development, even where enforcement proceedings are anticipated.[2] Questions involving development raise mixed questions of law, fact and indeed policy, so that judicial interference is justified only after the factual and policy issues are determined by the appropriate authority. The notion of judicial review as a last resort has been emphasised, perhaps because of judicial fears that the increasing demand for public law litigation is outrunning supply and also because of worries about the political role of the judiciary.[3]

In exceptional cases the court may have to confront the definition of development without a previous decision by the local planning authority. For example, under section 222 of the Local Government Act 1972 any local authority may institute legal proceedings in the interests of the inhabitants of its area. A local authority other than the local planning authority could use this power to seek an injunction restraining activities that it considers to be development. The injunction is a discretionary remedy and development without planning permission, although unlawful in the sense of contrary to statute, is not in itself an offence. An applicant for an injunction would therefore have to satisfy the court that the activities in question are overwhelmingly likely to be treated as development by the local planning authority and also that the statutory enforcement machinery is unlikely to provide an adequate remedy (see below, p. 183 and *Bedfordshire C.C.* v. *C.E.G.B.* [1985] J.P.L. 43).

Another example arises in connection with the termination of a business tenancy. Under section 30(1)(*g*) of the Landlord and Tenant Act 1954 a landlord may recover possession of a business tenancy if (*inter alia*) he intends to occupy the holding for his own business purposes. The landlord's intention must be genuine and capable of realisation within a reasonable time. Thus the issue may

[2] *Square Meals Frozen Foods* v. *Dunstable Corporation* [1974] 1 W.L.R. 59, 65, but see *R.* v. *Basildon D.C.* [1987] J.P.L. 863—construction of planning permission-enforcement notice not yet in existence. *Pyx Granite Co.* v. *M.o.H.* [1960] A.C. 260.

[3] See *Ferris* v. *Secretary of State* [1988] J.P.L. 777. (See further, p. 150).

depend upon whether the landlord's proposals constitute development requiring planning permission. The approach taken by the courts is to decide whether the

> "landlords have established a reasonable prospect... that planning permission is not required. This does not necessitate the determination by the court of any of the questions which may one day be submitted to the planning authority... "

(*per* Upjohn L.J. in *Gregson* v. *Cyril Lord Ltd.* [1963] 1 W.L.R. 41 at 48. See also *Westminster City Council* v. *British Waterways Board* [1984] 3 All E.R. 737, below, p. 72).

It is worth pointing out that the difficult question of whether an error of law is jurisdictional, thus making any resulting government action ultra vires and in theory void[4] does not seem to arise in the context of the definition of development. This is because an erroneous approach to the definition of development can invariably be exposed through statutory appeal or review machinery that undoubtedly embrace any error of law (above, pp. 48, 50). In any event planning decisions are administrative decisions and thus within the presumption created by Lord Diplock in *Re Racal Communications* [1981] A.C. 374 that all errors of law are jurisdictional.

The two limbs of development

Development is defined in section 22(1) as

> "the carrying out of building, engineering, mining, or other operations, in, on, over or under land" and "the making of any material change in the use of any buildings or other land."

The two parts of this formula must be kept separate because "operational," as we will henceforward call it, and "change of use" development sometimes have different legal consequences as do different kinds of operation or use. In particular there is a four-year time limit for issuing an enforcing notice in respect of operational development.

Section 22 goes on in subsections (2), (3) and (4) to give some special cases. Those in subsection (2) "shall not be taken... to involve development." Those in subsections (3) and (4) are declared to constitute development of particular kinds.

[4] *Anisminic* v. *Foreign Compensation* [1969] 2 A.C. 147; *Re Racal Communications* [1981] A.C. 374. See Aldous and Alder, *Applications for Judicial Review* (1985), Chap. 3.

The meaning of "operational" and "change of use" development will be considered in turn. The two parts of the definition are conceptually distinct. Operational development implies some physical alteration to the land, carried out by human beings. A material change of use can occur without any physical alteration to the land itself (*Parkes* v. *Secretary of State* [1978] 1 W.L.R. 1308). It does not follow that the two limbs are entirely separate. First, a fact situation could be dissected into separate operations and uses. For example, a change of use could involve the erection of buildings for the purpose of the use, in which case the commencement (or completion?) of the building operation could be evidence that the change of use occurred at the same time. Moreover, planning permission for a change of use does not automatically imply permission for any associated operations (*Wivenhoe Port* v. *Colchester B.C.* [1985] J.P.L. 396). (Compare section 33(2).)

A more difficult case is where the activities on the site are separate. For example, in *West Bowers Farm Products* v. *Secretary of State* [1985] J.P.L. 857 the landowner dug out a reservoir, this being development as an engineering operation. Large amounts of gravel were extracted which he sold off. It was held that the extraction must be regarded as a separate mining operation, thus requiring its own planning permission (with fee) and special procedural requirements peculiar to mining. The matter is one of fact and degree turning on the extent to which, *in terms of the effect on the character of the land, not the developers intention* the operation could be regarded as merely incidental to the main reservoir activity. Thus Nolan L.J. said (at 860) "The planning legislation is not impressed by the indivisibility of single processes, it cares also for their effects."

West Bowers concerned two kinds of operational development rather than the distinction between operational and change of use development but the same principle seems to apply. In *R.* v. *Surrey County Council* [1986] J.P.L. 828 the applicant had the benefit of a planning permission for quarrying operations granted in 1952. A condition authorised infilling subject to the approval of materials by the local planning authority. The applicant wished to tip commercial and industrial waste into the quarry. In an application for judicial review by a neighbouring landowner McNeil J. held that the local planning authority was entitled to treat the infilling activity as one within the scope of the previous operational permission. In this kind of case the distinction may be crucial because of the risks of dispoiling the countryside with what are effectively refuse tips (see below p. 89).

A similar principle applies where a single activity has to be classified either as an operation or a use. It cannot be both simultaneously. Thus in *Northavon D.C.* v. *Secretary of State* [1980] 40 P. & C.R. 32 the appellant drained his agricultural land by removing topsoil and replacing it by filling materials, including old builders rubble. If this was an operation it could be immune from control by virtue of the General Development Order 1988. However, if it were a use it would require planning permission as "tipping," an activity which is expressly designated as a use (see *Bilboe* v. *Secretary of State* (1980) 39 P.& C.R. 495). It was held that the proper test is that of the primary purpose of the landowner. Was this to provide a "last resting place for rubble" or merely to raise the level of the land for agricultural purposes? The trouble with this approach is that it imports a subjective element, which in planning cases the courts frequently disavow (below, p. 71). It is suggested, however, that the "objective" notion of "reasonableness" must be invoked here in two senses: (i) the matter is for the reasonable discretion of the local planning authority; (ii) they should apply a reasonableness test by looking at whether the treatment given to the land is a proper method of serving agricultural purposes. It is well established that, provided an act can be justified by reference to proper considerations, it matters not that some ulterior aim or desire—here getting rid of refuse—is incidentally achieved.

Another consequence of the distinction between different kinds of development is that it is difficult to identify any single conceptual or policy notion that underpins the concept of development. In *Coleshill Investments* v. *Secretary of State* [1969] 1 W.L.R. 746, Lord Wilberforce remarked (at 763) that "the Act appears to be drafted empirically rather than logically." That case concerned operational development and their Lordships were unable to find any core meaning capable of underlying the language of section 22. It was held that rather than look for a general notion of development, the facts should be examined on the basis of the particular categories singled out in the Act. However, it is arguable that the concept of development is geared primarily to what we described in Chap. 1 as the main policy behind the planning legislation, that is growth limitation. Development of both kinds embodies the notion of "change" in a physical sense and probably also only positive change. For example, the abandonment of a use is not development nor probably is the demolition of a building. Agricultural use is expressly excluded from the definition of development, because in 1947, when modern intensive farming methods were unforeseen, the notion of agriculture was associated with the status quo and the traditional ways of life idealised by Ebenezer Howard and the powerful lobbies that adopted his ideas.

"Building, engineering, mining or other operations"

As we have seen, this formula suffers from the lack of any common genus linking the three specified kinds of operation. Thus it was held in *Coleshill and District Investment Co.* v. *Minister of Housing* [1969] 1 W.L.R. 746 that the *ejusdem generis* principle cannot be used to identify "other operations," although the looser *noscitur a sociis* principle could be invoked. Thus "other operations" are activities similar to any of the specified three where the ingenuity of the local planning authority cannot quite stretch the terms to meet the facts.

"Operation" refers to a human activity which physically "changes the character of the land" (*Cheshire C.C.* v. *Woodward* [1962] 2 Q.B. 126; *Parkes* v. *Secretary of State for the Environment and the Peak Park Planning Board* [1979] 1 All E.R. 211). Thus the "mischief" to which the provision is directed is the creation of environmental blemishes.

Coleshill and District Investment Co. v. *Minister of Housing* is the leading decision on operational development, but unfortunately the House of Lords refused to lay down precise guidelines. Three notions were canvassed; first, "change," which was regarded as too weak to be helpful, and secondly, "positive construction," which elicited the most favourable response. This supports the government's opinion that demolition of a building as such is not development (Circular 49/67). The third notion—that development is "what a developer does"—was rejected for obvious reasons. Such a formula would, however, have the advantage of excluding from the ambit of planning control many small activities carried on by a private householder, interference with which lays a planning authority open to accusations on the theme of petty bureaucracy.

BUILDING OPERATIONS

The interpretation section (290(1)) provides that "building" includes "any structure or erection and any part of a building as so defined, but does not include plant or machinery comprised in a building." This is very wide. Any artificial object is a building as long as it is a "structure or erection." Size is immaterial if the object in question is a building for other reasons (*Buckingham C.C.* v. *Callingham* [1952] 2 Q.B. 515). It is tempting to apply the common law rules relating to fixtures and there is authority supporting this approach (*Cheshire C.C.* v. *Woodward* (above)). However, it is difficult to relate such an approach to the policy of planning legislation. Thus if a class of art students place a large, garishly-painted statue in front of their college premises this would not be a fixture (*Leigh* v. *Taylor* [1902] A.C. 157), but it is certainly something that a planning authority ought to control. The notion of fixture is relevant but not conclusive. Thus anything which is a fixture for the purposes of the law of real property as being physically attached to the land and intended to be enjoyed as a permanent feature of the land would also be a "building" for planning purposes. (Hoarding, radio masts and flagpoles are all capable of being buildings, but not purely temporary structures which can be removed without dismantling: see *James* v. *Brecon C.C.* (1963) 15 P. & C.R. 20).

Where the object is not a fixture, as for example in the case of a mobile crane or a caravan, the correct approach is to determine the function fulfilled by the object and the extent to which it impinges on its surroundings (*Barvis* v. *Secretary of State* (1971) 22 P. & C.R. 710; see also *Cardiff Rating Authority* v. *Guest Keen Baldwin's Iron and Steel Co. Ltd.* [1949] 1 K.B. 385. Thus size, mobility and degree of permanence are the relevant factors.

This test can be applied to the question whether parking a caravan constitutes development. This is usually treated, at least when the caravan is on wheels as a material change of use (see *Wealdon D.C.* v. *Secretary of State* [1988] J.P.L. 268). It is therefore not development for the owner of a dwelling-house to park his holiday caravan in his garden. On this view the parking of a caravan within the curtilage of a dwelling-house will, as a material change of use, only be development if it is used for a different purpose to that of the house itself. It will therefore be immune from control if used to provide extra accommodation in connection with the house. This is somewhat unreal, since the effect on the neighbourhood is the same in both cases and it is difficult to make a significant planning distinction between constructing a wooden extension to a house and placing a caravan in the garden. Difficulties also arise under a change of use analysis where additional caravans are brought on to an exercising caravan site. It is only exceptionally that an increase in the same activity will constitute development (see below, p. 77). These problems can be avoided by treating the parking of a caravan except on a purely transient basis as a building operation. Indeed for rating purposes a caravan is sometimes treated together with the land itself as one unit of occupation, the degree of permanence being the test (see *Field Place Caravan Park Ltd.* v. *Harding* [1966] 2 Q.B. 484).[5]

Returning to the meaning of "operation," it is clear that placing a building on land constitutes development, and it is provided that "building operation" includes alterations to and renovation of a building as well as "other operations normally undertaken by a person carrying on business as a builder" (section 290(1)). It is difficult to envisage anything done to a building that could not be described as putting it up, altering it or taking it down. It may be that the phrase is intended to catch preparatory activities such as levelling a site, but these can anyway be regarded as engineering operations. There must be a physical alteration to the building. Thus in *Kensington and Chelsea L.B.C.* v. *Secretary of State* [1981] J.P.L. 190 it was held that the nocturnal floodlighting of a historic building could not in itself constitute a building operation despite the impact on the appearance of the neighbourhood. This illustrates a possible weakness in the concept of development in that it does not concern impact as such. However painting the exterior of a building is development. (*Royal Borough of Windsor and Maidenhead* v. *Secretary of State* [1988] J.P.L. 410; see G.D.O. 1988 Sched. 2, Part 2.)

One important exception should be noticed. Under section 22(2)(a) "works for the maintenance improvement or other alteration of any building" are not development providing that they affect only the interior of the building or do not affect its external appearance. It is a question of degree for the planning authority whether a particular activity is merely an alteration, as opposed to a rebuilding which requires permission, even where the replacement is to the same specifications as the original (*Street* v. *Essex C.C.* (1965) 193 E.B. 537). Thus where a house is burned down any subsequent rebuilding will require planning permission. The building as a whole must be looked at rather than its separate parts so that "staged" rebuilding will not attract the benefit of the exception, nor of the general permission in the G.D.O. 1988 for certain alterations and improvements to a dwelling house (Sched. 2, Part I). Moreover, to see whether there has been any change in external appearance the end product must be compared with the appearance of the building immediately before the relevant operations began. Thus the restorer of a derelict country cottage cannot claim the benefit of the exception (see *Hewlett* v. *Secretary of State* [1981] J.P.L. 187).

---

[5] There are special controls over caravan sites in addition to ordinary planning controls: *Caravan Sites* v. *Control of Development Act* 1980; *Mixnams Properties* v. *Chertsey U.D.C.* [1985] A.C. 735.

The most notorious query in the definition of development and an examination question chestnut, is whether demolition constitutes development. The conventional wisdom is that it does not.

In *Coleshill and District Investment Co.* v. *Minister of Housing* [1969] 1 W.L.R. 746 the House of Lords held that the demolition of earthworks surrounding a disused ammunition dump was development. This was on the basis, alternatively, that the large-scale shifting of materials constituted an engineering operation, or that, treating the whole complex as a single entity, this was an external alteration to a building.

Their Lordships were not prepared to say whether demolition *per se* could be development. They took the view that the issue so formulated was too wide. Demolition is not *per se* excluded, but will be development only if it falls within some more specific category, for example, the demolition of part only of a building can be an alteration. The correct approach was to examine the facts of each case to see whether they fitted the language of section 22. Their Lordships did, however, incline towards the view that development implies a positive act, not something destructive. Given that one function of the highest appellate tribunal is to clarify points of principle, was not this approach excessively cautious? It is difficult to see how demolition can be thought of as equivalent in vagueness to terms like modernisation.

There are also dicta from the Court of Appeal that demolition is not development (*Iddenden* v. *Secretary of State* [1972] 1 W.L.R. 1433; *Howell* v. *Sunbury-on-Thames U.D.C.* (1963) 15 P. & C.R. 26; see also *L.C.C.* v. *Marks and Spencer Ltd.* [1953] A.C. 535).

The arguments in support of this are unconvincing. There is nothing in the notion of a building operation to restrict its natural meaning to positive acts. If partial demolition is development is there any reason to treat total demolition differently? It is true that in material change of use cases the cessation of a use is not development unless replaced by another use (see below, pp. 78). To hold otherwise would raise enforcement problems, since a person cannot be forced to carry on a use. This does not apply to demolition. Restoration of a building can reasonably be required by an enforcement notice, bearing in mind that a planning authority may be able to 'under enforce' by requiring less than full restoration (see below, p. 192). It is sometimes suggested that the specific prohibitions in sections 54–58 against the demolition of buildings listed as of special historic or architectural interest show that demolition generally is not to be controlled. This is fallacious. The controls over listed buildings equally prohibit external alterations to them, which do constitute development. It is moreover a criminal offence *per se* to demolish a listed building (section 55(1)). This is not the case with ordinary development. The listed building controls are thus more stringent supplements to the general law and have no necessary connection with the concept of development. Finally, demolition raises significant environmental problems. In the absence of necessary statutory implication and binding authority it is therefore suggested that demolition should always be regarded as development. Fears of undue infringement by the planners upon individual freedom can be allayed by granting permission under a general development order for harmless activities such as the demolition of domestic outbuildings.

It is relevant to note that for the purpose of the Factories Act 1961 "building operation" expressly includes the demolition of a building. The clear and comprehensive definition of building operation contained in section 76(1) of that Act could with advantage be adopted by the draftsmen of the planning legislation.

ENGINEERING OPERATIONS

Because of the wide meaning of "building" many activities normally regarded as engineering operations could equally be treated as building operations, for example, the construction of bridges. Engineering is a heterogeneous term, but its meaning must be limited by the context ("in, on, over or under land"), to what is known as civil engineering—activities which involve physical alteration to the land itself. The removal of the earthworks in the *Coleshill* case was treated as an engineering operation, as could be the infilling of a pit, the making of a swimming pool, and the laying out of a golf course (see also section 290(1)—formation and laying out of means of access to the highway).

MINING OPERATIONS

Mining operations are also undefined, but the interpretation section (section 290(1)) gives the word "mineral" a sufficiently wide meaning ("... all substances ... of a kind ordinarily worked for removal by underground or surface working, except peat cut for purposes other than sale") to permit the removal of any substance from the land to be treated as a mining operation with the probable limitation that "substance" excludes living things. Digging up a tree is not therefore a mining operation, and the Act provides special controls in respect of trees (sections 59–60). Mining also includes removing of material from spoil heaps and the extraction of minerals from disused railway embankments (section 22(3A).

There are special controls applicable to mining operations and in several planning contexts mining operations are treated as a special case.[6] Moreover, contrary to general principle a mining operation is occasionally treated as a use of land (*e.g.* section 51(1A)— Discontinuance Order).

An operation is a physical act. In the case of mining operations it has been held in *Thomas David (Porthcawl)* v. *Penybont R.D.C.* [1972] 1 W.L.R. 1526 that each "bite" of the shovel constitutes a separate operation for the purposes of the "four-year rule" under which an enforcement notice must be served within four years of the commencement of the operation in question. This analysis does not, however, apply to a building operation such as the construction of a house, where each individual act has meaning only as a contribution to a single end product. In *Copeland B.C.* v. *Secretary of State for the Environment* (1976) 21 P. & C.R. 403 planning permission was granted for the building of a house. An enforcement notice subsequently treated the failure to construct the roof according to specifications as a separate act of development. It was held that this was a breach of planning control in respect of the whole house, which was a single operation and the notice was therefore invalid. Lord Widgery C.J. pointed out that to divide the various acts involved in house-building into separate operations would lay open the way to all manner of eccentric omissions by builders. Similarly, building in excess of permitted height or bulk limits renders the whole development unlawful.

Material change of use

This aspect of development has given rise to much litigation. The central problem is to establish when a change of use becomes "material." Any variation in the activities carried out on land is a change in the use of that land. Not all such variations will be material and require planning permission. The word "material" has in the present context three meanings. First, "physical," as opposed to mental. A subjective change in the purposes of an occupier will not in itself normally constitute development. Thus where car repairs previously carried out as a hobby are continued on a commercial basis, this will not be development without a physical change, such as a marked increase in the level of activity (*Peake* v.

---

[6] Town and Country Planning (Minerals) Regulations (S.I. 1971 No. 756); Town and Country Planning (Minerals) Act 1981. G.D.O. 1988 Sched. 2, Parts 19–24. See Grant, pp. 487–748. 1971 Act, ss.30A, 51A–F.

Secretary of State for Wales (1971) 22 P. & C.R. 889). The mental element is not, however, always irrelevant (see below, p. 78).

Secondly, "material" means substantial. Trivial changes of use are ignored for planning purposes.

Thirdly, "material" means relevant. This is crucial. There is ample authority that a change of use is material only if it is the sort of change that raises considerations relevant to the purposes of planning legislation, for example whether it might affect the amenities of the neighbourhood or place an additional burden upon public services. The activities carried out on the land must be looked at and compared from the point of view of planning policy with what was happening before the change. The identity of the occupier is normally but not always irrelevant, as is the source of supply of articles used on the site and the destination of articles that leave the site. In *Westminster City Council* v. *British Waterways Board* [1985] A.C. 676 the local planning authority described a use as "local authority street cleansing depot." The use consisted of the storage and maintenance of vehicles and other equipment which left the depot each day to cleanse the city streets. The authority argued that if the appellants who were their lessors sought to recover possession under the Landlord and Tenant Act 1954 they would not be able to change to any other use without planning permission. The House of Lords rejected this argument. The descriptions of the use provided by the authority bore no relation to planning issues. The identity of the occupier authority did not matter, nor did the destination of the vehicles once they left the depot. The nature of the activities on the site itself is the primary consideration. Thus the street cleansing element was irrelevant. The proper description was "storage" and within that general description the landlords would be able to carry out a variety of beneficial activities (see also *London Residuary Body* v. *Secretary of State* [1988] J.P.L. 637).

The basic problem with this approach is that there is no consensus as to what are the purposes of planning.

Two preliminary points must be made. First, a material change of use does not take place merely because an activity is carried on in such a way as to cause harm to the amenities of the area (*e.g. Wealdon D.C.* v. *Secretary of State* [1988] J.P.L. 268). In other words before the question of materiality arises there must be an identifiable change. Secondly, the act of development is the *change* and not the use itself. This has crucial implications for an understanding of several problems (see, *e.g.* below, p. 79). Thus a change from use A to X to B could be development even if a change from A to B directly would not be development (see *Waverley D.C.* v. *Secretary of State* [1982] J.P.L. 105). Similarly, if planning permission is granted for a change from use A to uses B or C, a change from B to C would be unlawful. The permission is spent after the change from A to B. (See G.D.O. 1988, Sched. 2, Pt. 3, Class E.)

THE NATURE OF A USE

Attempts have been made to provide general formulae in order to explain what is a material change of use. For example, the phrase "changing the character of the land" is often used. This seems to mean no more than that the change must be substantial. Another common formulation is that the "particular purposes" of the occupier are irrelevant, but it is difficult to understand what this means unless it relates to the occupiers subjective intention. If the occupiers "particular purpose" raises planning considerations there seems to be no reason why it should not be relevant. Indeed, even subjective intention may be relevant (*e.g.* ancillary use cases, below, p. 81).

Sometimes a distinction is made between a change in "kind" and a change in "degree," the former being said always to involve development (see Circular 67/49). The concept of a change in "kind" appears to mean only that a different label can be attached as a matter of language to the new activity. It is doubtful, however, whether the subtle nuances of the English tongue bear any necessary relationship to distinctions relevant to a planner. There is a world of social distinction between "Tea Room" and "Snack Bar," but it is unlikely that a change in nomenclature made in order to attract a classier clientèle would justify the intervention of a planning authority. Changes in "kind" are moreover relative, since the classification of "kinds" varies with the point of view of the classifier. Thus a newsagent and a pornographic bookshop are both shops of the same kind to the person searching for a chemist, whereas a policeman would classify the facts differently. The identification of a change in "kind" is therefore merely a way of stating a conclusion that a given change is relevant from the point of view of planning policy. The "labelling" approach may be persuasive but it cannot be conclusive.

Perhaps the most common approach, but again not conclusive, is through the classical *per genus et speciem* principle. Broad categories of "use" are identified—residential, commercial, industrial, recreational, etc. and these are subdivided into more detailed categories—shops, light industrial, office, cinema and so on. However, the Act does not state as to how far this process should be taken before a change becomes too slight to be "material." A fundamental problem in change of use cases is to establish the *level of generality* at which the facts should be described. The process of subdivision can be extended indefinitely. Indeed, this approach seems to be no more than a variation of the "labelling" approach and thus is question begging.[7]

Any human activity can in theory be called a "use" of land. For example, it is likely that a private hotel which introduces a public discothèque commits a material change of use, but if topless dancers are subsequently introduced, can the planning authority by calling this a "use" of land, validly claim that planning permission is required? In *East Barnet U.D.C.* v. *British Transport Commission* [1962] 2 Q.B. 484, where a yard previously used for the storage of coal to be transported by rail was held not to undergo development when it became used for the storage of crated cars, also to be transported by rail. The reason was that the local authority could not show that the particular change had in itself any planning implications. (Compare *Lilo Blum* v. *Secretary of State* [1987] J.P.L. 278—livery stables to riding school held to be development because of local impact).

Other cases show the danger of relying on the *genus et speciem* approach. In *Birmingham Corporation* v. *Habib Ullah* [1964] 1 Q.B. 178, the Minister, in dealing with a case involving an increase in the number of families occupying a dwelling-house, thought that because the premises remained "residential" there could be no material change of use. It was held that the facts could be examined in detail and that development may occur if for example a dwelling-house became a house "let in lodgings." Such a distinction may raise planning issues and is therefore "material." In *Blackpool Borough Council* [1980] 40 P. & C.R. 104 an owner of a house in a select residential area let it out to family and friends, and occasionally on a commercial basis for family holidays. The Court upheld the Inspectors decision that this was not development. The fact that the arrangement could still be regarded as "residential" was not decisive, but the Inspector was right to have gone beyond that. She had considered the precise nature of the lettings and

---

[7] Labelling is often used in residential cases with confusing and inconsistent results unless it is remembered that the label is merely a matter of convenience. See, *e.g. Mayflower (Cambridge)* v. *Secretary of State* (1975) 30 P. & C.R. 28—bedsits to hotel. *Duffy* v. *Pilling* (1977) 33 P. & C.R. 85—multiple paying occupation. See also *Clarke* v. *M.H.L.G.* (1966) 18 P. & C.R. 82; *Mornford Investments* v. *M.H.L.G.* [1970] 2 All E.R. 253; *Hammersmith L.B.C.* v. *Secretary of State* (1975) 73 L.G.R. 288; *Lipson* v. *Secretary of State* (1976) 33 P. & C.R. 95. (See now Use Classes Order 1987, below, p. 87).

Labelling is important in construing a planning permission and other documents including in particular the Use Classes Order and General Development Order. Also in relation to enforcement notices. Chap. 9.

concluded that these were not casual holiday lodgings but restricted to families, and as such compatible with the existing character of the neighbourhood as stable and domestic as opposed to the "seaside landlady" ambience of other parts of Blackpool.

It is instructive to compare the facts of *Marshall* v. *Nottingham Corporation* [1960] 1 W.L.R. 707 with those of *Williams* v. *Minister of Housing* (1967) 18 P. & C.R. 514. In the former case land previously used both for the manufacture and sale of garden huts and other equipment became used for the sale of caravans and garden equipment not manufactured on the premises. This was held not to be a material change because the broad category of activity remained the same. In *Williams* the land was used as a market garden and a hut on the site was used for the retail sale of produce from the garden. It was held that where imported oranges were sold from the hut (amounting to about 10 per cent. of the business) a material change of use took place. *Williams* has been criticised (see Palk (1973) 37 Conv.(N.S.) at pp. 185–186), but it is consistent with *Marshall*. There is a difference from the point of view of planning policy between a landowner selling the produce of his own land and retail sales generally, because the encouragement of local horticulture is a legitimate concern of a planner. The introduction of sales from outside could be the thin end of an unwanted wedge. In the case of the sale of garden huts it was of no concern to the planner that these were not manufactured on the site (compare *Bromley (London Borough of)* v. *Haeltschi* [1978] J.P.L. 45, *Snooks* v. *Secretary of State* [1977] 33 P. & C.R. 1). Thus facts can be analysed in any degree of detail to discover considerations relevant to planning policy.

This approach invites local planning authorities to make value judgments about the social quality of a neighbourhood and indeed to apply prejudices about conventional life styles and family arrangements. For example, in *Guildford R.D.C.* v. *Penny* [1954] 2 Q.B. 112 Lord Evershed M.R. gave as an example of a material change of use, a hypothetical case where the Oval Cricket Ground was used "so as to provide . . . a great number of pitches on which boys or others could play cricket during the summer." . . . "It would be a cricket ground materially changed: it would no longer be a first class cricket ground but would be a cricket ground of a different kind." Admittedly in the Blackpool case the Inspector took into account such "environmental" matters as traffic disturbance and the upkeep of gardens, but there is a thin line between this and more general social judgments. For example, in *Panyani* v. *Secretary of State* (1985) 50 P. & C.R. 109 it was held that the use of self-contained flats to provide temporary accommodation for the homeless could be development. The label "hostel" was used by the inspector but this in itself was not decisive. Similarly in *Williamson* v. *Stevens* (1977) 34 P. & C.R. 117 it was held that a change from a gipsy caravan site to a site for general caravans could be development.

It is interesting to compare these cases with the debate in the U.S.A. concerning the practise of "exclusionary zoning" whereby local authorities seek to exclude from residential neighbourhoods people perceived as undesirables—for example, gypsies, hippies and those with unconventional life styles.

The U.S. Supreme Court has held that unorthodox life styles—in particular, communes—can be excluded in favour of upholding "family values, youth values, and the blessings of quiet seclusion and clean air."[8] The English cases could be regarded as embodying a similar set of values. On the other hand, in relation to low income families several State Supreme Courts in the U.S.A. have taken a remarkably radical approach, holding that a community has a positive obligation to accept its "fair share" of low income residents and must plan accordingly.[9]

As we have seen, the identity of the occupier is not normally relevant. In certain cases, however, identity is relevant.

In *Wilson* v. *West Sussex C.C.* [1963] 2 Q.B. 764 the Court of Appeal held that the phrase "agricultural cottage" denoted a cottage intended to be inhabited by agricultural workers. Danckwerts and Diplock L.JJ. took the view that if the cottage became occupied by non-agricultural workers a material change in the use of the land would take place. The rationale of this is similar to that in *Williams* (above). The preservation of agricultural land unpolluted by urban influences is a legitimate aspect of planning policy, as is the need for agricultural workers to live near their work (*cf. East Suffolk C.C.* v. *Secretary of State* (1972) 70 L.G.R. 595 and 1987 J.P.L. 232). It could also be argued that the occupation of a dwelling by people who do not work locally is development. This may be important in relation to the purchase of country cottages as holiday or second homes. (See also below, p. 131). Similarly a change from ordinary residential accommodation to sheltered accommodation for the elderly is development.

There is therefore considerable flexibility within the concept of material change of use. It is, for example, sometimes thought that

---

[8] *Village of Belle Terre* v. *Boraas* 496 U.S. 1 (1974) *Moore* v. *City of East Cleveland* 431 U.S. 494 (1977).

[9] See *Southern Burlington County N.A.A.C.P.* v. *Township of Mount Laurel* 336 A 2d 713 (1975). Ellickson and Tarlock, *Land-Use Controls, Cases and Materials* (1981), Chap. 8.

the planning authority cannot intervene where there is a modification of an industrial process so that it becomes more hazardous unless "operations" are involved in the modification or a change in the end product. This is fallacious. Safety is certainly a legitimate planning consideration (*Hidderley* v. *Warwickshire C.C.* (1963) 61 L.G.R. 266; *Stringer* v. *Minister of Housing* [1970] 1 W.L.R. 1281). Thus a change which takes the form of burning a new fuel could be held to be material. Indeed, in *Gray* v. *Oxfordshire County Council* (1963) 15 P. & C.R. 1 the Divisional Court thought that it was not possible to separate the notion of "kind" of activity from the methods of which that activity is carried out.

Intensification. Once it is accepted that changes in the character of the land which raise questions of planning policy are "material" then cases concerning the doctrine of "intensification" raise no particular difficulty. There are numerous authorities, albeit mostly in the form of *obiter dicta* in favour of the proposition that a marked increase in the same activity can constitute development. The intensification cases *could* provide an example, first, of the notion of growth containment as a basic planning concept and secondly, of an "impact" approach to planning that treats matters of density as sufficient to attract planning controls. In *de Mulder* v. *Secretary of State* [1974] D.B. 792 the court took the view that whatever the objections to the principle the authorities are now too strong to be overcome. In the *Guildford* case, (above), it was held that intensification could amount to development if it introduced new planning problems to the land. Thus safety, and the need for additional services, were relevant in deciding whether an increase in the number of caravans on a caravan site would constitute development. It also seems to follow that something might be lawfully held to be development in one locality but not in another.

However there are few cases where intensification was held on the facts to constitute development (see *Peake* v. *Secretary of State for Wales* (1971) 22 P. & C.R. 889; *Chrysanthou* v. *Secretary of State* [1976] J.P.L. 371; *Brooks & Burton Ltd.* v. *Secretary of State* [1977] 1 W.L.R. 1294.

The intensification doctrine is often criticised because of its uncertainty. For example in *Royal Borough of Kensington & Chelsea* v. *Secretary of State* [1981] J.P.L. 50, Donaldson L.J. emphasised the desirability of a "label" to describe the change of use and doubted whether intensification is development unless the change could be labelled. See also *Lilo Blum* v. *Secretary of State* [1987] J.P.L. 278. The intensification cases therefore reveal an incoherence in the concept of development which permits sharply different policies to be adopted.

DISCONTINUANCE OF A USE

Development involves a "change" of use. We must therefore consider how a use might come to an end. There are two distinct concepts: (i) abandonment; (ii) displacement.

Abandonment. It is settled that a use can be abandoned. Thus, in *Hartley* v. *Minister of Housing* [1970] 1 Q.B. 413 a site had a dual use with planning permission as a petrol filling station and for car sales. Owing to ill health the occupier ceased the car sales side of the business. Five years later car sales were resumed by a subsequent occupier. It was held that this resumption was a material change in the use of the land. The Court of Appeal laid down some important propositions. First, cessation of a use is not in itself development. Secondly, if a use has been abandoned then it ceases to exist. Thirdly, the resumption of an abandoned use constitutes a material change of use. Enforcement problems explain why the logically identical situation of a change from a positive to a nil use is not development.[10] Finally, abandonment is irrelevant where a use is *replaced* by another one. The previous use is automatically extinguished (below, p. 79). Abandonment applies only where the land is disused for a time immediately after the cessation of the use in question.

Where, however, land is disused but its previous use is not abandoned, then the previous use remains effective and its resumption does not require planning permission. The Court of Appeal held that abandonment is a question of fact and that evidence of intention is crucial. Two elements are required, a factual cessation of activity and the absence of an intention to resume at any specific time. Thus, if in *Hartley* the previous occupier had shown an intention to recommence the selling of cars when her husband's health improved, the use might have been preserved.

The court saw the matter in terms of a presumption in favour of abandonment which grows in strength proportionately to the length of time the land is disused. A positive intention not to resume will however constitute abandonment but only if it is unequivocal. Thus receiving, but not implementing, a planning permission for another

---

[10] The resumption of an earlier lawful use following a temporary use authorised by a planning permission does not need planning permission, s.23(3) (below, p. 201).

use, or offering the premises for sale, would not suffice. Other factors such as the state of repair of the premises are also relevant. Thus a neglected unoccupied dwelling house may not only cease to be a dwelling house capable of falling within the General Development Orders permission for alteration or improvements, but will also lose its existing use rights (see *Trustees of Castell-Y-Mynach* v. *Secretary of State* [1984] J.P.L. 40.[11]

It is sometimes said that because a planning permission as such cannot be abandoned (below, p. 172) a use cannot be abandoned if it has the benefit of a planning permission. This is not so. The law regarding abandonment is the same whether or not the use in question has the benefit of planning permission. The law about the abandonment of planning permission and the related point that a planning permission runs with the land concerns only permissions that have not been fully implemented (*Ibid.*). In the case of a use the act of development for which planning permission is required is a *change* between uses and not the use itself. Thus, once a change is made any planning permission is spent, but remains important as a record of whether that change was lawful. Whether the *use* that arises as a result of that change is later abandoned is a separate question. In *Pioneer Aggregates* v. *Secretary of State* [1985] A.C. 132 the House of Lords dealing with a planning permission for mining operations held that a planning permission as such cannot be abandoned but also that this had nothing to do with the abandonment of a use.

It also follows that changes from use A to use B to use A are nothing to do with abandonment, which applies only in the case of a change from a use to nothing (see *Young* v. *Secretary of State* (1983) 81 L.G.R. 389 at 397). Even if use B was purely temporary, a change of use has taken place so that a fresh planning permission is required (*Cynon Valley D.C.* v. *Secretary of State* [1987] J.P.L. 760). It is particulary important to emphasise that the concept here is one of change, not of abandonment, so that any intention to keep the earlier use alive is irrelevant (see *Grillo* v. *Minister of Housing Local Government* (1968) 208 E.G. 1201; *Postill* v. *East Riding C.C.* [1956] 2 Q.B. 386).

There is one special case. It was held by the Court of Appeal in *Webber* v. *Minister of Housing* [1968] 1 W.L.R. 29 that where there is a regular cycle of activities on a site viewed over a substantial period of time, as in the case of a seasonal alteration between agricultural and camping uses, then each use can be regarded as an

---

[11] See also *Balco* v. *Secretary of State* [1982] J.P.L. 177; *Maddern* v. *Secretary of State* 1980 J.P.L. 676; *Nichols* v. *Secretary of State* [1981] J.P.L. 890.

existing use of the land. Thus the cyclical alteration between them would not constitute development. It is as if they co-existed simultaneously. It is perhaps difficult to reconcile this reasoning with the basic statutory premise that what is forbidden is a *change* in a use and not a use in itself, but the practical advantage of the *Webber* principle is obvious.

Displacement Irrespective of the notion of abandonment a use can in certain circumstances be lost where a major physical upheaval takes place on the land which *as a question of fact* can reasonably be regarded as "creating a new planning unit" or "opening" a new chapter in the planning history of the site (*Jennings Motors* v. *Secretary of State* [1982] 1 All E.R. 471). If this happens existing use rights are lost. Indeed, at one time it was believed that the erection of a building on a site automatically wiped out even existing rights outside the new building. The position now seems to be that a new building covering substantially the *whole* site may have this effect, but it is unlikely that the addition of a small building would affect uses outside the building, provided that it is not inconsistent with them (*South Staffordshire D.C.* v. *Secretary of State* [1987] J.P.L. 635). Similarly, where a new building is erected on part of a site its use, unless a planning permission states otherwise, will be that of the site as a whole (*Hilliard* v. *Secretary of State* [1978] J.P.L. 840).

The "planning history" doctrine is therefore a principle of displacement by an inconsistant act. A. Oliver L.J. pointed out in *Jennings Motors* (above at 478) it is irrelevant whether the new act has planning permission unless the terms of the permission create the inconsistency (see below pp. 173–174).

It will not be easy to establish that a new chapter in the history of the site has occurred. It has been suggested that subdividing land terminates existing uses, leaving each new unit with a nil use. This idea has serious implications for the modern practise of letting retail or office developments on the basis of subdivided units. It seems, however, that this would be the case only if the change creates inconsistency with the existing use or counts as development in its own right. For example, in *Wakelin* v. *Secretary of State* [1978] J.P.L. 769, a lodge originally occupied as servants quarters in connection with a large dwelling house on the same site, was sold for the purpose of ordinary housing. This was held to constitute development, not because of the sub-division as such but because of section 22(3)(*a*) (below, p. 89) and because the existing use was that of a large individual household. This kind of subdivision has a clear impact on the character of a neighbourhood. By contrast in *Winton* v. *Secretary of*

State [1982] 46 P. & C.R. 205 a building was originally used for breeze block manufacturing. Following its subdivision each part was separately occupied, one part being used for sheet metal working, the other for converting cars to right hand drive. It was held that the Secretary of State was wrong to conclude that development had automatically occurred. The new uses must in each case be compared with the previous breeze block making use.

The "new chapter" doctrine is therefore not the same as the "planning unit" in its geographical sense (below, p. 84). It would be preferable to use different terminology to elicit different concepts.

MULTIPLE USES

We have discussed the general nature of a material change in the use of land. The courts have developed special principles to deal with the situation where more than one use exists on a site.

Ancillary uses. There may be one or more main uses together with other related uses which are subordinate and incidental to a main use. These subordinate uses are called "ancillary." They are not recognised as uses in their own right but will in law partake of whatever is their "parent" use. In *Trentham* v. *Gloucestershire C.C.* [1966] 1 W.L.R. 506, where a building on a farm was used for the storage of agricultural equipment, the use of the whole site was held to be agricultural with no "storage" element. The Court of Appeal held that when the building became used for the storage of builders' materials a material change of use had taken place from "agricultural" to "storage." A feature of an ancillary use is that the legal use of the ancillary activity may change without any physical change in the activity itself if the major use ceases (see *Jones* v. *Secretary of State* (below); *Clarke* v. *Minister of Housing* (1967) 18 P. & C.R. 82). Conversely the physical activity may change drastically without there being a material change of use. Suppose that in the *Trentham* case (above) the building used for storing farm equipment was turned over to a farm office the use in law would remain agricultural (*Brazil Concrete* v. *Amersham R.D.C.* (1967) 18 P. & C.R. 396; *Vickers Armstrong* v. *Central Land Board* (1957) 9 P. & C.R. 33).

An ancillary use must be distinguished from the case where a second use on the site is unrelated to the main use but is too small, sporadic or temporary to be regarded as "material" (see *Biss* v. *Smallburgh R.D.C.* [1965] Ch. 335). If the parent use ceases, an ancillary use will become a use in its own right and development may occur (below). By contrast the cessation of the major use will not affect the status of an insubstantial use which can always be ignored. A use can also be ancillary to operational development (see *R.* v. *Surrey C.C.* (above, p. 64)). Similarly an operation can be ancillary to a use so that if buildings were erected more than four years ago for the purpose of a material change of use, an enforcement notice can require that these be demolished notwithstanding the four year embargo upon enforcement in respect of building operations (*Murfitt* v. *Secretary of State* (1980) P. & C.R. 254).

It is generally believed that a use cannot be ancillary to a parent use on another site. For example in *Lewis* v. *Secretary of State* [1971] 23 P. & C.R. 125 workshops were used for an haulage business on another site. The haulage business closed down but the workshops continued in use, now being used to repair vehicles generally. It was held that no development had taken place. By contrast in *Jones* v. *Secretary of State* (1974) 28 P. & C.R. 362 workshops had been used for manufacture and repair of trailers in connection with the appellant's haulage business *on the same site.* The same happened as in *Lewis* but this time it was held that development had taken place. The manufacture and repair use was previously ancillary to haulage but had now lost its parent thus undergoing a notional change of use from haulage to manufacturing.

These cases are difficult to reconcile with *Swinbank* v. *Secretary of State* [1987] J.P.L. 781. There it was held that the storage of farm tractors for use on a different planning unit was ancillary to the agricultural use of the main unit and could not therefore be the subject of an enforcement notice because agricultural use is not development (below, p. 86). The *Swinbank* decision seems contrary to principle (*e.g. Westminster City Council* v. *B.W.B.* (above, p. 72)) and also inconsistent with any coherent planning policy based upon geographical separation of incompatible uses.

It is not clear whether an ancilliary use must be something that is *normally* incidental to the present use or whether an unusual ancilliary purpose would qualify.[12] The answer depends not upon logic but the extent to which local authorities should be trusted to make value judgements about personal idiosyncracies.

Finally, an ancillary use may as a matter of fact expand to become

---

[12] See *Wealden D.C.* v. *Secretary of State* [1988] J.P.L. 268. Compare *Hussain* v. *Secretary of State* (1971) 23 P. & C.R. 330—slaughter according to muslim custom not ancillary to butchers business but depended on the notion of "ordinarily incidental" in the Use Classes Order. See Use Classes Order 1977 Art. 3(3).

independent of its parent and thus take on its own legal identity. See *Peake* v. *Secretary of State for Wales* [1971] 22 P. & C.R. 889.

One ministerial application of the ancillary use doctrine is dubious. In Circular 67/49 the Minister stated that he would not treat as a material change of use a situation where a "professional man—say a doctor or a dentist" uses rooms in a private dwelling for consultation purposes. Not only has this principle been applied arbitrarily, as where use of part of a dwelling-house for a tailoring business, and by an architect for professional purposes were both treated as development (see [1970] J.P.L. 674, but see now Circular 2/86 and [1978] J.P.L. 685), but the circular itself appears to be misconceived. Use as a doctor's surgery has no functional connection with use as a dwelling-house and is thus not ancillary. It makes nonsense of the doctrine to hold that merely because two uses are conveniently operated on the same site one is ancillary to the other. The use of part of a doctor's dwelling-house as a surgery is properly treated as the introduction of a separate independent use.

Concurrent uses. This is where a site has more than one independent use. Here each use whether or not geographically separated must be looked at separately. There is one special feature of this class of case. This is where one or two more concurrent uses encroaches upon the territory of the other as a result of expansion. If this occurs a material change of use takes place (*Wipperman* v. *Barking Borough Council* (1965) 17 P. & C.R. 225), and it makes no difference whether the uses were physically intermingled or separate. This principle has been criticised (see Palk (1973) 33 Conv. 168), but it is suggested that it is merely an example of the operation of ordinary principles. In *Bromsgrove D.C.* v. *Secretary of State* [1978] J.P.L. 747, Forbes J. regarded the *Wipperman* principle as an example of intensification and applicable only where the encroaching use absorbs the whole site. This is inconsistent with the earlier decision in *Brooks* v. *Gloucestershire C.C.* (1967) 66 L.G.R. 386, where part of a dwelling-house was used as a shop, the shop part later encroaching into the territory of the dwelling-house. It was emphasised that the principle is not based upon intensification but upon displacement. This analysis is desirable from a policy point of view since the balance of uses on a site may raise planning issues. In *Philglow* v. *Secretary of State* [1985] J.P.L. 318 it was held that some degree of expansion is required although not necessarily enough to cover the whole site. However in that case there was no displacement at all. One of two uses merely stopped. (See also *De Mulder* v. *Secretary of State* [1974] Q.B. 792).

THE UNIT OF DEVELOPMENT

Before deciding whether development has taken place the authority must identify the unit of land in relation to which the facts must be analysed. The most natural unit and the one applicable in the majority of cases is the area occupied by a single occupier or by joint occupiers in a common enterprise. If some other unit is chosen then this may produce a different result. Thus in *James* v. *Secretary of State for Wales* [1966] 1 W.L.R. 135 part of a site was occupied by caravans and planning permission was sought for an increase in the number of vehicles so as to encroach on to another part of the site. If the appropriate unit was the land actually covered by caravans, then encroachment on to neighbouring land would certainly constitute a change in the use of that land. If however the whole site occupied by the developer could be considered, the problem becomes one of intensification and it would be more difficult to establish development.

The unit problem also arises in connection with enforcement notices. In *Thomas David (Porthcawl) Ltd.* v. *Penybont R.D.C.* [1972] 1 W.L.R. 1526 mining operations took place only on part of the unit occupied by the developer. Nevertheless it was held that an enforcement notice could validly prohibit the extension of operations over the rest of the unit. An enforcement notice need not extend to the whole unit, but cannot go beyond it, and must not artificially divide up a unit by serving more than one notice where to do so would be more onerous than if a single notice were issued. (*De Mulder* v. *Secretary of State* 1974 Q.B. 792).

The unit problem usually arises in connection with multiple user. Choosing the wrong unit here may well affect the question whether development has taken place. In *Williams* v. *Minister of Housing* (above, p. 75) if the hut were to be regarded as a separate unit then development could not have taken place at all since at all relevant times retail sales would have been the use of that unit.

The law governing identification of the unit of development is reasonably clear. As usual the question is primarily one of fact for the planning authority who must direct their attention to two possible units. The primary unit is the whole area occupied by the developer. The nature of his estate or interest in the land is irrelevant. Thus in *Johnstone* v. *Secretary of State* (1974) P. & C.R. 424 a row of lock up garages owned by a single owner but occupied separately was held to constitute separate units of development. However if one occupier occupies areas of land that are geographically separate each site is a separate unit (see *Duffy* v. *Secretary of State* [1981] J.P.L. 811; *Swinbank* v. *Secretary of State* [1987] J.P.L. 781).

In all cases there is a presumption, which is particulary strong in the case of a dwelling-house, that the unit of occupation is also the unit of development (*Burdle* v. *Secretary of State* [1972] 1 W.L.R. 1207). This has been the unit chosen in the overwhelming majority of cases. The presumption can be rebutted if there are geographically and functionally separate "units of activity" within the primary unit. A common example arises where part of an area of land is used as a caravan site and the rest for agricultural purposes. It is a question of fact whether the caravan site is sufficiently distinct geographically to be a separate planning unit. Such matters as the existence of fences and similar boundaries are of evidential value. In "ancillary use" cases there is no separate "unit" problem since if a use is ancillary to another use within the same area of occupation the whole will, *ipso facto*, comprise a single unit of development. Unrelated uses will not however produce separate units unless there is a clear geographical separation. In *Brooks* v. *Gloucestershire C.C.* (1967) 66 L.G.R. 386, part of a manor house used as a residence was also used as a shop and restaurant, but the whole was treated as a single unit even though the commercial activities were confined to certain rooms. This can be explained on the basis of the strong presumption against subdividing a dwelling-house.

Brooks shows the danger of over-emphasising the importance of the conceptual "unit' question. In *Brooks* it made no difference which of the two possible units was selected. This is because of the *Wipperman* principle that encroachment by one use on to the territory of another is, in itself, a material change of use (see above, p. 83). Thus even if the shop part of the house had been treated as a separate unit, development would still have taken place when this extended into the residential part. (See also *Richmond Borough Council* v. *Secretary of State* [1987] J.P.L. 509).

Even in intensification and enforcement notice cases, it will be unusual that a unit other than that of occupation is selected and even more unusual that it will be decisive. It is suggested that in order to avoid multiplying concepts it would be preferable in all cases to have regard only to the area of occupation. The contrary authorities consist mainly of *obiter dicta*. Indeed, judicial statements can be found which seem to assume that the area of occupation is the only appropriate unit (*Brazil Concrete Ltd.* v. *Amersham R.D.C.* (1967) 18 P. & C.R. 396, 399; *Vickers-Armstrong* v. *Central Land Board* (1957) 9 P. & C.R. 33, 37; but see Palk 37 Conv.(N.S.) at pp. 174–176 for criticisms of this approach).

Special Cases

ACTS WHICH ARE NOT DEVELOPMENT

Section 22(2) lists six acts which "shall not be taken to involve development of the land."

One of these we have already noticed. This is the "maintenance, improvement or other alteration" to a building which affects only its interior or which does not materially affect the external appearance. This concession has been slightly modified in that *underground* extensions to a building commenced after December 5, 1968 are excluded and thus being clearly an alteration to the land constitute development.

Two more concern routine maintenance work by certain public authorities.

The fourth exception, "use within the curtilage of a dwelling-house for any purpose incidental to the enjoyment of the dwelling-house as such," is superfluous in the light of the development by the courts of the doctrine of the ancillary use. However, its inclusion casts doubt upon the validity of the courts' approach, indicating as it does that the notion of ancillary uses was intended by Parliament to apply only to dwelling-houses.

Fifthly, the use of any land for agriculture or forestry purposes (including buildings occupied with the land) does not constitute development. Two things should be said about this important exception to planning control. First it is only the use which is within the exception and agricultural *operations* require planning permission. However, the General Development Order 1988 grants permission for many such operations. Secondly, it is questionable whether so generous an exemption is justifiable. Changes between different kinds of agricultural use, for example, from market garden to battery chicken rearing, may raise environmental issues which a planning authority should be able to evaluate. Indeed some agricultural processes are more akin to industrial activities and by exempting them from planning controls the Act produces the risk that local authority policy may be frustrated as regards the balance of uses within its area. Similarly it is questionable whether forestry should be assimilated with agriculture and exempted from control since the practice of foresting unspoilt countryside raises its own environmental problems. The law as conceived in 1947 is firmly based on the rural myth ideology (above p. 15) and has not adjusted to changing circumstances. (See Scrase [1988] J.P.L. 447).

"Agriculture" is defined in detail in the Act (section 290(1)). It includes horticulture, fruit growing, seed growing, dairy farming, the breeding and keeping of livestock (including any creature kept for the production of food, wool, skins or fur, or for the purpose of its use in the farming of the land), the use of land as grazing land, meadow land, osier land, market gardens and nursery grounds, and the use of land for woodlands where that use is ancillary to the farming of land for other agricultural purposes. Although the definition is inclusive and not therefore exhaustive it has been construed literally. As in other "use" contexts the state of affairs on the land itself including buildings must be examined, the destination of products from the land being immaterial. Thus the grazing of horses for use in sporting activities elsewhere is agricultural (*Sykes* (1981) P. & C.R. 19) but not where horse training and showjumping is carried out on the site (*Belmont Farms* v. *Secretary of State* [1962] 13 P. & C.R. 417). Similarly large scale slaughter of foxes on the site is not within the definition (*Gill* v. *Secretary of State* [1986] J.P.L. 397), but breeding foxes for slaughter elsewhere is (*North Warwickshire B.C.* v. *Secretary of State* (1985) P. & C.R. 47). If agriculture has a core meaning it seems to involve the production of living materials for consumption, to which processing must be merely incidental.

The Use Classes Order 1987. Finally, the Secretary of State can exempt from the definition of development any change of use within any class designated by him in a statutory instrument (section 22(2)F). This permits central government to remove large areas of activity from local authority control.

The Use Classes Order is therefore a device for relaxing planning controls in favour of market forces. It also helps to reduce the number of planning applications (see *Home* [1987] J.P.L. 167). The Order only applies once a use has been implemented and excludes from the definition of development any further change within the same class of use as specified in the Order.

The order in force is the Use Classes Order 1987 (S.I. 1987 No. 764. See Circular 11/87). It creates 16 classes of use, for example, shops, professional and financial services, restaurants, offices, various industrial uses, hotels and hostels, residential uses, public amenities. Certain uses of a particulary sensitive nature are specifically excluded from all classes. These include, theatres, amusement arcades, launderettes, petrol filling stations, car sales, taxi or car rent businesses, scrapyards and the like (see Art. 6). It is worth noting that restaurants and "takeaway" hot meals shops are now within the same use class (A3) which is distinct from A1 "shops," although the latter includes cold food takeaway shops such as sandwich bars.

Class C1 is of particular interest in the light of what we have said about matters of social character as being relevant to the definition of development. It comprises the use as a dwelling house (a) by a single person or by people living together as a family, or (b) by not more than 6 residents being together as a single household (including a household where care is provided for residents).

Provided that these requirements are fulfilled it follows that changes of a social kind that otherwise could be development are now lawful. For example a developer could convert a row of terraced houses in a seaside resort into units of sheltered housing for the elderly each unit housing six people.

The Use Classes Order can be excluded by an express condition attached to a planning permission (below, p. 179) or by a planning agreement (below, Chap. 7), the latter having the advantage that there is no right of appeal to the central government. The Order cannot be excluded by a planning permission drafted to define a particular use (*e.g. Carpet Decor Guildford Ltd.* v. *Secretary of State* [1981] J.P.L. 806—storage of papers).

The Order must be construed in its planning and historical context, but not liberally in favour of bringing borderline cases within it.[13-14]

If a given change of use falls within any one class it cannot be development even if it is a change by way of intensification (*Brooks and Burton* v. *Secretary of State* [1977] 1 W.L.R. 1294). The language of the order is conclusive. Conversely, there is no rule that a change between use classes is always development.[15] Ordinary principles must be applied (*e.g. Rann* v. *Secretary of State* [1980] 40 P. & C.R. 113). For example, it could be argued that a change of use

---

[13-14] *e.g. Tessier* v. *Secretary of State* (1975) 31 P. & C.R. 161—sculptor's studio; *Newbury D.C.* v. *Secretary of State* [1980] 1 All E.R. 731; "repository." *Firkhurst* v. *Secretary of State* [1982] J.P.L. 448.

[15] Certain changes between specified use classes have automatic planning permission under the General Development Order. The existence of the Order may indirectly condition the judge's approach to more general questions. See *London Residuary Body* v. *Secretary of State* [1988] J.P.L. 637 and Encyclopaedia Vol. 3, para. 313–387.

from solicitors office (Class A2) to barristers chambers (B1) is not development, although the fact that there is no public access to the latter provides a contrary argument. Similarly changes from, say, a grocers shop (A1) to a wine bar (A3) to a takeaway sandwich bar (A1) may all require planning permission even though the grocers shop and sandwich bars are within the same use classes.

The 1987 Order raises difficulties of construction particularly between Class A1 (shops), Class A2 financial and professional services to the visiting public, and Class B "business including offices." Multi-disciplinary law practices would seem to be safe within A2 but a large bank is more questionable (see *Norris* [1987] J.P.L. 819). In general the Order allows more flexibility in relation to business users by grouping together offices and light industry which has no harmful effects on local amenity (B1). It also distinguishes between offices which contribute to the life of a town centre (Class A2) and other business activities (Class B1).

It appears to be irrelevant to the operation of the Use Classes Order whether the initial use was a lawful use. This only matters of course where the initial use has become immune from enforcement due to lapse of time. (Compare G.D.O. below p. 95).

ACTS WHICH ARE DEVELOPMENT

Section 22(3), which is expressed to be "for the avoidance of doubt," defines two cases where development does take place.

(i) The deposit of refuse (sub-section 3(*b*)). This is a material change of use even where the site is already used for the same purpose unless neither the surface area of the deposit is extended nor its height so as to exceed the level of the surrounding land.[16]

(ii) "Use as two or more separate dwelling-houses of any building previously used as a single dwelling-house" (sub-section 3(*a*)). The problem is to establish what makes a "separate" dwelling-house. The phrase "separate dwellings" is also found in the Rent Acts, and has been defined in that context to mean a situation where there is no sharing of living accommodation, even though a toilet and bathroom may be shared (see *Neale* v. *Del Soto* [1945] K.B. 144; *Cole* v. *Harris* [1945] K.B. 474; *Goodrich* v. *Paisner* [1957] A.C. 65). It is doubtful whether the same test is appropriate in a planning context where the nature of the shared facilities seems irrelevant. It

[16] Special controls over waste deposits include the need for consent to the deposit of hazardous substances. (Housing and Planning Act 1986, Part IV) maintenance of waste land; 1971 Act, s.65 (as amended). See also Control of Pollution Act 1974, s.3—deposit of waste other than agricultural or quarry refuse without a licence (in addition to planning permission).

has been held that multiple occupation even by families living separately does not itself turn a single house into "separate dwellings" for planning purposes (*Ealing Corporation* v. *Ryan* [1965] 2 Q.B. 486; see also *Birmingham Corporation* v. *Habib Ullah* [1964] 1 Q.B. 178). In the *Ealing* case the Divisional Court found it unnecessary to decide whether the Rent Act test should apply in a planning context and indicated that further argument upon the scope of the planning legislation would be desirable, assisted by a representative of the Minister as *amicus curiae*.

However, in *Wakelin* (1978) 46 P. & C.R. 214, the Court of Appeal took the view that occupation by separate households is sufficient to attract sub-section (3)(*a*) on the basis that this involves the creation of separate planning units. There a lodge was originally occupied by the staff of an adjoining dwelling-house. The owner now wished to lease the lodge for residence unconnected with the main house and this was held to be development. The planning authority could therefore intervene by permitting separate occupation only by persons related to the residents of the main house. Lord Denning M.R. treated the whole complex as one building so as to attract sub-section 3(*a*), but the others preferred to rely on the sub-section only as an analogy.

It seems therefore that the *Ealing* and *Habib Ullah* cases are no longer good law, although they can be distinguished in that the relevant activities took place within a single building.

Finally, section 22(4) provides that the use of any external part of a building for the display of advertisements constitutes a material change of use where the part in question is not normally used for such purposes. Were it not for this provision such displays would probably be regarded as operational development.[17]

Conclusion

It is difficult to discover from the cases on development any coherent judicial policy in favour of private property rights. On the contrary the courts have allowed considerable discretion to planning authorities to determine what development means within their own policy framework. The concept of the planning unit and the insistence upon the notions of positive act and change are

---

[17] Additional controls over the display of advertisements apply under ss.63–64. Compliance with regulations made under s.63 is deemed to be a grant of planning permission; See Town and County Planning (Control of Advertisement) Regulations (S.I. 1969 No. 1532). See also Housing and Planning Act 1986, s.45; Town and County Planning Act 1971, ss.109, 109A.

perhaps the most important inhibiting factors. One policy thread which does seem to underline the cases, and which in a broad sense serves the interests of property owners, is that traditional and conventional modes of community life can be used as a reference point against which to measure a change of use, thus reinforcing the notion of planning law as essentially a conservative instrument as opposed to a vehicle for achieving distributive justice.

5. Applications for Planning Permission

The need for planning permission

Once it has been established that a proposed activity constitutes development it must be decided whether an application must be made for planning permission. Even if this is the case the developer may prefer to carry out his development without permission (bearing in mind that no penalty is attached to this in itself), and to wait for the authority to take enforcement action. This it may never do since there is no systematic method of monitoring development. If enforcement action is taken the developer can appeal to the Secretary of State against the enforcement notice. This can be a long drawn out process and may result in a grant of planning permission (below, p. 204). Whether the risk is worth taking depends partly upon economic factors, bearing in mind that several years may elapse between commencing the unauthorised development and being required to cease.

EXEMPTIONS

There are several cases where express planning permission is not required. Some of these are statutory and designed to cater for technical problems. Others implemented in the main through delegated legislation are the result of central government intervention and can be regarded as devices to limit the scope of local authority power (see McAuslan, (1981) 4 *Urban Law and Policy* 215 at 243–260).

Section 23 provides for six cases where no planning permission is needed. All concern the reversion to previous uses of land. Three are of limited importance involving transitional situations where a landowner was prejudiced by the introduction of planning controls in 1947 (section 23(2) (3) (4) (7)).

The other three illustrate the basic principle that it is a *change* of use and not a use itself which requires planning permission.

Exemptions are given in respect of the return to the "normal" use of land after (i) the expiry of a temporary planning permission (section 23(5)) or (ii) a permission granted by development order subject to limitations (section 23(8)) (see *Cynon Valley D.C.* v. *Secretary of State* [1987] J.P.L. 760 below, p. 179). The "normal" use includes only a use which either had planning permission or which did not require planning permission. It does not include a use commenced in breach of planning control even if immune from enforcement (section 23(6)). The developer may revert to the latest use that was in fact "normal" before the limited or temporary permission was implemented. Thus intervening uses must be disregarded if they are either temporary or unlawful. The normal use must be implemented as soon as the use that was authorised by the temporary permission ceases.[1] Section 23(9) exempts from the need for planning permission a resumption of the "lawful" use immediately proceeding a use in respect of which an enforcement notice has been issued. The difference in wording seems to be the result of defective consolidation but section 23(9) has nevertheless been strictly construed against the landowner.[2]

Permission by development order. Planning permission can be granted by a development order. This is a statutory instrument made by the Secretary of State subject to parliamentary veto (section 287(2)). Development orders can either grant planning permission or specify procedural and substantive requirements for applications for permission (section 24, 31).[3] They can either be special or general. A special development order grants permission in respect either of a specific development or of a prescribed area or description of land (section 24(3)(*b*)). It might be used for example where a proposal raises political issues which deserve parliamentary debate. Thus proposals in respect of the third London airport and the application to extend

---

[1] See *Smith* v. *Secretary of State* (1984) 47 P. & C.R. 194. This need not be immediately after the expiry of the temporary *permission* but the normal use could be lost by lapse of time (*ibid.*).

[2] See below, p. 201. See also Purdue [1984] J.P.L. 6; *Kingdom* v. *Secretary of State* [1988] 1 Q.B. 257; *LTSS Print and Supplies* v. *Hackney L.B.C.* [1976] 1 Q.B. 633. "Lawful" does not include uses which are time barred from enforcement. See also *Young* v. *Secretary of State* [1983] 2 A.C. 662.

[3] Planning Permission by Private Act is of course possible. This may be necessary in the case of complex developments affecting harbours which may include interference with navigational rights or waters outside the jurisdiction of the L.P.A.

the Windscale nuclear processing establishment were dealt with by special development orders (see S.I. 1978 No. 523). Looked at from a more sinister point of view, special development order procedure avoids the obligation to hold a public inquiry which would arise where there is an appeal against the refusal of an express planning permission (see *Essex C.C.* v. *Ministry of Housing* (1967) 18 P. & C.R. 531). Special development orders are also used to give effect to proposals for development within their territories made by urban development corporations (L.G.P. and L.A. 1980, section 148).

A general development order (of which the current example is the General Development Order 1988 (hereinafter called the G.D.O.) applies to all land, but may make different provision with respect to different descriptions of land (section 24(3)(a)). Permission is given for 23 classes of development. Particulars of these are given in the standard textbooks and they will not be discussed in detail here.[4] In general the G.D.O. applies mainly to relatively minor activities by public and private bodies but statutory undertakers are given large privileges as also are airport operators, the British Coal Corporation and telecommunications developers.

Under article 4 of the G.D.O. the Secretary of State, the local planning authority or, under Art. 6, the minerals authority (county council) may withdraw the benefit of any G.D.O. permission in relation to a particular piece of land or to an area. This means that the landowner must make an application for planning permission. If permission is then refused compensation is payable (section 165(2)). Most directions made by the local planning authority require the approval of the Secretary of State. Art. 5(1). Directions made by the minerals authority can be vetoed by the Secretary of State (Art. 6(5)). This is a useful device for retaining stringent controls in special cases (see, *e.g. Thanet D.C.* v. *Ninedrive Ltd.* [1978] 1 All E.R. 703). An article 4 direction just like any other revocation of permission cannot be made once the development in question has been implemented: (*Cole* v. *Somerset C.C.* [1957] 1 Q.B. 23; see (1987) J.P.L. 663).

The effect of the G.D.O. is fundamentally different from that of the Use Classes Order (above p. 87). The latter is concerned with defining development whereas the G.D.O. grants planning permission. In particular a G.D.O. provision applies

---

[4] See Encylopaedia Vol. 2–833; Moore *A Practical Approach to Planning Law* (1987) Chap. 7.

only where a use to which it relates is itself lawful irrespective, apparently, of whether it is immune from enforcement due to lapse of time. (*Asghar* v. *Secretary of State* [1988] J.P.L. 476).

The Secretary of State may attach conditions or limitations to a development order (section 23(4)).

Deemed planning permission. There are special cases where planning permission is "deemed to be granted." These mainly involve development by public authorities in cases where authorisation from a government department is required including cases where the authorisation is merely for the acquisition of the relevant land (section 40). The department in question may, but does not have to, direct that planning permission is deemed to be granted. Other special cases include (i) development permitted under the pre-1947 planning legislation provided that it was begun before April 1, 1974 (Sched. 24, para. 19(1)(2)); (ii) the display of certain kinds of advertisement in accordance with regulations (section 64). In this case the Secretary of State can remove the benefit of deemed consent by designating the area as one of special control (section 63(3); see Telling pp. 225–230).

Crown land. The Town and Country Planning Act 1971 does not bind the Crown, there being neither express language nor necessary implication to rebut this general presumption (see *Minister of Agriculture* v. *Jenkins* [1963] 2 Q.B. 317). This seems to have little rationale apart from constitutional tradition, and difficult cases may arise as to whether a particular public body is or is not holding land on behalf of the Crown. Thus central government departments do not require planning permission, although in practice local planning authorities are consulted, according to a set of administrative rules (see Circulars 7/77; 2/81). These correspond broadly to ordinary planning procedures but are more favourable to the Crown (see Grant, pp. 236–237).

The Crown's immunity is purely personal and does not attach to the land as such. Development by other persons in their own right on land owned by the Crown is in principle subject to planning control. However, there are further provisions applicable to any land in which the Crown or the Duchy of Cornwall possesses an "interest." This could include for example land over which the Crown has a reversion, or even perhaps the benefit of a covenant or easement. Section 266 applies the normal development control regime to interests in such land other than interests held by the Crown and for this purpose "interest" includes a licence in writing (Town and Country Planning Act 1984, section 4). Section 266(3) prohibits enforcement action in respect of development originally carried out by or on behalf of the Crown where the land was Crown land at the date of the development and other enforcement action requires Crown consent. (s.266(2)(a). However under the Town and Country Planning Act 1984 section 5, the Crown may enter into an agreement with the local planning authority concerning material changes of use by the Crown. Such an agreement has effect as if there were a planning permission with a condition requiring discontinuance of the use if the land ceases to be occupied by the Crown for that purpose. The agreement binds third parties as a local land charge (section 5(4)) but binds those with private interests in the land at the date of the agreement only if actually notified of it by the local planning authority (section 5(3)).

Problems arise when the Crown wishes to dispose of land and seeks planning permission for the purpose of a disposal in order to realise the full market value of the land. There were administrative procedures under which a government department could obtain an advisory opinion from the local planning authority as to whether planning permission would be granted. But in *R. v. Worthing D.C. ex p. Burch* [1984] J.P.L. 261 this practice was exposed as an unlawful fetter on the discretion of the authority. The matter has now been dealt with by statute. The Town and Country Planning Act 1984 permits the Crown to apply for planning permission in respect of proposals to develop the land after it ceases to be Crown land or where the development is to be carried out by virtue of a private interest in the land (section 1(3)). Permission may be sought only for the purpose of disposing of the land.

The 1984 Act also makes provision for development carried out otherwise than by or on behalf of the Crown at a time when no person is entitled to occupy the land by virtue of a private interest (section 3). Development carried out in such cases (*e.g.* by trespassers on the verges of trunk roads) is subject to a "special enforcement notice" procedure broadly similar to the ordinary enforcement regime. The consent of the Crown is required (see *Encyclopaedia of Planning Law and Practice* 2–2190).

Enterprise zones and simplified planning zones. These devices were introduced with the aim of stimulating market forces by relaxing planning controls, and in the case of enterprise zones by creating tax havens.[5] They are broadly similar to the zoning ordinance technique familiar in the U.S.A. and other common law jurisdictions but with the crucial difference that they do not allow any class of development to be prohibited. A zone can prescribe: (i) activities that are automatically permitted; (ii) activities permitted subject to conditions; and (iii) activities requiring ordinary planning permission.[6] A "scheme" is produced by a district or London borough council, new town corporation or urban development corporation following publicity and consultation processes analogous to those for "local" plan making.[7] Once adopted and, in the case of an enterprise zone confirmed by the Secretary of State, the scheme operates as a grant of planning permission.

There are several important differences between enterprise zones and simplified planning zones. Enterprise zones involve greater central government control and less safeguards for the individual. They also confer various privileges, most of them of a fiscal nature, not directly related to planning. They have been described as analogous to the "freeport" concept as exemplified in Hong Kong designed to create a "micro state" where the forces of free enterprise are unleashed with minimal distortion of the market by bureacratic controls.

The initiative to create an enterprise zone comes from the Secretary of State in the form of an "invitation" to the relevant local authority to propose a scheme. The scheme must be adopted by the authority and then designated by the Secretary of State (L.G. and P.A. 1980, Sched. 32). Designation takes the form of a statutory instrument, so that apart from a general obligation, subjectively framed and imposed on the adopting body, to give adequate publicity to its proposals and to consider representations, (relating only to whether planning permission should be granted) there is no obligation to hold any kind of inquiry or hearing. Nor is a map or any other particular form required, the matter being regulated entirely by terms of the Secretary of States' "invitation" (*ibid.* Sched. 32, para. 1(5)). The Secretary of State may designate the enterprise zone authority as the local planning authority

---

[5] Local Government Planning and Land Act 1980, Sched. 32 (enterprise zones); Town and Country Planning Act 1981, section 24A–E (Simplified Planning Zones). See "Enterprise Zones" Department of Environment 1980; Lloyd and Botham, 7 *Urban Law and Policy* 33.

[6] *Ibid.* section 24B(1) 6 (S.P.Z.). L.G.P. and L.A. 1980, Sched. 32, para. 17(3) (4) (6) (Enterprise Zone).

[7] L.G.P. and L.A. 1980, Sched. 32, paras. 2, 3; T. and C.P.A. 1971, Sched. 8A. (Above p. 2).

98 APPLICATIONS FOR PLANNING PERMISSION

(paras. 5(7), 20(1)). With the consent of the Secretary of State the authority may exempt specific developments, or classes of development, or classes of development within a specified area from the general permission conferred by the scheme. Conditions can also be attached and matters reserved for specific approval.

The zone provisions seem more flexible and responsive to public participation than the power to grant planning permission by way of development order (above) particularly in relation to the combination of local and central powers, although the ultimate balance of power falls squarely on the side of the central government.

In theory any area of land within the territory of a district council, a London borough or an urban development corporation could be designated as an enterprise zone. In practice enterprise zones are intended to be used on a small scale in areas that are suffering grave social and economic problems or which are depopulated, for example, some inner city areas. It is questionable whether the concept is effective to stimulate economic activity. On the one hand, enterprise zones are necessarily superimposed upon an existing pattern of development and so may bring windfall benefits to businesses already located in the zone without stimulating increased activity. On the other hand, an enterprise zone may disadvantage areas immediately outside the zone. There is evidence "that the development that has occurred so far owes more to public sector intervention, expenditure and subsidies, rather than to the relaxation of regulations and controls." (See Lloyd and Botham *op. cit.*, n. 5 above).

Simplified planning zones were introduced by the Housing and Planning Act 1986. They embody the same basic principle as enterprise zones but without the non-planning privileges associated with enterprise zones and with less overt central government involvement. Unlike an enterprise zone a simplified planning zone scheme (S.P.Z.) must consist of a map and written statement (Sched. 8A, para. 1). When adopted or approved this automatically grants planning permission for any development specified in the scheme or of any class so specified (section 24A(2)). Local planning authorities must consider and keep under review the question whether it is "desirable" that part or parts of their area become S.P.Z.'s. They must make a scheme if they decide it is desirable (section 24A(4)).

S.P.Z.'s can be used for a variety of purposes. They can encourage particular kinds of development or grant permission for all development subject to exceptions. They are particularly appropriate for large tracts of disused or lightly used land or where co-ordinated development is desired.

Certain categories of land or development cannot be included in S.P.Z.'s. These comprise areas designated under various statutory powers for conservation purposes and also county matters and areas designated as green belts in the development plan.[8] An S.P.Z. is adopted by the local planning authority after publicity and consultation procedures similar to those applicable to local plans but unlike the case with enterprise zones the approval of the Secretary of State is not required.[9] However, where objections are duly made a public local inquiry must be held and in other cases may be held (*ibid.* Sched. 6, para. 8). S.P.Z.'s are thus very similar to local plans, but with the effect of directly granting planning permission for development therein specified. Indeed, conflict could arise between an S.P.Z. and the local plan actually in force. The S.P.Z. would necessarily prevail since local plans have no binding force. Other development rights are not affected and the S.P.Z. prevails over any restrictions in earlier planning permissions (*ibid.* section 24B(2)). S.P.Z.'s are similar to American zoning ordinances found in the U.S.A. and may therefore encounter similar problems—rigidity—distortion of land values, susceptibility to vested interests—to those that are well charted in the American literature.[10] On the other hand, English planning is dominated by central government so that pressures from private vested interests may be less of a factor than in the localised American system.

Although the formal involvement of the central government is not a prerequisite to the adoption of an S.P.Z. there are several powers available to the Secretary of State for the purpose of compelling local planning authorities to prepare S.P.Z.'s in a form congenial to the central government. The overall effect of these seems to be that the Secretary of

[8] *Ibid.* section 24E; T. and C.P. (S.P.Z.) (Excluded Development) Order (S.I. 1987 No. 1849).
[9] These are calling in and default powers: T. and C.P.A. 1971, Sched. 6, paras. 10 and 12. All proposals must be sent to the Secretary of State (*ibid.* para. 5(3)). Alterations to schemes approved by the Secretary of State must also be approved by him (*ibid.* para. 2(1)). See also below, n. 11. The Secretary of State must hear objections but need not hold a public inquiry (*ibid.* para. 11(3)). See Town and Country Planning (S.P.Z.) Regs. 19/87 S.I. No. 1750. See also [1987] J.P.L. 609.
[10] See, *e.g.* Babcock, *The Zoning Game* (1979); Elickson and Tarlock, *Land Use Controls—Cases and Materials* (1981), Chaps. 3 and 4.

State can both prevent and impose the adoption of a scheme.[11]

It has often been argued that the thrust of recent legislation has been to weaken the discretionary powers of local planning authorities and to strengthen central government powers. The balance of the legislation has also been tipped in favour of developers.[12] It remains to be seen how the S.P.Z. concept will be used. If it plays a minimal role of legitimising development that conforms with the local plan it might well achieve the advantage of reducing bureaucratic procedures. On the other hand, there is no necessary correlation between the S.P.Z.'s and prevailing structure or local plans. In the case of enterprise zones the structure or local plan must be reviewed and if necessary altered to take account of an enterprise zone scheme (L.G.P. and L.A. 1980, Sched. 32, para. 24).

The decision makers

As we have seen, many different persons and bodies participate in the planning process. The range of factors actually taken into account, might vary considerably depending upon whether the effective decision maker is an elected local body, a committee, a professional local official, a civil servant or a Minister. There is considerable flexibility as regards the delegation of powers within the planning system, a factor which may contribute to the confusion and incoherence sometimes associated with British planning law. There is also considerable overlap between central and local responsibilities, the role of central government going well beyond those of supervisor and co-ordinator.

Primary responsibility for planning permission (and enforcement) decisions rests with district councils or London borough councils (L.G.A. 1972, Sched. 16, para. 15). In certain cases other bodies may exercise these powers. These include county councils, urban development corporations, housing action trusts, and the Secretary of State.

---

[11] He can direct the making or alteration of a scheme if, after a request by any person, the local authority refuses to do so or delays beyond 3 months (T. and C.P.A. 1971, Sched. 8A, para. 3). See also paras. 7 and 13(1)— (regulations governing form and content). See also n. 9 above.

[12] See Loughlin (1981) 44 M.L.R. 422; Loughlin, *Local Government in the Modern State* (1986) pp. 136–143; McAuslan (1981) 4 *Urban Law and Policy* 215–268; Loughlin in *Law, Legitimacy and the Constitution* (ed. McAuslan and McEldowney) Chap. 4.

COUNTY COUNCILS

In the case of county councils the range of "county matters" was greatly reduced by the Local Government Planning and Land Act 1980. County matters are broadly confined to minerals and waste disposal matters and most matters affecting national parks.[13] In particular, applications that contravene the development plan are no longer decided at county level, although in some cases the district council must consult the county (see below, p. 117). Similarly the county no longer has power to give "directions" to the district council. This, depending upon the political perspective of the observer could be regarded as a manifestation of any of the following ideals: (a) "returning power to the people;" (b) weakening long term strategic planning; and (c) strengthening the process of central government *vis-à-vis* local authorities.

The decision whether a matter is a county matter is a subjective one for the district council (L.G.A. 1972, Sched. 16, para. 15(2)). Thus all applications must be submitted to the district council, who, if it appears to them to be a county matter, must then send a copy to the County within seven days (*ibid.* paras. 15(3) 3A). Judicial review is severely limited. Under para. 51(1)(*a*) "determination or a certificate granted, made or issued or purporting to be granted, made or issued by a local planning authority . . . shall not be called into question in any legal proceedings or in any proceedings under the Town and Country Planning Act 1971 that are not legal proceedings on the ground that the permission etc. should have been granted . . . by some other local planning authority." This ouster clause, because it employs the word "purport," does not seem to be susceptible to the reasoning embodied in *Anisminic* v. *Foreign Compensation Commission* [1969] 2 A.C. 147 under which an ultra vires government act being a nullity does not prima facie fall within an ouster clause. However, the Court of Appeal has held that the clause does not apply where *neither* body has power to grant the planning permission in question nor, obviously, where there is some other defect (*Co-Operative Retail Society* v. *Taff-Ely D.C.* (1980) 34 P. & C.R. 223).

A County Council may delegate any of its planning functions to the district council (L.G.A. 1972, section 101). In some cases non-statutory "development control" schemes have been made in order to regulate decision-making and consultation between county and district levels.

---

[13] L.G.A. 1972, Sched. 16, para. 32. Special arrangements apply to National Parks and there is a strong non-elected element. See L.G.A. 1972, section 182(4); Sched. 11, para. 16; Sched. 17 (Encyclopaedia 2–1646,7).

URBAN DEVELOPMENT CORPORATIONS

Urban development areas are designated as such by statutory instruments made by the Secretary of State.[14] Urban Development Corporations (U.D.C.) preside over them. They make no pretence at being democratic bodies but are entirely comprised of appointees of the Secretary of State and charged with the duty to secure the regeneration of their area (L.G.P. and L.A. 1980, sections 135, 136 and Sched. 26). They can be paid but are not Crown servants or agents (*ibid.* section 135(6). In making appointments the Secretary of State is obliged to take into account the desirability of securing the services of people with local knowledge, and must consult local authorities relevant (Sched. 26, para. 2). He can therefore "pack" a U.D.C. with developers. A U.D.C. can carry out development itself subject to the approval of the Secretary of State exercisable by special development order (section 148). The Secretary of State may also designate an U.D.C. as local planning authority (section 149). This ousts the jurisdiction of all other planning authorities. The Secretary of State may also direct an U.D.C. how to exercise its powers (section 138). However, the U.D.C. must consult with relevant local authorities and prepare a code of practice for doing so (*ibid.* section 140(1)).[14a]

THE SECRETARY OF STATE

As well as acting as an appellate body (below, Chap. 10) the Secretary of State may exercise first instance development control powers, thus enabling the central government to pre-empt local decisions.

The Secretary of State can "call in" any applications or class of applications for planning permission to decide himself (section 35). Similar procedural requirements concerning consultation apply as to local decisions (see below, p. 116) but unlike the local authority the Secretary of State is bound if requested by either the applicant or the local planning authority to hold an inquiry (*ibid.* section 35(5)).

---

[14] "If he is of the opinion that it is expedient in the national interest," L.G. and P.A. 1980, section 134.
[14a] Housing Action trusts can also be designated as L.P.A.s and apply for planning permission on a similar basis—Housing Act 1988 ss. 66, 67.

The Secretary of State has a discretion whether or not to call in
any application and can direct that any application for planning permission be notified to him with a view to deciding whether or not to
make a calling-in direction (section 31(1)(e)).[15] The calling-in
power is generally exercised only where the issues are of more than
local importance such as large out-of-town shopping centres,
applications inconsistent with the structure plan (below, p. 119) or
where conflicts of interest are likely (see Circulars 71/76, 96/77,
2/81, 21/86 [1987] J.P.L. 110). Reasons need not be given for the
decision whether or not to call in an application.[15a] A local planning
authority could pre-empt a calling-in direction by granting planning
permission themselves, although this could be prevented by the
Secretary of State making a further direction restricting the grant of
planning permission (section 31(1)a; G.D.O. Art. 14). Such a
direction has been held to be "unquestionably" mandatory (*Co-op
Retail Services Ltd.* v. *Taff-Ely B.C.* [1980] 39 P. & C.R. 223 at
245–246, 253–254). There is no appeal against the decision of the
Secretary of State on a called-in application (section 35(6) which
can be challenged only under the "six weeks time limit" procedure
(above, p. 47). Because of this it may be that natural justice
requires all relevant matters, for example the nature of any
conditions which the Secretary of State has in mind to attach be
disclosed at the inquiry.

Local authority land and development

Land owned by local planning authorities is not exempt from
planning controls as such. Where a local planning authority wishes
to develop land within its area whether or not owned by it or where
other persons wish to develop land owned by a local planning
authority there is an obvious conflict of interest. The position is
governed by section 270 which states that "the provisions of this Act
specified in Part V of Schedule 21 shall have effect subject to"
modifications made by the Secretary of State. According to
Webster J. in *Steeples* v. *Derbyshire County Council* [1985] 1

[15] See G.D.O., 1988, Arts. 14(1), 17. He is not generally required to give a hearing
before deciding whether to "call in" an application: *R.* v. *Secretary of State ex p.
Southwark L.B.C.* [1987] J.P.L. 587. Applications may also be drawn to the
Departments' attention by M.P.'s or members of public. For notification
directions see below, n. 24. See also Barker and Couper (1984) 6 *Urban Law and
Policy* 363 at 417–430, pointing out that the calling in process is random and
spasmodic.
[15a] Above p. 3. However at this stage he should not consider the merits of the
application. *Lakin Ltd.* v. *Secretary of State for Scotland* [1989] J.P.L. 339.

W.L.R. 256 this excludes the normal planning regime *except* those provisions specified in Sched. 21, Pt. V as modified by the Secretary of State. These include the main development control rules, but not the provisions for publicity and notification embodied in sections 26 to 28 (below, p. 118).

Where the local planning authority wishes to obtain planning permission then under the Town and Country Planning General Regulations 1976 (No. 1419) two resolutions are required, first, a resolution to seek permission, and secondly, following consultation and publicity requirements broadly analogous to those governing ordinary planning applications, a resolution to carry out the development. This must not be earlier than 21 days after the first resolution is placed in the register of planning applications thus ensuring some publicity (see *R. v. Doncaster M.B.C. ex p. B.R.B.* [1987] J.P.L. 444; see below, p. 125). The second resolution takes effect as if it were a grant of planning permission by the Secretary of State (Reg. 5) (see Grant, p. 240). The recommendation of the Dobry Report (1974) that all applications by local planning authorities should be publicised has not been implemented.

Unlike other planning permissions, a permission deemed to be granted under this procedure is personal to the authority and does not survive a disposal of the land (Reg. 7) except where from the very beginning the authority does not propose to carry out the development itself (Reg. 5(6)). The power to make either or both resolutions can be delegated to officers (Reg. 6, *R. v. Lambeth B.C.* [1986] J.P.L. 201).

As we shall see the "bias" rule of natural justice has only a limited application (below, p. 107). However, the Secretary of State may call in any application (Reg. 7(1))[15a] and the local planning authority is bound by his directions. Any application which consists of or includes proposals for the alteration or extension of a listed building must be referred to the Secretary of State (Reg. 7(a)).

Where development is proposed jointly by a local planning authority and a private developer it is uncertain when the special procedure must be used. The language of section 270(1) is inconclusive. It may be that where the land is wholly owned by the local planning authority, including ownership as joint tenant or landlord the special procedure must be used, but not where the authority is proposing to develop land in which they do not hold the whole interest jointly with a private developer (see *Sunbell*

[15a] There is a duty in the case of proposals that depart from the Development Plan to notify the Secretary of State (see Town and Country Planning Development Plans (England) Direction 1981, para. 8(1)).

Properties v. *Dorset C.C.* (1979) 25 E.G. 1123; *cf.* Grant, p. 239).

Delegation

Local planning authorities have wide and flexible powers to delegate powers to committees, sub-committees, officers and other local authorities (L.G.A., 1972, section 101). They cannot, however, delegate to individual councillors and there cannot be a committee of one (*R. v. Secretary of State for the Environment ex p. Hillingdon L.B.C.* [1986] 1 W.L.R. 192).[16] Indeed, it is arguable that a committee must comprise at least three persons. In the case of a committee or sub-committee its functions can similarly be delegated downwards (*ibid.* section 101(2)). The delegator itself can revoke its delegation in any particular case (*ibid.* section 101(4)). Planning committees must comprise at least two-third elected members but otherwise any person who is not disqualified from being a member of a local authority may sit on a committee.

Section 101 seems to exhaust a local planning authority's power of delegation.[17] Other forms of delegation whether direct or indirect for example acting under directions from some other body are therefore unlawful (*Lavender* v. *M.o.H.* [1970] 1 W.L.R. 1231). In many cases however the L.P.A. must obey directions from the Secretary of State and in special cases the applicant must obtain the prior consent of another body.[18]

The Secretary of State may, at common law, act through any official in his department and the courts seem unwilling to impose

---

[16] It is therefore unlawful to delegate to a committee chairman, although *West Glamorgan C.C.* v. *Rafferty* [1987] 1 All E.R. 1005 at 1009 suggests that such a decision can be ratified. (But see *Co-Op Retail Services Ltd.* v. *Taff Ely D.C.* [1980] 39 P. & C.R. 223 at 239). Internal procedural decisions can be taken by chairman: *R.* v. *Brent Health Authority ex p. Francis* [1984] 3 W.L.R. 1317. See Jones [1987] J.P.L. 612. Officers can also make decisions having been required to consult with Chairman and even, apparently, subject to chairman's approval. *Fraser* v. *Secretary of State* [1988] J.P.L. 344 (*sed. quaere.*).

[17] See *Provident Mutual Life Assurance Assoc.* v. *Derby Corporation* [1981] 1 W.L.R. 173: non-discretionary matters of administrative machinery can be delegated. See particularly p. 182. Delegation can be implied by conduct. See below, p. 111 and *Cheshire C.C.* v. *Secretary of State* [1988] J.P.L. 30.

[18] G.D.O. 1988 Arts. 14, 15—The application is suspended pending consideration of the matter by the Secretary of State. L.G.A. 1972, Sched. 16, para. 17. See also Petroleum and Submarine Pipe Lines Act 1975, section 36; Health Services Act 1976, section 15. See further n. 24.

any limitations upon his discretion so to do (*Re Golden Chemical Products* [1976] Ch. 300). This is sometimes explained pragmatically on the basis that such delegation is administratively unavoidable, thus converting the rule into an example of a more general principle (see Lanham (1984) 100 L.Q.R. 587). However, the rule applies only to civil servants within a central government department (*Nelms* v. *Roe* [1970] 1 W.L.R. 4) and is explicable on the basis of the convention of ministerial responsibility (*Carltona* v. *Commissioner of Works* [1943] 2 All E.R. 560). The Secretary of State thus acts unlawfully by accepting even partially binding directions from other departments (*Lavender* v. *M.o.H.* (above)).

Urban development corporations are in a curious position. They can be local planning authorities but are not "local authorities" for the purposes of local government law generally. They cannot therefore apply for injunctions to enforce planning control (*London Docklands Development Corporation* v. *Rank Hovis McDougal Ltd.* (1986) 84 L.G.R. 101. Nor it seems can they take advantage of the power to delegate to officials under s.101. Planning decisions must be enforced by at least a quorum of the corporation. (See L.G.P. and L.A. 1980 Sched. 26, para. 13).

A decision-maker can always delegate fact finding and make recommendations but must be provided with sufficient information to make a general decision as opposed to being a rubber stamp (see *Jeffs* v. *N.Z. Dairy Board* [1967] 1 A.C. 551). Decision-making powers within a local authority can be delegated in a variety of ways so as to preserve the overriding control of the council (see Grant, pp. 247–251). For example, in some cases, only decisions to *refuse* permission are delegated. Alternatively, the council or the main committee may reserve the right to decide prescribed categories of case, for example, where an officer's recommendation is overridden. Some councils have a procedure whereby any councillor can challenge a committee or sub-committee decision within a time limit. Decision-making is normally delegated to a committee but only exceptionally is there full delegation to officials.

Conflicts of interest

The internal decision-making structure within a local authority may also vary considerably (see Craig, *Administrative Law* (1983) Chap. 6). Some authorities possess separate development control and planning sections, others combine their planning and engineering departments. A few have specialist enforcement officers. The majority have a planning committee while some have development committees dealing with additional matters other than planning such as traffic management, property sales, and even housing repairs. The ideological perspective of the purpose of development control may be influenced by the particular administrative arrangements. In particular, conflicts of interest could arise between the planning and entrepreneurial activities of a local planning authority, for example, where it wishes to dispose of its own land for development in competition with private-sector proposals.

The "bias" rule of natural justice has often been invoked in this connection. It is clear that over and above statutory provisions requiring disclosure of interests (Grant, pp. 258–260) the existence of a personal financial interest on the part of a member of the relevant committee or an official would invalidate a planning permission (*R.* v. *Hendon R.D.C. ex p. Chorley* [1933] 2 Q.B. 696). Other interests such as family connections may also invalidate a decision, the test being whether a reasonable man in possession of all the facts known to the reviewing court would consider there to be a reasonable suspicion of bias, (a lower standard than the rival "real likelihood" formulation).[19] Political partisanship as such does not invalidate a decision unless a participant has entirely prejudged the issue.[20] Furthermore, the reasonable man test does not apply where there is a conflict between two or more lawful objectives of the local planning authority including conflicts involving financial gain.

In *R.* v. *St. Edmundsbury B.C.* [1985] 1 W.L.R. 1168 a local planning authority had agreed to sell land to a supermarket company and to help it to obtain planning permission. This did not invalidate a subsequent grant of planning permission to the company despite allegations of bias from rival applicants for permission. The decision is explicable on the basis that by entrusting planning functions to multi-purpose local authorities rather than to independent judicial tribunals, Parliament must necessarily have contemplated this kind of bias. However, the court's reasoning was couched in the language of a distinction between judicial and administrative bodies. It was held that the sole test in the case of an administrative body was whether the authority "despite its interest or its action, was activated by a genuine and

---

[19] *R.* v. *Liverpool City J.J.* [1983] 1 All E.R. 490; See Foulkes, *Administrative Law* (1987), pp. 256–262.

[20] *R.* v. *Amber Valley D.C. ex p. Jackson* [1985] 1 W.L.R. 298. *R.* v. *Waltham Forest D.C. ex p. Baxter* [1987] 3 All E.R. 671; *R.* v. *Rushmoor B.C. ex p. Cranford*, (1981) *The Times*, November 28. See 1983 P.L. 29. These cases illustrate that the courts adopt a wide and non-interventionist approach to the permissible objects of the planning system.

impartial exercise of its discretion," *i.e.* a test of actual bias (see also *R.* v. *Sevenoaks D.C.* [1985] 3 All E.R. 226). The reasoning of Webster J. in *Steeples* v. *Derbyshire C.C.* [1985] 1 W.L.R. 256 where the traditional "reasonable man" was applied was rejected. However, on the facts *Steeples* is probably correct in that the authority seems actually to have fettered its discretion by undertaking to take all reasonable steps to obtain planning permission and agreeing to compensate the developer if it failed to do so. Moreover, these cases concern alleged bias on the part of the authority itself. The position, even in the case of an administrative body, is different where conflicts of interest exist in relation to individual members or officers.

A characteristic of local government committees is that it is possible (subject to the rules governing membership (above)) for officials and elected members to participate on equal terms. Typically members will be briefed by officials about particular applications, will be given a summary of decisions taken by officials under delegated powers and offered recommendations in respect of other applications, but without having detailed information before them. Elected councillors may therefore be at a disadvantage *vis-à-vis* their officials. Indeed, their part-time roles accentuate this. In practice the recommendations of officials are overruled only exceptionally, although where this happens the decision is likely to be influenced by short term ad hoc or political considerations, this being perfectly lawful (see *Cardiff Corporation* v. *Secretary of State* (1971) 22 P. & C.R. 718 at 722–723). Now that planning orthodoxy leans towards pragmatism as opposed to determinist theory (above, Chap. 1) the ideologies of professional planners and elected members may be more compatible than was the case a decade ago.

As regards the constitutional relationship between members and officials there is no analogy with that between ministers and civil servants. There is no relationship analogous to ministerial responsibility between individual members or even committees and officials and the duty of officials is owed to the authority as a whole. Thus, at common law an individual councillor has no right to see council papers except on a "need to know" basis.[21] On the other hand, just as the authority cannot be bound by official advice, nor can it be bound by any mandate from its electorate, although a mandate is a relevant factor which can be taken into account (*Bromley L.B.C.* v. *G.L.C.* [1983] 1 A.C. 768).

---

[21] See *Birmingham City D.C.* v. *'O'* [1983] 1 A.C. 578; *R.* v. *Hackney L.B.C. ex p. Gamper* [1985] 2 All E.R. 375; Birkinshaw [1981] P.L. 545. See L.G.A. 1972, section 100F—right to information except "exempt information."

OFFICIAL ADVICE—ESTOPPEL

We have seen that officials exercise considerable influence upon decision-making. Problems arise when a statement made by an official conflicts with the decision ultimately taken by the authority. For example, a citizen may be informally told that he does not need planning permission only to find that the council subsequently takes enforcement proceedings. Assuming that the official has not warned him of this possibility, and that it is reasonable for him to rely upon the official's assurance, there are two possible legal remedies open to him.

First, he may sue in tort upon the basis of a negligent misrepresentation by the official (*Davy* v. *Spelthorne B.C.* [1984] A.C. 262). There is no need to establish that the official voluntarily assumed responsibility for his statement. As we have seen, development control duties are not as such owed to individual citizens so as to create a cause of action in tort (above, p. 43). Nevertheless it is arguable that there is a special enough relationship between an applicant and a planning official to create a duty in respect of injuries including economic loss, that are a foreseeable result of a false representation (see also Moore, *A Practical Approach to Planning Law*, (1987) p. 121).

Secondly, he may argue that the official's representation binds the authority by virtue of an estoppel. This is more difficult and the cases conflict. In general, the doctrine of estoppel has only a limited application to public law and is essentially a private law doctrine (see *Newbury D.C.* v. *Secretary of State* [1981] A.C. 578).

The citizen must show first, that a statement of fact, or, in equity, a promise, was made by the official; secondly, that it was reasonable for him to rely upon and that he did rely upon the statement; and thirdly, that he incurred loss or detriment in acting upon the statement. Arguably this third requirement does not apply in case of equitable estoppel where the official makes a promise as opposed to a statement of fact (see *Alan* v. *El Nasr* [1972] 2 Q.B. 189).

There is a fundamental objection to the estoppel argument based upon the principle that a public authority cannot disable itself from exercising its statutory functions, nor can it increase its statutory powers by its own acts (see *Maritime Electric Co.* v. *General Dairies* [1937] 1 W.L.R. 465). Responsibility for planning functions is vested in the council, and if it were to be bound by the unauthorised statements of its officials the intention of Parliament would be frustrated. This principle was applied in *Southend Corporation* v. *Hodgson (Wickford) Ltd.* [1962] 1 Q.B. 416. The Divisional Court held that the council was not bound by its engineer's erroneous assurance the respondents' proposed use as a builders yard did not need planning permission. The council's statutory discretion whether to take enforcement action was not to be hindered.

There has been a judicial assault on this principle. In several cases (but in none was the point essential) it was held that estoppel can make an unauthorised decision binding upon an authority (*Robertson* v. *Minister of Pensions* [1971] 1 K.B. 227; *Lever Finance Ltd.* v. *Westminister Corp.* [1971] 1 Q.B. 222; *Norfolk County Council* v. *Secretary of State* [1973] 1 W.L.R. 1400). If these are correct then the public interest that planning decisions be made upon the basis of all relevant factors would give way to the interest of a private individual outside the statutory framework.

To allow estoppel a wide scope has undesirable consequences. First, it might prejudice the position of third parties such as neighbours in that a decision may become binding without compliance with statutory procedures designed to protect them. Secondly, officials may be inhibited from giving informal advice by the fear of binding their authority (see *Brooks and Burton* v. *Secretary of State* (1976) 75 L.G.R. 285, 296).

In *Wells* v. *Minister of Housing* [1967] 1 W.L.R. 1000 estoppel was given a more limited scope. The authority determined a planning application without complying with certain formal requirements (see below, p. 112). The decision was nevertheless held to bind the authority on the ground that the requirements in question were not essential. There is no reason why the doctrine of estoppel should not apply in this kind of case. Ultra vires is not involved and there is therefore no conflict of principle. Lord Denning M.R. said in *Wells* at p. 1007, that "a public authority cannot be estopped from doing its public duty, but I do think it can be estopped from relying on technicalities." The requirements of the estoppel doctrine and in particular that of reasonable reliance militate against any tendency to take this too far. Strict adherence to formalities would produce "an architect's nightmare and a bureacrat's morass to the advantage of nobody" (*per* Sachs L.J. in *Lever Finance* (above) at p. 232) but on the other hand "the local planning authority is not a free agent to waive statutory requirements in favour of (so to speak) an adversary: it is the guardian of the planning system" (*per* Russell L.J. (dissenting) in *Wells* at p. 1015).

This compromise approach was applied by Sachs L.J. in the *Lever* case (above), although Lord Denning M.R. with whom Megaw L.J. agreed relied upon estoppel alone. An official informed the developer that certain variations in its plans would not require planning permission. There had been a long-standing practice to allow such decisions to be made by officials, but on this occasion the council purported to overrule the official. It was held that the council was bound by the official's decision. However, there was statutory power to delegate such matters to officers (see now L.G.A. 1972, section 101). No such power existed in 1962 when the *Southend* case was decided. The council had not delegated in writing as the Act required, but, on the basis of the *Wells* case, this could be treated as a minor procedural requirement, the defect being cured by application of estoppel principles. No question of vires was therefore in issue.

Finally, in *Western Fish Products Ltd.* v. *Penrith D.C.* [1981] 2 All E.R. 204 the Court of Appeal confined the operation of estoppel to two exceptional situations, first, where there had been implied delegation, and secondly, to cases such as *Wells* involving minor procedural requirements. The doctrine that estoppel cannot fetter the exercise of a statutory discretion was reaffirmed. The case concerned a claim that the plaintiff was led to believe (during conversations) that it had existing rights in respect of a proposed development. It was held on the facts that there had been neither a representation nor detrimental reliance, but even if there had been the authority could not be estopped. Official status above is not enough to justify the citizen relying upon a statement. There must be something more, for example an established practice of delegation amounting to an implied delegation (see *Cheshire C.C.* v. *Secretary of State* [1988] J.P.L. 30).

The views expressed about the general scope of estoppel were *obiter*, and the conflict with *Lever Finance* remains (see *Ward* [1978] J.P.L. 594). In particular it is unclear whether the delegation exception applies where there is no statutory power to delegate at all. It is submitted that it does not. The existence of a well-known practice concerns the question whether it is reasonable for the citizen to rely on the statement made by the official, not whether the power to delegate exists. On this view the delegation exception is really an example of the broader notion of condoning minor irregularities, *i.e.* the absence of express formal delegation. Indeed it may be difficult to rely upon any kind of implied delegation in view of L.G.A. 1972, s.100G. This requires local authorities to publish a list stating which powers are delegated to officers.

Even where estoppel cannot operate, representations by officials must at least be taken into account when decisions are made. Thus an assurance may create a legitimate expectation that the authority will have to justify overriding by reference to some other lawful consideration (below, p. 142).

This approach if taken to extremes would involve the court

indulging in a political balancing act. For example, in *Laker Airways* v. *Trade Department* [1977] Q.B. 643 at 707 Lord Denning M.R. accepted that the government cannot be estopped from exercising its powers "but . . . it can . . . be estopped when it is misusing them; and it does misuse them if it exercises them in circumstances which risk injustice or unfairness to the individual without any countervailing benefit to the public."

This statement is curious in that if there is a misuse of power the question of estoppel is surely irrelevant. The estoppel issue concerns the *valid* exercise of power in the face of an unauthorised assurance that the power would be exercised in a different way. The need to take prior representations into account in exercising a discretion is another matter altogether and concerns procedural fairness. It is submitted that the courts should intervene in the case of an unauthorised representation only where the authority (a) refuses to hear the affected party and (b) can offer no justification for overriding the assurance.

It is often discussed whether, irrespective of negligence, compensation should be awarded to a person who, for example, erects a building in reliance upon an unauthorised assurance thus giving some of the benefits of an estoppel without overriding the public interest (but see Craig, *Administrative Law*, (1983) pp. 582–583). The argument here is that the public benefit should be paid for, bearing in mind that the level of compensation would be less than the overall benefit to the public, quite apart from the benefit of justice being achieved. The cost to be set against this lies in the risk of inhibiting officials from giving "off-the-record" advice (see Rutherford, etc. [1986] J.P.L. 981 and Circular 142/73).

Kinds of applications

Several different kinds of application can be made in relation to a planning permission.

SECTION 53 DETERMINATIONS

Under section 53 any person who proposes to carry out any operations or to make any change of use may apply to the local planning authority for a determination whether development is involved or whether planning permission is required in the light of the (sic) development order and of any enterprise zone or simplified planning zone scheme. A simple procedure is supplied requiring a written application together with basic plans and a description of the proposals, and where relevant of the existing or latest use of the land. (G.D.O. 1988 Art. 9). A section 53 application can be combined with an application for planning permission. In *Wells* v. *M.o.H.* [1967] 1 W.L.R. 1000 at 107–108 Lord Denning M.R. described the effect of a section 53 determination as equivalent to an unconditional grant of planning permission. This is somewhat misleading (*e.g.* abandonment principles, below, p. 172) although as with a planning permission a section 53 determination must be registered with the local planning authority (section 53(2); see further below, p. 170).

Section 53 does not apply to activities already implemented, nor to such matters as the construction of an *express* planning permission.

A valid section 53 determination will bind the authority even after a change in the law (see *English Speaking Union of the Commonwealth* v. *City of Westminster L.B.C.* (1973) 26 P. & C.R. 575) not because of estoppel but simply as an exercise of statutory power.

This suggests that procedural formalities should be strictly followed. However, apart from a strong dissent of Russell L.J. in *Wells* v. *M.o.H.* [1967] 1 W.L.R. 1000 the courts have taken a relaxed view, holding for example that an exchange of letters could constitute a valid determination (*English Speaking Union* (above)). Moreover in *Wells* the majority held that a formal application for planning permission could constitute an implied application under section 53 for a determination that planning permission is not required. This raises strong public policy objections (see the dissent of Russell L.J.) and seems to be inconsistent with the language of section 53. Moreover the House of Lords has held that the converse does not apply. Therefore an applicant who applies for and receives planning permission cannot be estopped from subsequently claiming that his activities do *not* constitute development (*Newbury D.C.* v. *Secretary of State* [1981] A.C. 578). It could be that the principle in *Wells* depends on estoppel and is thus within the exception recognised by the Court of Appeal in *Western Fish* (above, p. 111) under which "minor" procedural irregularities can be waived. In *Western Fish* their Lordships expressed misgivings about *Wells* but regarded themselves as bound. Again, this group of cases hardly evidences judicial enthusiasm for private property interests (see Grant, pp. 209–210).

APPLICATIONS FOR PLANNING PERMISSION

Application can be made for:

(i) full planning permission which can be retrospective;
(ii) in the case of building operations, "outline" planning permission. Section 42. G.D.O. 1988, Art. 7;
(iii) for extensions of existing permissions which have neither been implemented nor lapsed (Town and Country Planning (Applications) Regulations 1988 (S.I. 1988 No. 1812);
(iv) for development without complying with conditions attached to an existing planning permission (Section 31A, Sched. 11, para. 4). Under this procedure the authority may vary the conditions but cannot consider other matters.
(v) for approval of reserved matters following an outline planning permission (above) or approval of details or consents required by a condition (*e.g. R. v. Surrey C.C. ex p. Monk* (1987) 53 P. & C.R. 410), G.D.O. 1988 Art. 8.

The application procedure is regulated by the G.D.O. 1988, the Town and Country Planning (Applications) Regulations 1988 (above), and by directions issued by the Secretary of State, (sections 24, 25, 31). Applications must be on forms issued by the authority and accompanied by plans and such other information as the authority directs "to enable them to determine the application" (section 25). A fee is payable in accordance with regulations.[22]

Application procedure

COMMON LAW

English law recognises no general obligation to notify, consult or publicise in relation to government decisions. A decision-maker is master of its own procedure subject to the elementary notions of "fairness" or natural justice. It is questionable whether the common law rules of natural justice apply to applications for planning permission so as to give an applicant any specific procedural rights to be heard over and above those provided by

---

[22] See Town and Country Planning (Fees for Applications and Deemed Applications) Regulations S.I. 1983 No. 1674. These are geared to administrative costs. See S.I. 1987 No. 101. No fee is required for approval of details or consents required by a condition.

legislation and administrative directives. On the one hand natural justice is no longer confined to decisions that are analytically judicial in character nor those affecting legal rights in the strict sense. Therefore early dicta, for example in *Hanily* v. *M.o.H.* [1952] 2 Q.B. 444 are no longer reliable. An applicant claiming a right to a hearing—which would entail a right to comment upon the material before the authority—must now establish a "legitimate expectation" in the sense of something in the statutory context or the surrounding circumstances, which would make it unfair not to give a hearing. This could include for example a previous practice of giving hearings or a specific undertaking given to the applicant (*Council of Civil Service Unions* v. *Minister for the Civil Service* [1985] A.C. 374). Any claim to a legitimate expectation to be heard is weakened by the following considerations.

(a) A planning permission does not remove existing rights but is a discretionary privilege (see *McInnes* v. *Onslow-Fane* [1978] 1 W.L.R. 1520).

(b) There are usually opportunities for extensive hearings at appeal stages.

(c) The existence of statutory requirements (above) might impliedly exclude any common law rights.[23]

In the administrative context the right to be heard requires only a minimal standard of fairness and certainly does not include a right to examine all the evidence. For example, in *R.* v. *Sheffield Corporation* (1979) 37 P. & C.R. 1 it was held that there was no obligation formally to consult with the occupants of a caravan site in respect of which an application was made as long as the authority took their views into account.

Nevertheless a hearing may be required in special cases. These might include, for example, cases where the local planning authority leads the applicant to believe that permission will be granted or where the applicant's personal intentions or conduct are relevant, or where substantial objections have been received from local residents in a controversial matter (see *R.* v. *Great Yarmouth B.C.* [1988] J.P.L. 18). In these cases the applicant may be entitled to make representations and to see and comment on representations made by others. Indeed it could be argued that the incidence of appeals—a notorious cause of delay in the planning system— might be significantly reduced if greater openness were adopted at local level.

[23] *Bates* v. *Lord Hailsham* [1972] 1 W.L.R. 1373. Procedural rules contained in delegated legislation do not have this effect (see below, p. 215). See also *Gaiman* v. *National Association for Mental Health* [1971] Ch. 317.

It is also arguable that a person who can show that an application bears particularly hard upon him so as, for example, to interfere with his amenities or to reduce the value of his property would have a right to a hearing to the extent of requiring the authority to consider a written representation. In this connection it has been held that a planning authority is obliged to take into account the impact of a development upon the private rights of neighbours and a right to be heard may follow from this (*Stringer* v. *Minister of Housing* [1970] 1 W.L.R. 1281).

There is no general statutory requirement to publicise applications for planning permission nor to take into account representations from the public (see below, p. 118). However, in practice the majority of local planning authorities advertise all applications. This goes beyond the minimal requirements of the general law, although it may be that an established practice of publicity creates a legitimate expectation of a right to make representations and that any representations made must be fairly dealt with (but see, *R.* v. *Monmouth D.C. ex p. Jones* [1986] J.P.L. 686; *R.* v. *Secretary of State ex p. Kent* [1988] J.P.L. 706).

In any event the courts are not impressed with the notion that a right to be heard invokes participation in decision-making as such but regard hearings as primarily concerned with the impact of a decision upon the interests of the person claiming to be heard. There is no right to be heard in relation to aesthetic, professional, or policy value judgments (below, p. 211).

STATUTORY HEARING PROCEDURES

Requirements to consult, publicise or notify are imposed by the Act, by the G.D.O. and by directions issued by the Secretary of State under the G.D.O.[24] Consultation is a two way process requiring a genuine exchange of information and sufficient time to produce a reasoned reply (see *R.* v. *Secretary of State for Social Services ex p. A.M.A.* [1986] 1 All E.R. 164). In the planning

---

[24] Section 31. G.D.O. 1988, Arts. 11, 12, 13–15, 17–19, 21. See, *e.g.* Town and County Planning Development Plans (England) Direction 1981, Circular 2/81; Town and Country Planning (Aerodromes) Direction 1981; Town and Country Planning (Housing Accommodation) Direction 1952 (Grant 230). Town and Country Planning (Shopping Centres) Direction 1986; Circular 21/86. See also Local Government, Planning and Land Act 1988, section 138 (Urban Development Corporations); Town and Country Planning Act 1971, Sched. 11, paras. 5 and 7 (Listed buildings and conservation areas) Circular 8/87. Directions have the force of law but are not statutory instruments and so escape publicity and Parliamentary controls. They may be contained in circulars but are different in legal terms from the rest of the circular.

context *consultation* is required only with other public authorities.[25] *Notification* entitles the notified party only to be informed of the general nature of the application. The only general notification requirement imposed directly on the authority is to notify parish and community councils if they so request.[26] Other notification duties are imposed upon the applicant for planning permission (below).[27] Publicity requirements exist only in special cases (below, p. 118) and there is a limited right of public access to local authority meetings and associated documents under the Local Government (Access to Information) Act 1985 (see Eyre [1987] J.P.L. 311).

Notification requirements. An applicant for planning permission must certify either that he is the owner of the land or that he has notified the owner in which case the owner has a right to make representations (section 27). The same applies to agricultural tenants (section 27(3)) and, in the case of mining operations, to owners of mineral rights (other than oil, gas and coal, or gold and silver) (section 27(1)A, B). These provisions are desirable because any person can apply for planning permission in respect of any land. Injustice could arise where, say, a purchaser having the benefit of a planning permission, but not notifying the owner of this, acquires the land at less than market price (see Moore, *A Practical Approach to Planning Law*, (1987) pp. 105 *et seq.*).

A fundamental difficulty of English property law is that land ownership (except in the case of surplus land owned by public bodies, (see L.G.P. and L.A. 1980)) is not a matter of public record so that it may be impossible to discover the owner's identity.[28] There is an alternative certificate procedure designed for this kind of case including a requirement for local newspaper publicity (section 27(2)). In the case of permission for underground mining operations a site notice must also be posted (section 27(2)A)).

---

[25] L.G.A. 1972, Sched. 16, para. 19(2). County councils G.D.O. 1988, Art. 18—Public Authorities affected by particular kinds of development; 1971 Act, section 29(5)—caravan site licencing authority; G.D.O. 1988, Art. 15 (highway authority notification); *Ibid.* Art. 21—parish council notification, *Ibid.* Art. 20—county matters. Permitted time: 14 days (G.D.O. 1988, Arts. 18(4), 19. See also advisory code (Encyclopaedia, 2–855).

[26] L.G.A. 1972, Sched. 16, para. 20.

[27] There are also notification requirements relating to the powers of the Secretary of State to call in applications or restrict grants of planning permission (above, p. 103).

[28] "Owner" for this purpose means a freeholder or lessee with at least seven years to run (s.27(7)). See G.D.O. 1988 Arts. 11, 12, 13.

Publicity requirements. Publicity requirements and their correlative duty to take into account representations received from the public (section 29(3), (4)) fit uneasily into the system of representative democracy embodied in the planning legislation. The advantages of publicity in legitimising and informing decisions can be balanced against the risks of domination by well resourced pressure groups and selfish short term local interests. Professor McAuslan's version of "participation" as representing the voice of opposition has little support in terms of legal protection. Publicity requirements are minimal, largely negative and couched in discretionary terms.

There are miscellaneous publicity requirements. They include:

1. "Bad Neighbour" development (section 26). This means development (which is presumably believed to be offensive) specified in the G.D.O. (Art. 11 and Sched. 4). The duty is imposed upon the applicant and requires a site notice to be placed for at least 7 days and a newspaper advertisement (of any size) specifying a period of at least 21 days for objections. Certificates must be furnished with the application stating that the statutory requirements have been satisfied or that all reasonable steps have been taken to do so.

2. Development which would *in the opinion of the authority* affect the character of a conservation area or the setting of a listed building (section 28). Here the duty is imposed directly upon the local planning authority and requires site notices and local newspaper publicity in the same way as bad neighbour development.

3. "Departure Applications." This is based on directions issued by the Secretary of State (section 31(1)(*b*)) and concerns applications which in the *authority's opinion* conflict with, or prejudice the implementation of the development plan and which they do not propose to refuse or where conditions are proposed to overcome the problem (Town and County Planning (Development Plans) (England) Direction 1981, Circular 2/81.) In the case of conflicts with the structure plan there are further procedural requirements (below).

The only publicity requirement is to insert a local newspaper advertisement (of any size) specifying a period of at least 28 days for objections. Even this can be dispensed with if the application has been advertised in pursuance of other planning requirements.

In all these cases the local planning authority is enjoined not to consider the application until the expiry of the 21 day period. People who made representations under these provisions

in context to "owner certificate" people have no procedural rights
at the appeal stage[29] nor in relation to "called in" applications.

DEPARTURE APPLICATIONS

There are complex procedural requirements relating to departure
applications. They derive from several sources[30] and do not easily fit
within the general principle that the development plan is only one of
the factors that a local planning authority must take into account
(section 29(1); see below, pp. 143–145. There are three levels of
procedural requirement relating to departure applications. These
are increasingly more stringent depending upon the seriousness of
the matter. They do not apply where the authority proposes to
refuse permission or to impose conditions that will prevent the
conflict in question. The requirements have been somewhat relaxed
in recent years with the implication that the link between positive
planning and development control is becoming increasingly
tenuous.

They can be summarised as follows (Town and Country Planning
(Development Plan) (England) Directions, 1981, Circular 2/81):

1. Publicity for some departure applications (above).

2. Applications that in the opinion of the authority would
materially conflict with or prejudice the implementation: (i) of any
policy or general proposal in a *structure plan*, or (ii) in certain cases
of any proposal in a local plan made by the county council, or (iii)
proposed alterations in a structure plan or county local plan to
which publicity has been given.

In these cases the County Council has the right to be consulted
(L.G.A. 1972, Sched. 16, Art. 19). There is a non-statutory code of
practice, the theme of which is to minimise consultation (see
Circular 2.81).

3. Applications which in the opinion of the authority would
materially conflict with or prejudice the implementation: (i) of any
of the policies or general proposals in the structure plan in force, or
(ii) any modification to a local plan made by the Secretary of State
or, in cases involving development by a local planning authority
(above, p. 103), of the provisions of *any* development plan. In these

[29] "Bad neighbour" objectors no longer have a right to appear at the inquiry in
relation to "called-in" cases. See below, p. 220.
[30] Section 31(1)(b). G.D.O. 1988, Art. 17; Town and Country Planning
(Development Plans) (England) Directions 1981 (Circular 2/81). Town and
Country Planning General Regulations S.I. 1976, No. 1419 (local planning
authority development). L.G.A. 1972, Sched. 16, para. 192(a).

cases the Secretary of State must be notified to give him 21 days to decide whether to call in the application.

It has been held that the requirements of the development plan direction concerning consultation and publicity are only directory and that failure to comply does not invalidate a planning permission (below, p. 123). The reasoning is based upon the subjective element built into these requirements, the fear of uncertainty, and the fact that there is no general duty to comply with a development plan in the first place.[31]

OTHER PROCEDURAL REQUIREMENTS

In order to comply with European Community law there is an obligation in certain cases imposed on the applicant for planning permission to provide an "environmental statement" indicating the potential impact of the proposal on the local environment. The local planning authority must itself carry out an "environmental assessment." Projects of this kind include oil refineries, power stations, railways etc. In addition many private industrial developments are included "if they are likely to have significant effects on the environment." A right of appeal to the Secretary of State is provided in relation to this question.[31a]

The other main procedural requirement is the duty upon the local planning authority to notify the applicant of the decision within a period of eight weeks from the date when the application was received (G.D.O. 1988, Arts. 23, 24). Failure can be treated as a deemed refusal of permission and thus enables the applicant to appeal to the Secretary of State (section 37). The eight week period can be extended by agreement and permission can be *granted* outside the eight weeks.

---

[31] *R.* v. *St. Edmunsbury B.C.* [1985] 1 W.L.R. 1168; *R.* v. *Carlisle City Council* [1986] J.P.L. 206 (below, p. 123); See also *Co-Operative Retail Services* v. *Taff-Ely B.C.* [1980] 39 P. & C.R. 223; *Edinburgh Corporation* v. *Simpson* (1960) S.C. 313 at 319. But see *R.* v. *Doncaster M.B.C.* [1987] J.P.L. 444 (local authorities own application). On the other hand, section 29(1), which confers a general power to grant permission is expressed to be "subject to the following provisions of this Act." Section 31(1)(*b*) confers powers exercisable through the G.D.O. and directions to impose conditions on departure applications. This would seem sufficient to permit the Development Plan Direction to remove the authorities' jurisdiction during the 21 days or if it fails to comply with the Direction. See *contra* Grant, p. 235. A direction under G.D.O. 1988, Art. 14 could prohibit a grant of planning permission: *R.* v. *St. Edmunsbury B.C.* (above).

[31a] Town and County Planning (Assessment of Environmental Effects) Regulations 1988. (S.I. 1988, No. 1199. Circular 15/88. W.O. 23/88.) See E.C. Directive 85/337. G.D.O. 1988 Art. 14(2).

Finally there is, as we have seen (above, p. 53), a duty to give reasons in writing for refusing permission, for refusing approval of reserved matters or for conditions. The statement of reasons must include any directions given by the Secretary of State or other authority. There seems to be no obligation to give reasons for withholding agreement or consents in other cases (*e.g.* where a condition requires that the local authority approve materials for subsequent works).

Breach of procedural requirements

The law relating to the effect of a failure to comply with statutory procedural requirements is in considerable confusion. There are clear policy conflicts. On the one hand there is the concern to ensure that public authorities comply with procedural restrictions imposed by Parliament presumably for good reason. Against this there is an understandable judicial reluctance to strike down a government decision on technical grounds, particularly where, as with a planning permission, the decision is embodied in a public document that future landowners must rely upon who would not be able to check whether the proper procedures have been followed. The simplistic distinction between property and public interest ideologies is quite inadequate in this context. Procedural defects are typically raised by pressure groups or disappointed rival applicants for planning permission. In general the courts are taking a broader, less legalistic approach than was the case 10 years ago.[32]

Confusion may arise because of a failure to distinguish three separate but related issues. First, the nature of the procedural requirement, secondly, the question whether the requirement has actually been broken, and thirdly, the consequences of a breach in the particular case. In *O'Reilly* v. *Mackman* [1982] 3 All E.R. 1124 at 1127 Lord Diplock's approach to procedural irregularities was as follows:

> "Where the legislation which confers on a statutory tribunal its decision-making powers also provides expressly for the procedure it shall follow ... it is a question of construction of the relevant legislation ... whether a particular procedural provision is mandatory, so that its non-observance ... makes the decision itself a nullity, or whether it is merely directory, so that the statutory tribunal has a discretion not to comply with it

[32] See, *e.g.* "Development Control 30 Years On," *J.P.L.*, *Occasional Papers* (1979), pp. 74, 75.

if, in its opinion, the exceptional circumstances of a particular case justify departing from it."

This distinction between mandatory and directory requirements once provided the dominant judicial approach. A mandatory requirement is an essential requirement. Whether a particular requirement is mandatory depends upon the interpretation of the particular statutory provisions: "the importance of the provision that has been disregarded and the relation of that provision to the general objective intended to be secured by the Act (*Howard* v. *Boddington* (1877) 2 P.D. 203 at 211). The court will look at such matters as the effect on persons affected of a failure to comply with the procedure, and whether the procedure is attached to a power or a duty. In the case of a duty they are more willing to treat a requirement as directory than in the case of a power (*Cullimore* v. *Lyme Regis Corp.* [1962] 1 Q.B. 718).

Within this framework considerable confusions have arisen. For example, do we assess whether a procedural requirement is mandatory or directory by examining the statutory provision in the light of the facts of the particular case as suggested by Lord Hailsham in *London and Clydesdale Estates* v. *Aberdeen D.C.* ([1979] 3 All E.R. 876) or do we attempt to look at the matter in general terms first (see *R.* v. *Secretary of State for Social Services ex p. A.M.A.* [1986] 1 All E.R. 164). Does breach of a requirement that is merely directory have any effect at all upon the validity of the decision? (see *James* v. *M.O.H.* [1965] 3 All E.R. 602). Conversely, does breach of a mandatory requirement always make a decision a complete nullity? (*London and Clydesdale Estates* (above)).

The courts will sometimes condone the breach even of a mandatory procedural requirement if there has been "substantial compliance" (*Coney* v. *Choice* [1975] 1 W.L.R. 422). This reflects the fact that there is often a discretion as to how to comply with a procedural requirement (*e.g.* "adequate publicity.") Moreover the judicial review remedies are themselves discretionary and this may ultimately be more important than formal classification.

In *London and Clydesdale Estates* v. *Aberdeen D.C.* (above) Lord Hailsham thought that the distinctions between mandatory and directory, void and voidable were inadequate to explain the "spectrum of possibilities open" to the court. Indeed there are enough devices at hand to give the judge a virtually unfettered complete discretion to decide how to deal with a procedural breach. There are certainly many more possibilities than Lord Diplock's dictum suggests and it seems futile to assign these rigidly between the two categories of mandatory and directory. Absolute notions of nullity have not been applied in English administrative law. The better distinction is between defects that are *capable* of resulting in nullity and those that are never much more than voidable. Even a decision tainted by a mandatory breach has been held capable of legal consequences (*e.g. London and Clydesdale Estates* (above) — ultra vires certificate not the name as "no certificate" for compensation purposes).

In the planning context the courts have until very recently applied the mandatory/directory distinction, but even after deciding (often at great length) that a requirement was mandatory have recognised that they had a discretion not to quash. They have been particularly influenced by the importance of third parties being able to rely upon an ostensibly valid planning permission.[33]

The reasons offered for treating some procedural requirements as mandatory and others as directory seem obscure. In *Main* v. *Swansea D.C.* [1985] 49 P. & C.R. 26 it was held that the "certificate" procedure required by section 27 for notifying owners of planning applications was mandatory. This is not surprising and the same seems to apply to the "bad neighbour" and conservation area publicity requirements imposed by sections 26 and 28 (above) (see *Steeples* v. *Derbyshire C.C.* [1984] 3 All E.R. 468). However, in *Main* the court emphasised that the mandatory, disectory distinction was not crucial and exercised its discretion not to quash because of delay.

On the other hand, the consultation and publicity requirements relating to applications that depart from the development plan have been held only directory, or in the alternative the court has exercised its discretion not to quash because no serious injustice was in fact experienced (above, p. 120). The rationale for this appears to be twofold: (i) the subjective nature of these requirements—the authority must form an "opinion" about whether the application departs from the plan; (ii) the fact that the procedural duties about development plans stem from section $31(1)(b)$ and rules made under it, whereas independently of section 31, an authority is empowered by section 29(1) to depart from the development plan (see above n. 31). The courts have also taken account of the commercial disadvantages of setting aside a planning permission. In *R.* v. *Carlisle City Council* [1986] J.P.L. 206 the court distinguished between "prior notification" requirements in connection with an

---

[33] *e.g. Main* v. *Swansea City Council* [1985] 49 P. & C.R. 26 at 34–37, 39; *R.* v. *St. Edmunsbury B.C.*, n. 31, above; *R.* v. *Carlisle City Council*, n. 31 above; *Co-Operative Retail Services* v. *Taff Ely B.C.* (1980) 39 P. & C.R. 223 at 238–239, 246. See also *R.* v. *Secretary of State for Social Services ex p. A.M.A.* [1986] 1 All E.R. 164; *Coney* v. *Choice* [1975] 1 W.L.R. 422.

application for planning permission and consultation requirements in a departure application. The former should be treated strictly as mandatory, the latter can be regarded as directory. Macpherson J. thought that consultation requirements do not "go to the root" of an application. He also exercised his discretion in favour of the Council on the basis that no one had suffered harm.

Finally, compliance with the eight week time limit for notifying applicants of a decision on a planning application has been held to be directory only (*James* v. *M.o.H.* [1966] 1 W.L.R. 135).

It is suggested that the approach based upon mandatory and directory requirements is hopelessly inadequate. The following approach seems to be preferable. It is based on two tests.

1. Has the procedural requirement actually been breached? The questions of "substantial" compliance and subjectivity should arise at this stage. The statutory language will also be significant as indicating an intention to treat the requirement strictly and to this extent the old notion of "mandatory" may still survive.

2. Should the court exercise its discretion not to quash? In connection with this the court must take into account the circumstances of the particular case including the seriousness of the breach question of administrative convenience, the conduct of the applicant and third party reliance.

In *Brayhead (Ascot)* v. *Middlesex C.C.* [1984] 2 Q.B. 303 the Divisional Court held that a failure to give reasons for the imposition of a condition although subject to mandamus did not render the condition void at all. This is sometimes taken as meaning that the duty was only directory. However, the court expressly held it to be mandatory (at pp. 313–314). The essential point seems to be that the duty to give reasons can be separated from procedural requirements relating to the decision making process itself so that there is no purpose to be served by treating the validity of a permission as contingent upon the giving of reasons.

In two recent cases the courts seem to have moved towards an analogous approach. Both cases concerned the local planning authority's power to grant itself planning permission (above, p. 103). In both the court stressed the desirability of strict procedural compliance but because of the particular local circumstances rather than *a priori* legal principles. *R.* v. *Lambeth L.B.C. ex p. Stamp* ([1987] J.P.L. 441) concerned a proposal for a synthetic athletics track affecting a conservation area. The required newspaper advertisement had failed to specify the period for objections. The Court of Appeal rejected the mandatory/directory approach as unhelpful, was reluctant to apply the *St. Edmundsbury* and *Carlisle* cases (above, n. 31) and preferred two broad tests, first, how important is the procedural requirement, and secondly should the court give relief in its discretion. On this basis the planning permission was quashed because of the intense public interest in the application. *Lambeth* was followed in *R. v. Doncaster M.B.C. ex p. British Railways Board* ([1987] J.P.L. 444). This concerned procedural flaws in a local authority's resolution to grant itself planning permission for a "departure application." It was held that in controversial cases where an authority is in effect giving itself planning permission it is particularly important to comply strictly with procedures.

In the procedural cases both common law and statutory, the judges are at their most flexible. There is no evidence that administrative legality is valued for its own sake. Nor on the other hand is there much deference to property rights in the narrow sense. Administrative efficiency, commercial certainty and "legitimate expectations" seem to be the main considerations coupled with a willingness to look into the substance of a particular transaction in considerable detail. In the absence of legislative guidelines the judges have been forced into the political role of balancing competing policies but have on the whole performed this in the light of non-controversial principles.

6. The Discretion of the Authority

General considerations

Planning permission may be refused, granted unconditionally or granted subject to such conditions as the authority thinks fit (section 29(1)). The Act requires authorities to have regard to the provisions of the development plan and to "any other material considerations" but without specifying what these are (section 29(2)). There are also specific statutory provisions authorising certain kinds of conditions (below, p. 152). The grounds upon which the exercise of discretion can be challenged in the courts have been formulated in several different ways. Inconsistent terminology is one of the bugbears of this subject and there is little agreement as to how to classify the various grounds of judicial review or indeed as to the theory behind them (above, Chap. 1). Both the Scylla of over-simplification and the Charybdis of using differing language to mean the same thing need attention.

The grounds of review can broadly be summarised under three heads: (1) Taking irrelevant factors into account; (2) failing to take relevant factors into account including, in particular, the fettering of a discretion and (3) unreasonableness or "irrationality."

These grounds of review are not peculiar to so-called discretionary powers but are common to every exercise of statutory power. Indeed, as we saw in Chapter 1 the notion of discretion is difficult to pin down. Many questions of statutory interpretation are discretionary in the sense that the decision maker, whether court or official, has a choice as to how to apply the words of the statute to the facts. In as much as the courts allow freedom of choice to an official, for example, in deciding whether a particular activity is or is not development (above, Chap. 3), then the official is exercising discretion. Arguably the notion of discretion as such is superfluous and a more useful distinction is between *duties* on the one hand and powers on the other. A duty exists where the official is *required* to do something, *e.g.* take a particular factor into account or apply a

126

fixed rule. The function of judicial review is therefore to impose duties, the effect of which is to circumscribe official power. Power in this sense means the legal capacity to make an effective decision, either as to whether a state of affairs exists, *e.g.* has "development" occurred, or as to whether planning permission should be granted or a condition imposed.

Some kinds of government power are said to be "non-justiciable." This means firstly that judicial review may be expressly excluded by statute. As we have seen this is not generally so with development control, except where the Act provides its own special review machinery (above, pp. 47–48). A non-justiciable decision is also one which has some inherent quality that persuades the court not to intervene. There are several reasons why this might be so, for example, foreign relationships, deference to a very high-level political body, or lack of judicial experience.

These factors do not usually arise in the development control context. Decisions that are wholly non-justiciable are uncommon and relate mainly to the royal prerogative (see *Council of Civil Service Unions* v. *Minister for the Civil Service* [1984] 3 W.L.R. 1174). They must be distinguished from cases where judicial review is available in principle but where for policy reasons the courts adopt a lower than normal level of review or will not interfere with particular aspects of the decision. In these latter cases the court will not determine what factors are or are not relevant or what is "reasonable" upon any ground short of bad faith or deliberate misconduct. Decisions involving highly specialised or politically sensitive considerations such as national security, decisions where judicial interference might affect the proper discharge of a government function, or decisions subject to Parliamentary approval fall into this category.[1] In the planning context, aesthetic and economic value judgments play a major part in decision making and the courts adopt a policy of not interfering with these.

It is often said that judicial review is concerned with the "decision making process" rather than with its substance.[2] This is misleading.

---

[1] In *Leech* v. *Parkhurst Prison Deputy Governor* [1988] 1 All E.R. 495 the House of Lords seemed to be resistant to the idea that any area of statutory power is inherently unreviewable but preferred to rely on the discretionary nature of the remedies in particular contexts. *Gouriet* v. *U.P.O.W.* [1978] A.C. 435—A.G.'s power to seek injunction; *Nottingham C.C.* v. *Secretary of State* [1986] 1 All E.R. 199; *R.* v. *H.M. Treasury ex p. Smedley* [1985] 1 All E.R. 589. Permission for development may also be sought through a private Act of Parliament thus excluding the courts entirely: see *Picken* v. *B.R.B.* [1974] A.C. 765.

[2] *e.g. Chief Constable of North Wales Police* v. *Evans* [1982] 1 W.L.R. 1155. See further Chap. 2 above.

The notion of relevance is certainly concerned with the way in which a decision is made in the sense that the court is concerned to identify the factors that must be taken into account and not generally with the weight to be given to any particular factor. However "substance" is important even here. The court will not set aside a decision even where an irrelevant factor has been taken into account or a relevant factor overlooked unless the defect actually affects the substance of the decision. For example, the weight of the other relevant considerations may be such that the authority would have made the same decision anyway, in which case the court will not disturb the decision. Conversely if *unreasonable* weight is given to a relevant factor the court might interfere.[3] For example in *South Oxfordshire D.C.* v. *Secretary of State* [1981] 1 W.L.R. 1902 it was held not only that other planning permissions relating to the applicant's land should be taken into account but that less weight must be given to expired permissions than to live permissions.

An extreme example is provided by *The London Residuary Body* v. *Secretary of State* [1988] J.P.L. 637. The Secretary of State had granted planning permission for a change of use of County Hall from the headquarters of the G.L.C. to offices. The Inspector at the enquiry decided that there was considerable need for the building for government purposes but no significant need for offices and recommended refusal of permission. Nevertheless the Secretary of States' decision was upheld in principle and was set aside only because he had not given adequate reasons. He was entitled to apply a general presumption in favour of granting permission and for political reasons to prefer this to the need for the existing use. (See p. 644–646).

There is a presumption in favour of granting planning permission. This means that a clear reason must be given why a proposal is harmful. However, this presumption does not affect the basic principle of judicial review that government decisions are presumed to be valid unless the challenger can show the contrary. Thus as long as the reasons given are prima facie adequate it will be presumed that all relevant factors have properly been taken into account unless the applicant can show otherwise.[4] Nor does the

---

[3] *Pickwell* v. *Camden L.B.C.* [1983] 1 All E.R. 602 at 621; *R.* v. *Secretary of State for Social Services ex p. Welcome Foundation Ltd.* [1987] 2 All E.R. 1025; *West Glamorgan C.C.* v. *Rafferty* [1987] 1 All E.R. 1005; *R.* v. *I.L.E.A. ex p. Westminster City Council* [1986] 1 W.L.R. 28. *Chichester D.C.* v. *Secretary of State* [1981] J.P.L. 591. *R.* v. *Westminster City Council ex p. Monahan* [1988] J.P.L. 537 at 559. *Simplex Holdings Ltd.* v. *Secretary of State* [1988] J.P.L. 809.

presumption mean that a legal burden of proof as regards *facts* is placed on the authority. Once it has given a clear reason why a proposal is damaging it can insist that an applicant show an overwhelming case for receiving permission. (See *Cranford Hall Parking Ltd.* v. *Secretary of State* [1989] J.P.L. 169.)

Taking irrelevant factors into account

The question of irrelevant considerations has two aspects. First the factors which are taken into account must be "planning considerations," meaning that they must be related to the objectives of the planning legislation. We saw in Chapter One that the various professional groups who operate the planning system adopt their own versions of this, and that these bear no necessary relationship to the law. The Act gives little clue to what purposes Parliament intended and the courts have correspondingly construed the Act broadly and in a sense neutralised it. It seems that any political or social purpose related to land use is in principle relevant to planning.

Secondly, the authority must not take into account any consideration unrelated to the particular development for which permission is sought. This is particularly important in connection with the imposition of conditions upon a grant of planning permission, but probably applies also to grants or refusals of planning permission. Although each planning application is separate, the authority must take into account the whole planning context including, where appropriate, alternative sites (below, p. 137), rival applications, other analogous uses, the history and existing use of the site and the undesirability of opening the floodgates to other applications.[5]

RELEVANT TO PLANNING

There are dicta suggesting the courts regard planning as exclusively concerned with the protection of the physical environment and the conservation of traditional "amenity" values (*e.g. Copeland B.C.* v.

---

[4] *Bradley* v. *Secretary of State* [1983] J.P.L. 43 at 47; c.f. *Steinberg* v. *Secretary of State* [1989] J.P.L. 258—*aliter* where special duty imposed by statute to consider conservation area. See also Circular 14/85.

[5] See *South Oxfordshire D.C.* v. *Secretary of State* [1981] 1 All E.R. 954; *Clyde and Co.* v. *Secretary of State* [1977] 1 W.L.R. 926; *Collis Radio* v. *Secretary of State* [1975] L.G.R. 211; *Granada Theatres* v. *Secretary of State* [1981] J.P.L. 278; *Yns Mons Isle of Anglesey B.C.* v. *Secretary of State* [1984] J.P.L. 646.

Secretary of State [1976] 31 P. & C.R. at 403). There is no doubt that environmental protection and amenity are proper concerns of planning. Indeed, planning authorities are entitled to make purely aesthetic judgments about matters of design,[6] a proposition that is difficult to justify coherently. In the U.S.A. "aesthetic planning" raises serious concerns about freedom of expression.[7] Planning powers involve the resolution of conflicts between competing values. "Amenity" considerations cannot be applied in isolation but must be balanced against the whole range of social, economic and moral considerations, for example, employment, housing need, shopping, education, transport, private property rights, and personal hardship.

Apart from two questionable cases concerning financial matters (below) the author has been unable to discover any reported case where the courts have declared any social or economic factor relating to the physical use of land as irrelevant to planning. On the contrary, the courts seem to endorse the proposition that the Act is politically neutral (except in the sense that it is power conferring) and can be used to achieve any public goal. *Clyde and Co.* v. *Secretary of State* [1977] 1 W.L.R. 926 provides an example. The Court of Appeal held that planning permission for office development could be refused solely to preserve the site for social housing (see also *Bradwell* v. *Secretary of State* [1981] J.P.L. 276).

The overriding principle is that a planning consideration must be a consideration related to physical land use (*Great Portland Estates* v. *Westminster City Council* [1985] A.C. 661). Within this broad formulation any political, social or economic consideration can be relevant. Whether any given consideration *is* relevant in a particular case depends upon the facts of that case (*Stringer* v. *M.o.H.* [1970] 1 W.L.R. 128). Since every human activity involves the use of land, this principle does not seriously limit the freedom of an authority to take into account a wide range of factors. In other words, planning powers are a vehicle for elected bodies to carry out political purposes of any kind and the courts defer to the discretion of the authority.[8] If furtherance of a particular goal is lawfully within the

---

[6] *Winchester City Council* v. *Secretary of State* [1978] J.P.L. 467; see Circular 31/85.
[7] *City of Pasiac* v. *Paterson Bill Posting Co.* 62.A.267 (1905); *Metromedia Inc.* v. *City of San Diego* 610 P.2d.407; *State ex rel. Stayanoff* v. *Berkeley* 458 S.W. 2d/305.
[8] See above, pp. 12–22. Thus the conflict between the "cost/benefit analysis" view—of planning and the "redistributist" view is beside the point—since both are legitimate political ideologies that governments are free to apply under the Act. See Loughlin (1980) 3 *Urban Law and Policy* 171. See also Reade [1982] J.P.L. 8. McAuslan's argument that the law limits development control powers by reference to a private property ideology is today reflected in government policies more than judicial decisions (*Ideologies of Planning Law* (1981) Chap. 6). See also Sneddon [1988] J.P.L. 6.

sphere of planning it is irrelevant that the same goal also falls within some other statutory power (*Hoveringham Gravels* v. *Secretary of State* [1975] Q.B. 574).[9]

Sometimes the central government takes a more restrictive view of the purposes of planning. For example, there seems to be no legal objection to a local planning authority attaching a condition to a planning permission that requires that the occupants of a residence must have local connections (albeit the term "local connection" could fail for uncertainty unless carefully defined).[10] A policy favouring local housing needs by excluding outsiders who wish to buy second homes in the countryside seems to be within the lawful sphere of planning (see *Fawcett Properties* v. *Bucks. C.C.* [1961] A.C. 636). On the other hand, on appeal the Secretary of State would be entitled to strike out such a condition for policy reasons. The same applies to a policy of discouraging the conversion of buildings into retirement homes.

An economic policy that has no land use implications at all is not relevant to planning. In circular 22/80 the government enjoined local planning authorities to favour "small businesses." It is difficult to see what planning considerations are involved in the choice between two otherwise identical applicants for a retail development, the one being a multi national enterprise, the other a family business. By contrast the "traditional business' ideology upheld in *Great Portland Estates* (above) had land use implications relating to convenience, access to suppliers, and the amenities appropriate to a metropolis. The question is essentially one of causation relating to the extent to which hypothetical consequences can be taken into account.

Similarly, the regulation of competition or the safeguarding of moral standards are not as such relevant to planning. However, proposals threatening existing businesses have obvious land use implications, as do proposals to carry out immoral or socially unpopular activities. It would be unreal to examine these factors in isolation from the commercial or moral context (*Finlay* v. *Secretary of State* [1983] J.P.L. 803—sex cinema). An ambivalent example is provided by *R.* v. *Westminster City Council ex p. Monahan*

---

[9] See also *Westminster Bank* v. *M.O.H.* [1971] A.C. 508; but *cf.* Pearce L.J. in *Fawcett Properties* v. *Bucks C.C.* [1959] 2 All E.R. 231 at 336. Compare *Esdell Caravan Parks Ltd.* v. *Hemel Hempstead R.D.C.* [1965] 3 All E.R. 737.

[10] See *Wakelin D.C.* v. *Secretary of State* (1978) 46 P. & C.R. 214—relatives; *Bizony* v. *Secretary of State* [1976] J.P.L. 306 building only used by "day visitors." *Allnatt Properties* v. *M.O.H.* [1964] 15 P. & C.R. 288. "Local industry" held invalid on other grounds, *Shanley* v. *Secretary of State* [1982] J.P.L. 80—uncertainty. See Loughlin *loc. cit.* n. 8 above, at 181–183, c.f. [1989] J.P.L. 253.

[1989] J.P.L. 107. It was held that the financing of improvements to the Royal Opera House was a relevant planning consideration, not apparently because of the value of opera per se, but because there were *physical* improvement to the building—perhaps a distinction without a difference.

The impact of proposals upon the private amenities of neighbours is also relevant. Planning law does not create any individual rights of action but does permit the private interests of neighbours to be taken into account as material considerations. To this extent planning law overlaps with the law of nuisance (*Stringer* v. *M.o.H.* [1971] 1 All E.R. 65).

We can illustrate the application of the irrelevant considerations doctrine by discussing two related issues, the relevance of personal circumstances, and the cost of the proposed development.

PERSONAL CIRCUMSTANCES

All planning decisions have personal consequences for individuals. Generally speaking, purely personal factors, such as the character, finances, or behaviour of the applicant cannot be taken into account. For example, planning permission for the expansion of a restaurant could not lawfully be refused on the ground that it happens to be a meeting place for criminals. There must be a causal connection between the character of the use and patterns of behaviour. We saw in Chapter Three that the introduction of short term residents into a conventional "stable family" residential area can constitute development, so that the pattern of family behaviour is a planning consideration. Similarly, in *Great Portland Estates* v. *Westminster City Council* (above) the House of Lords upheld a policy of protecting businesses of a kind that added to the "diverse character, vitality and functioning" of Westminster. As well as environmental considerations this causal link could take the form of creating a special need for services or public amenities, requiring a distinctive use of space, or creating a desirable combination of uses, for example the question of retirement homes in seaside resorts.

The Act provides for personal planning permissions (section 33(1)) and there may be cases where personal circumstances are directly relevant to the use of the land. For example, planning permission could be granted for a "takeaway food" establishment personally to a named proprietor who has a good track record of discouraging nuisance.

A special case is that of personal hardship. This could arise, for example, if an applicant is refused permission for a more profitable use and therefore compelled to continue an existing but less profitable or even uneconomic use. Similarly a desirable activity which the landowner cannot otherwise afford to carry out might be facilitated by granting permission contrary to green bill policy (see *Essex C.C.* v. *Secretary of State* [1989] J.P.L. 187). Personal hardship, even though not itself a land use matter, can be taken into account, but only as an exceptional circumstance to be weighed against the normal land use factors.[11]

THE COST OF DEVELOPMENT

The notion that a planning consideration is any land use consideration helps to explain the controversial issue of whether the cost of a proposed development can be taken into account. Is the financial viability of a project legally relevant? The cases are reasonably coherent and are perhaps best represented by the dictum of Woolf J. in *SOSMO Trust* v. *Secretary of State* [1983] J.P.L. 806. There His Lordship said that "what could be significant was not the financial viability or lack of financial viability of a project but the consequences of that financial viability or lack of financial viability." Costs are therefore relevant if they raise other land use issues. In *SOSMO* the appellants argued that if they were refused permission for office development their site would remain derelict due to lack of finance. Woolf J. held that the Secretary of State should have taken that factor into account since the prospect that land may be unused is clearly a planning matter. Costs may also be relevant where alternative sites for necessary but environmentally unpopular projects are canvassed (below) or where profits may be diverted to desirable land use activities (*R.* v. *Westminster City Council ex p. Monahan* (above) or in "hardship" cases.[12] In *Clyde and Co.* v. *Secretary of State* [1977] 1 W.L.R. 926, permission for office development was refused on the ground that the existing use of the property for housing was preferable. One factor was whether the property could economically be used to meet the housing needs of the area. Their Lordships took the liberal view,

---

[11] *Great Portland Estates* v. *Westminster City Council* [1984] 3 All E.R. 744 at 750, *per* Lord Scarman; *New Forest D.C.* v. *Secretary of State* [1984] J.P.L. 178.

[12] Including cross-subsidisation of mixed uses. *Calfane* v. *Secretary of State* [1981] J.P.L. 879. See also *Kent Messenger* v. *Secretary of State* [1986] J.P.L. 376 *Miller* v. *Secretary of State* [1980] J.P.L. 264; *Sears Blok* v. *Secretary of State* [1980] J.P.L. 523; *Godden* v. *Secretary of State* [1988] J.P.L. 99. *Brighton B.C.* v. *Secretary of State* (1980) 39 P. & C.R. 46—*sed quaere* the relevence test (below p. 136). See also *R.* v. *Beverley B.C.* [1989] J.P.L. 183—cost relevant where delay led to losses. Contract, *Wain Leisure Ltd.* v. *Secretary of State* [1989] J.P.L. 190—loss of chance of grant not relevant.

that as long as there was a "fair chance" (*per* Cairns L.J. at 936) that housing development could economically be carried out, the Secretary of State's decision must be upheld.[13] *Clyde* cannot easily be reconciled with an individualistic judicial bias.

In other cases the costs factor worked in the applicant's favour, but it is difficult to infer from these any judicial bias in favour of the interests of private property. Indeed, *Sovmots Investments Ltd.* v. *Secretary of State* [1977] 1 Q.B. 411 suggests the contrary. Forbes J. thought that in principle costs were always a relevant consideration but that it was for the Secretary of State to decide whether to treat costs as relevant in any given case. This is rather different from saying that the *weight* to be given to the cost issue is for the Secretary of State. If the decision whether or not to take costs into account is itself discretionary the courts power to intervene becomes one based upon "reasonableness" rather than relevance and is therefore minimal. This provides an example of the court's unwillingness to impose specific standards upon authorities in respect of the thoroughness of their methods of investigation (below p. 213). Other cases do not easily fit Forbes J.'s approach. Indeed in *Niarchos* v. *Secretary of State* (1977) 35 P. and C.R. 259 Sir Douglas Franks held, not only that the cost question was relevant but that the Secretary of State's decision was "unreasonable" because he apparently gave inadequate weight to the question of cost. *Niarchos* comes very close to the court substituting its own policy view for that of the authority and in this respect has been strongly criticised (Forbes J. in *Bell and Colville* v. *Secretary of State* [1978] J.P.L. 823).

The cost of a development is not always relevant. In *J. Murphy and Co.* v. *Secretary of State* [1973] 1 W.L.R. 560 Ackner J. held that the question of cost is never relevant, but partly retreated from this later.[14] In *Walters* v. *Secretary of State* (1978) 77 L.G.R. 248 Sir Douglas Frank Q.C. thought that the Secretary of State should not have taken into account the possibility that a development may not be completed because it

---

[13] The "fair chance" test has been criticised in favour of a "balance of probabilities" approach. See *Westminster City Council* v. *British Waterways Board* [1984] 3 All E.R. 737 at 742. See also *Finn* v. *Secretary of State* [1984] J.P.L. 734; *Vikoma International* v. *Secretary of State* [1987] J.P.L. 38. The fair chance approach seems more in keeping with the rationale of judicial review.

[14] *Hambledon and Chiddingfeld B.C.* v. *Secretary of State* [1976] J.P.L. 552—cost of supplying caravan site drainage relevant. Expense of soundproofing not relevant. See also, *Wain Leisure* (above n. 12).

is financially impracticable, this being a matter that should be left to the judgment of the market. Walters has been doubted on this point. (*SOSMO Trust* above).

Residual doubts can be raised. Are local authorities and civil servants competent to make assessments about matters of the market? Is the question whether the cost of development is excessive to be answered in the light of the applicant's particular financial circumstances or according to an "objective" "reasonable developer" test? (See *Monahan* (above)). There has been much academic discussion about the costs issue. In particular, it has been suggested that traditional legal analysis has failed to produce a coherent and consistent solution, but that analysis of the *results* of the cases in terms of economic efficiency can do so. Economic analysis is claimed to expose a judicial preference for leaving judgments about market forces to the private sector and against imposing "loss" upon the private landowner.[15]

There are difficulties with the economic analysis approach. For example, what is the theoretical justification for examining only the result or facts of a given judicial decision and excluding what the judge said and the legal context. For example, at least two cases which support the "private profit" thesis have been judicially criticised, (*Walters* and *Niarchos* (above)). Secondly, whatever pattern of economic effect emerges it is purely descriptive and cannot serve as a guide to future decisions. There has been much criticism of "black-letter lawyers" but economic analysis seems often to be equally rigid. Thirdly, economic analysis does not seem to explain the result of all the cases. In particular, the decision in *Clyde* overrides the interests of the landowner perhaps to the extent of imposing loss in favour of wider social gains and to some extent entrusts the market judgment to the authority. Finally, in one sense, "loss" is always the result of a refusal of planning permission. Indeed, loss can also be caused by a *condition* that restricts the exercise of existing rights, but as we shall see, the courts have consistently upheld such conditions (below, p. 147).

The ordinary methods of case analysis seem to produce a reasonably coherent principle linked to the notion of social utility. Since this form of discourse is the form adopted by the practice of lawyers and officials it is difficult to see what theoretical basis there can be for resorting to the tools of economic analysis as a substitute.

In conclusion, the assumption that planning has identifiable economic or social objectives seems to be based upon a

---

[15] See Loughlin (1980), 3 *Urban Law and Policy* 1–22. Stevens and Young, *ibid.* (1985) 7.

misconception as to the function of the word "planning." Unlike such terms as "housing," "planning" does not refer to any specific subject-matter but is a method. Planning is the technique of guiding and regulating change and can relate to any purpose. It is a method of achieving objectives, and carries no implication as to what these objectives should be.

Relevance to the proposed development

A factor must not only be relevant to planning generally but also relevant to the proposed development. This test is particularly important in relation to a condition attached to a planning permission. Section 30(1)(a) authorises conditions to be attached relating to land under the control of the applicant other than land in respect of which the application is made, but this must be "for the purposes of or in connection with the development authorised by the permission" (see below, p. 151). In one sense the courts have taken a restrictive view of relevance in this context. It is not sufficient that the condition in question be related to the *land*, the subject of the application. It must be related to the specific kind of development in respect of which permission is sought. In *Newbury D.C.* v. *Secretary of State* [1981] A.C. 578 a temporary planning permission was granted for the use of an old aircraft hanger for the storage of rubber goods. A condition was attached requiring the removal of the hanger at the expiry of the permission. There is no doubt that the condition related to a lawful planning purpose, but it was held to be invalid because the development was for a use of an existing building so that the demolition of the building bore no logical relationship to the use.[16]

What of a permission for the building of a new factory on condition that a factory of the same kind owned by the applicant elsewhere in the town be closed down? Such a condition could be relevant to planning and is also related to the proposed development in terms of need. It is submitted that it would be valid even if it has no direct physical impact on the development land (*cf. Pyx Granite Co. Ltd.* v. *M.O.H.* [1959] 1 Q.B. 554).

Similarly, a condition that required the removal of a building in an overdeveloped neighbourhood could also be valid. Conversely, a permission for a factory, subject to a car park large enough for the new factory *and* the applicant's existing factory would not be valid.

---

[16] See also *Elmbridge B.C.* v. *Secretary of State* [1989] J.P.L. 277; *Gill* v. *Secretary of State* [1985] J.P.L. 710; *Dudley Bowers* v. *Secretary of State* (1986) 52 P. & C.R. 365.

However, it would not matter that an amenity required by a condition incidentally conferred an unrelated benefit provided that it be justified entirely on the basis of a need generated by the development. For example, a permission for a residential development could require the incorporation of a shop even if the shop was available to the general public. This is an aspect of the general principle that an irrelevant consideration will not in itself invalidate a decision unless it has a measurable effect on the substance of the decision. Thus, a condition that requires something to be done over and above the needs of the development would be void. The *Newbury* case (above) illustrates this. Their Lordships left it open whether a condition relating to a change of use could ever require the removal of an existing building. Provided that the necessary degree of relevance is established there seems to be no reason why it should not, *e.g.* where the building would otherwise not conform to the development plan (see Lord Scarman at 619–621).

The "relationship to the proposed development" test also applies to the decision to grant or refuse planning permission. In *R. v. Westminster City Council ex p. Monahan* [1989] J.P.L. 107, the Court of Appeal held that in deciding whether to grant planning permission for the commercial redevelopment of part of the Covent Garden area, the L.P.A. could take into account that the profits generated by the commercial development were needed to finance physical improvements to the Royal Opera House. This was arguably sufficiently related because the area as a whole was to be redeveloped. A majority of the Court stressed that all matters considered must be relevant to the proposed development.

If the decision to grant planning permission were not subject to the relevence requirements then the authority would have a powerful bargaining counter capable of distorting the local planning system. This raises the general issue of "planning gain" (below p. 148).

Another example is provided by the case of "alternative sites." Should a planning authority consider the possibility that there are alternative and better sites for the proposed development before granting permission? If the law required planning authorities in all cases to root around for alternative sites the law could justly be accused of insensitivity to the realities of administration. The principle that has emerged is one of reasonableness. The authority has a general discretion whether to investigate alternative sites, but in certain kinds of case it should attempt to do so.

The Court of Appeal has set out the tests to be applied in *G. L. C.*

v. *Secretary of State* [1986] J.P.L. 193. This involved a "called-in" application for office development on a site within the territory of the London Docklands Development Corporation. One issue was the pressing need for housing in the area and it was alleged that the Secretary of State should have examined the possibility of alternative sites. Oliver L.J. said that a comparison with other possible sites was appropriate in cases having the following characteristics:

1. The presence of a clear public convenience or advantage in the proposal under consideration.

2. The existence of adverse affects or disadvantages to the public or to some section of the public in the proposal.

3. The existence of an alternative site for the same project which would not have those effects.

4. A situation in which there could only be one permission granted for such development or at least only a very limited number of permissions.

Subsequently, in *Vale of Glamorgan B.C.* v. *Secretary of State for Wales* (1986) 52 P. & C.R. 418 Woolf J. emphasised that the relevance of an alternative site is a matter for the discretion of the local planning authority or the Secretary of State. The court would interfere only if their decision was unreasonable. His Lordship emphasised that "The fact that a particular landowner wanted to develop his land in a particular way should not be frustrated because there was other land owned by someone else which would be more suitable in planning terms for that particular use."

Examples of cases where alternative sites may be particularly relevant include airports, mining projects, petrochemical plants, power stations and gypsy encampments, but nor normally dwelling houses, offices or superstores.[17] However, in the case of superstores alternative applications may be relevant, since the need for the store compared with the effect on existing commercial centres is often a central issue. In practice, applications for superstores are frequently called in by the Secretary of State and multiple applications are sometimes considered at a single inquiry (see Circular 21/86). In *R.* v. *Carlisle City Council* [1986] J.P.L. 206 the Council had authorised the development of a superstore on its own land. It was alleged that the Council should have considered the details of the applicants proposals for a superstore on another site by holding what amount to a judicial contest between the two sites. It was held that the Council was under no duty beyond the need to

---

[17] See Encyclopaedia 2. 877/1. See also *R.* v. *Vincent* [1987] J.P.L. 511; *Trust House Forte* v. *Secretary of State* [1980] J.P.L. 834.

consider the broad outlines of the alternative proposal which were in fact before it (see also *R.* v. *Doncaster M.B.C.* [1987] J.P.L. 444). The authority is not generally obliged to take the initiative to seek out alternative sites. It is enough to consider whether evidence of alternative sites is necessary and to deal with the alternatives placed before it.[18]

Failing to take relevant factors into account

DISCRETION AND RULES

It is more common for a planning decision to be challenged because of a failure to consider relevant factors than because of taking into account irrelevant factors. As we have seen, the range of relevant factors is wide. In particular, the "costs" cases and the "alternative sites" cases often arise because the authority has chosen to narrow and simplify the range of factors it wishes to consider. This is one of the risks of the bureaucratic process. The courts are therefore required to enforce standards of thoroughness and fairness at the expense of certainty and economy of effort.

Policy guidelines outside the development plan setting out the factors to be considered and the weight to be given to various considerations are a common administrative device. These typically take the form of circulars emanating from the Secretary of State but can also take the form of White Papers speeches, Parliamentary written or oral answers, and reports of eminent bodies.[19] Unless expressly or by necessary implication authorised by statute, policy statements have no binding force but can and sometimes must be taken into account. It is clear that Circulars emanating from the Secretary of State *must* be taken into account, since these indicate the attitude likely to be taken in an appeal. In the case of unofficial reports and proposals the authority has a discretion (see cases cited above, n. 19).

---

[18] *Rhodes* v. *M.H.L.G.* [1983] 1 All E.R. 300; *Sir Brandon Rhys Williams* v. *Secretary of State* [1985] J.P.L. 29; *R.* v. *Carlisle City Council* [1980] J.P.L. 266. This is an aspect of a more general question (below p. 213).

[19] See *Dinsdale Developments* v. *Secretary of State* [1986] J.P.L. 276—after dinner speech; *Westminster City Council* v. *Secretary of State* [1984] J.P.L. 27—*draft* circulars not relevant. See also *Pye* v. *Secretary of State* [1982] J.P.L. 557. Compare *Richmond on Thames L.B.C.* v. *Secretary of State* [1984] J.P.L. 24— P.A.G. report relevant. See generally Table of Abbreviations Encylopaedia 20 520/2/1/ Grant, Chap. 7. The main Department of Environment policy statements are now published together as guidance notes. See [1988] J.P.L. 146.

The courts approach to general policies embody the following principles. They add up to judicial concern to preserve the discretionary nature of the development central system coupled with a willingness to ensure that general policies are applied coherently and fairly. This area of law will illustrate the delicate balance between rules and discretion.

1. A discretion cannot be fettered by a general policy.[20] This is a fundamental tenet of English administrative law. An authority is free to adopt a policy, but in the absence of statutory authority cannot apply any policy rigidly without considering whether an exception should be made in the circumstances of the particular case. A policy in a circular can therefore embody presumptions of any strength short of an absolute rule. The mechanics of this are well illustrated by the cases concerning green belts and other policies relating to housing development. There is a general presumption in favour of granting planning permission which is even stronger where there is less than a five years supply of land available for housing, but with a contrary presumption in the green belt. The circulars also prescribe the method by which demand and supply should be calculated. The weight of these presumptions is a matter for the decision maker who must preserve a flexible approach even within particular presumptions and must justify a refusal of planning permission.[21]

2. A departure from a policy must be specifically explained[22] and there may be exceptional cases where a policy cannot be departed from against the interests of an individual (below, p. 142).

3. The interpretation of a circular or development plan is a

---

[20] *e.g. Stringer* v. *M.O.H.* [1970] 1 W.L.R. 1281; *Lavender* v. *M.O.H.* [1970] 1 W.L.R. 1231; *Surrey Heath D.C.* v. *Secretary of State* [1987] J.P.L. 199. In *Coleshill Investments* v. *M.O.H.* [1969] 1 W.L.R. 746 Lord Wilberforce suggested (at 765) that a circular that had been consistently relied upon for a long time acquires "vitality and strength." It is suggested that this situation is best regarded as creating a legitimate expectation (below, p. 142).

[21] See Circulars 15/84, 22/84, 14/85; P.P.G. 3 *Cranford Hall Parking* (above p. 129); *Gransden D.C.* v. *Secretary of State* [1986] J.P.L. 519; *Bolton D.C.* v. *Secretary of State* [1987] J.P.L. 580; *Wigan D.C.* v. *Secretary of State* [1987] J.P.L. 575; *Pye Estates* v. *Secretary of State* [1982] J.P.L. 577; for a summary see *Wycombe D.C.* v. *Secretary of State* [1988] J.P.L. 111; see Nott and Morgan [1984] J.P.L. 623; Baldwin and Houghton [1986] P.L. 239 (which perhaps overstates the legal significance of circulars). *Hooper, Pinch and Rogers* [1988] J.P.L. 225.

[22] *Wigan, Gransden* (above, n. 21). *Rockhold Ltd.* v. *Secretary of State* [1986] J.P.L. 130; *Westminster City Council* v. *Great Portland Estates* [1985] A.C. 661 at 673. *Reading B.C.* v. *Secretary of State* (1986) 52 P. & C.R. 385.

matter of law for the court.[23] This permits the court to interfere if it disagrees with the authority's interpretation and not merely on the basis of unreasonableness.

This very high level of review can be defended by the desire to ensure that central government policies are uniformly treated by all local authorities. On the other hand, circulars are not always drafted with the precision appropriate for judicial analysis and this particular power of the court could well be regarded as an attempt to impose the values of the legal profession upon the equally legitimate practices of administrators. However, the courts have emphasised that a broad approach to the interpretation of non-statutory documents should be taken.[24]

4. Where policies conflict the authority can choose between them, provided that both conflicting policies are genuinely considered. It is not permissible, for example, to treat a development plan as superseded by some other policy *Surrey Heath D.C.* v. *Secretary of State* (above, n. 20).

5. Local planning authorities can rely upon informal plans prepared by their officials. Such informal plans are often known as "bottom drawer" plans and are made without the statutory processes of publicity, objections, and inquiry (see above, p. 2). In *Great Portland Estates Ltd.* v. *Westminster City Council* [1985] A.C. 661 the House of Lords held that all policies referred to in the development plan must be stated in the plan itself. The development plan referred to office development and went on to state that particular policies for this could be specified in subsequent non-statutory plans. Their Lordships held that this was unacceptable but did not outlaw non-statutory plans altogether. Lord Scarman who gave the main speech emphasised that a development plan is not a rigid blueprint. Non-statutory guidance could, for example, relate to matters of procedure, or interpretation, or create exceptions to the policies in the plan. It appears, however, that if a development plan exists the local planning authority cannot create substantive policies outside its framework. The *Great Portland Estates* case therefore strengthens the participatory element in the planning process.

6. Circulars cannot alter existing legal rights nor affect the question of what considerations are legally relevant. (*R.* v.

---

[23] *Waverley D.C.* v. *Secretary of State* [1987] J.P.L. 202; *Surrey Heath and Bolton* cases (above, n. 21). *Wycombe D.C.* v. *Secretary of State* (above, n. 21). *Rockhold Ltd.* v. *Secretary of State* (above n. 22) *E.L.S. (Wholesalers)* v. *Secretary of State* [1987] J.P.L. 844.

[24] *Chelmsford D.C.* v. *Secretary of State* [1986] J.P.L. 112. *Mid Bedfordshire D.C.* v. *Secretary of state* [1984] J.P.L. 631.

Westminster City Council ex p. Monahan [1988] J.P.L. 557 at 561.)

POLICIES AND CONSULTATION

In principle the authority is free to alter or depart from established policies. It is clear, and indeed essential to the workings of a democracy, that a public authority cannot be estopped from changing its policies (see *Laker Airways* v. *Department of Trade* [1977] Q.B. 643).

In recent years, however, the courts have developed the doctrine of "legitimate expectation." This gives the citizen who relies upon a published policy a limited amount of protection. The legitimate expectation doctrine started life as a device for determining when a citizen is entitled to a hearing but later expanded in scope to the point synonymous with a right to review generally.[25] In cases where the citizen is not charged with wrongdoing or threatened with the deprivation of an existing legal right, he may still be entitled to a hearing if a previous administrative practice or a specific undertaking upon which he has relied raise an expectation from which it would be unfair to resile. The legitimate expectation doctrine, (see *e.g. Costain Homes* v. *Secretary of State* [1988] J.P.L. 701) often goes no further than to confer locus standi, or a right to be heard.

However, there are dicta that the same principle might actually prevent a policy being altered except if required by an "overwhelming public interest."[26] If this is correct then a planning policy embodied in a circular could in theory be enforced against the Secretary of State. However, the policy statements involved in the relevant cases were specific under-takings addressed to individuals concerning their individual interests whereas policy statements in planning circulars are usually couched in the form of general guidelines and are not represented as conferring specific entitlements. In these circumstances the element of reasonable reliance would be difficult to establish, and it would probably be sufficient for the authority to publicise its change of policy and to consider

---

[25] *e.g. Council of Civil Service Unions* v. *Minister for the Civil Service* [1984] 3 W.L.R. 1174; *O'Reilly* v. *Mackman* [1983] 2 A.C. 237; *In Re Finlay* (below).

[26] *R.* v. *Home Secretary ex p. Khan* [1985] 1 All E.R. 40 at 46; see also *A.G. of Hong Kong* v. *Ng Yuen Shiu* [1983] 2 A.C. 629; *I.R.C.* v. *Preston* [1983] 2 All E.R. 300; *H.T.V.* v. *Price Commission* [1976] I.C.R. 170.

representations.[27] In *Re Finlay* ([1985] A.C. 315) Lord Scarman emphasised that the legitimate expectation doctrine depends upon the particular statutory context. In that case a group of prisoners were held not to have a legitimate expectation capable of preventing the parole policy from being altered to their disadvantage, but only one that the policy of the day would be properly applied in their cases. It is not clear from His Lordship's speech what particular element in the statutory context negated the "legitimacy" of prisoners' expectation. It could be that their Lordships perception of parole policy did not embrace the idea that the views of individual prisoners were of relevance because parole policy concerns general political questions.

Apart from general policies there are other devices with which discretion may unlawfully be fettered. We have already discussed estoppel (above, Chap. 5) and will discuss the important topic of fettering discretion through agreements between planning authorities and developers in the next chapter.

THE DEVELOPMENT PLAN

The Act expressly requires that the provisions of the development plan to be taken into account, but does not require the plan to be binding (section 29(1)). We have seen that there are special procedural requirements where an application for planning permission is inconsistent with the development plan (above, pp. 119–120).

As regards structure plans there is a further duty to seek to achieve the general objectives of the plan (L.G.P. and P.A. 1980, section 86(3)) but this has been held to be satisfied merely by evidence that the structure plan was in fact considered (*R. v. Royal County of Berkshire* [1985] J.P.L. 258).

Two main issues arise:

(1) A development plan cannot be questioned in "any legal proceedings" after the expiry of a six weeks time limit (section 242 (above, pp. 47–48)). Suppose an irrelevant policy is inserted into a plan. Once the time limit has expired does this become valid, thus requiring the authority to take it into account and preventing anyone from challenging the relevance of the policy. It could be argued that the validity of the development plan as such is a different matter from the relevance of particular policies contained

---

[27] *Fourth Investments* v. *Secretary of State* [1988] J.P.L. 620. *R. v. Secretary of State for the Home Dept. ex p. Ruddock* [1987] 2 All E.R. 518. *Wigan and Bolton* cases (above n. 21). See Hadfield (1988) 39 N.I.L.Q. 103.

within it. An authority must take the development plan into account, but must reject particular policies in it if they are irrelevant to planning or unreasonable. Indeed, a development plan must be taken into account only in as far as it is material to the application. Thus in *Westminster Renslade Ltd.* v. *Secretary of State* (1984) 48 P. & C.R. 255, it was held that not all policies contained in a development plan are necessarily relevant to planning permissions. In that case the policy concerned the provision of public car parking facilities not related to the particular development. It was held that this objective although mentioned in the development plan could not be achieved by means of planning control but only through the powers of the local authority in another capacity. However, in *Westminster Corporation* v. *Secretary of State* [1986] J.P.L. 27, it was held that a provision requiring "planning gain" contained in a development plan (see below, p. 157) could not be challenged. Mr. David Widdicombe Q.C. thought that the vires of the plan could not be examined by the court. It could, however, be examined by the Secretary of State in appeal proceedings because such proceedings are not "legal proceedings." The approach taken in *Westminster Renslade* seems preferable.

(2) Should a development plan in the course of revision be taken into account? The argument here is that if the authority fails to take a possible alteration to the plan into account its decision upon a planning application might pre-empt and frustrate the plan. Conversely, if the authority relies upon an alteration this may prejudice objections to the plan. Freezing applications until the content of a plan is known may also cause difficulties.

The courts take a non-interventionist approach which accentuates the gulf between plan-making and development control. The matter is for the discretion of the authority subject to a duty to give a reasonable and "site-specific" reason for their decision. They must not adopt a rigid general policy of refusing applications that are inconsistent with a plan or pending the crystallisation of a plan.[28] On the other hand, the authority is free to pre-empt a plan, by granting planning permission which may be out of line with its proposals. Conversely, permission could be granted or refused in reliance upon an uncompleted plan even in the face of public

---

[28] See *Myton* v. *M.o.H.* (1965) 16 P. and C.R. 24; *Thornville* v. *Secretary of State* [1981] J.P.L. 116; *Link Homes* v. *Secretary of State* [1976] J.P.L. 430; *Arlington Securities Ltd.* v. *Secretary of State* [1989] J.P.L. 166—importance of development justified waiting for plan; *Wyre Forest D.C.* v. *Secretary of State* [1989] J.P.L. 270—evidence uncertain, plan should be awaited.

objections to the plan.[29] Furthermore, provided that the plan is considered, other policies can be preferred to those in the plan itself (*Surrey Health D.C.* v. *Secretary of State* [1987] J.P.L. 201).

Unreasonableness

In many cases the terms unreasonableness and irrelevance overlap in the sense that decision is unreasonable because it is based upon some irrelevant consideration. However, the two notions are distinct and it is important to keep them so. For example, in *Hall* v. *Shoreham R.D.C.* [1964] 1 W.L.R. 240 and *R.* v. *Hillingdon Borough Council ex p. Royco Homes* [1974] Q.B. 720 conditions attached to planning permission were held to be invalid for unreasonableness. In both cases the language of "relevance" and reasonableness was used somewhat indiscriminately. In *Hall* the condition required the developer to dedicate a highway to the public at his own expense and in *Royco* to use private housing to carry out the statutory functions of a local planning authority. In neither case could it plausibly be argued that an irrelevant factor had been taken into account. In *Hall* the authority was concerned with traffic needs, in *Royco* the provision of public housing. Both these considerations are considerations relevant to the grant or refusal of planning permission and are not therefore outside the purposes of planning (see *Clyde and Co.* v. *Secretary of State* [1977] 1 W.L.R. 927). In both cases the court was saying something quite different. In *Royco* the authority was attempting to shift its own statutory responsibilities upon the private developer. In *Hall* the authority was requiring the developer to give up all control over part of his land and effectively to dedicate it to the public. In both cases the court disapproved of the principle that the private sector should bear the *whole* cost of providing public services that were imposed by statute upon public authorities (see further below, p. 148). The court was therefore concerned with the morality of the *means* and not with the purposes as such.

Hall v. *Shoreham R.D.C.* is also explicable on the basis that the condition amounted in effect to compulsory acquisition

---

[29] See *R.* v. *City of London Corp. ex p. Allen* (1980) 79 L.Q.R. 223. *R.* v. *Fulham and Hammersmith L.B.C.* [1981] J.P.L. 684, 869. The plan could, however, give rise to a "legitimate expectation" *Wigan M.B.C.* v. *Secretary of State* [1987] J.P.L. 575; *R.* v. *Carlisle City Council* [1986] J.P.L. 206.

without compensation whereas the purpose of development control is purely regulatory.[30]

This leads us to the reason why we should separate "irrelevance" from "unreasonableness." Where a court holds that an irrelevant factor was taken into account the authority must go back and make its decision again, this time on the basis of the relevant factors. It is open to the authority to make the same decision as before so long as it is not influenced by an irrelevant consideration.

By contrast in cases of "unreasonableness" such as *Hall* and *Royco* the authority is prohibited from making that particular decision altogether. Thus "unreasonableness" plays a special part in the machinery of judicial review and comes near to embodying a set of constitutional values.

To allow judicial review for unreasonableness also comes close to inviting the courts to intervene with the merits and of a decision. In order to avoid this danger the courts have consistently emphasised that unreasonableness has a special narrow meaning unrelated to the hypothetical standards of the man on the Clapham omnibus. A decision is unreasonable only if it is arbitrary or capricious or "so unreasonable that no reasonable authority could ever have come to it."

This formula derives from the judgment of Lord Greene M.R. in *Associated Provincial Picture Houses* v. *Wednesbury Corporation* [1948] 1 K.B. 23, 229–231. However it is doubtful whether it does any more than emphasise that unreasonable means "very unreasonable," and it may be that the United States doctrine, that a decision will not be set aside if its merits are "fairly debatable" is preferable. In *C.C.S.U.* v. *Minister for the Civil Service* [1985] A.C. 374 at 410 Lord Diplock proposed the notion of "irrationality." This describes one kind of unreasonableness but understates the extent of the courts powers.

The courts have set aside decisions as unreasonable which could only by a gross distortion of language be described as capricious or irrational, such as a statutory instrument which purported to exclude the jurisdiction of the courts (*Customs and Excise Commissioners* v. *Cure and Deeley* [1962] 1 Q.B. 340). Do the local authority decisions in *Hall* and *Royco* really deserve to be

---

[30] See [1964] 1 All E.R. 1 at 8, 14. These cases could be interpreted as being about "ulterior purposes." See, *e.g. Emery and Smythe, Judicial Review* (1987) pp. 177–183. This seems largely semantic since any unreasonable aim could be like this. For other cases which seem to contemplate a distinction between relevance and reasonableness, see *Wheeler* v. *Leicester City Council* [1985] 2 All E.R. 1106; *West Glamorgan C.C.* v. *Rafferty* [1987] 1 All E.R. 1005. See also *Shanley* v. *Secretary of State* [1982] J.P.L. 380.

stigmatised as "irrational"? The courts will regard as "unreasonable" a decision which they think either unduly harsh, or which without express or necessarily implied statutory authority violates what they regard as basic values. They will even interfere if they think that an undue burden has been placed upon a section of the community (see *Bromley L.B.C.* v. *G.L.C.* [1983] 1 A.C. 768). One value that attracted the unreasonableness doctrine was that of the protection of private property rights. This can be seen at work in *Hall* (but see pp. 32–39, above).

More recently the application of the presumption against deprivation of existing rights has been restricted. The presumption against deprivation of property rights begs the question, what is meant by a "right?" This was recognised in *Hall* by Wilmer L.J. who emphasised that since there is no general right to develop land it cannot be argued that the presumption applies in all cases where the use of land is severely restricted ([1964] 1 All E.R. 1 at 67).

In *Westminster Bank* v. *Minister of Housing* [1970] 2 W.L.R. 645, the Bank had been refused permission to extend its premises because of the prospect of a future road widening scheme. The scheme could also have been implemented under the Highways Act by paying compensation to the bank. Lord Reid emphasised that there is no general right to compensation for the refusal of planning permission and that therefore the applicant had not been deprived of anything. It was moreover reasonable for an authority to choose the cheapest method of proceeding and thereby to avoid paying compensation (see also *Mixnam's Properties Ltd.* v. *Chertsey U.D.C.* [1965] A.C. 735, 754–755). There are also Divisional Court cases holding that a planning condition can deprive the developer of "existing rights" over his land.[31] Existing rights are those conferred by the planning legislation itself and include activities which are not development, activities exempt from the need for permission, activities covered by an earlier permission and activities time-barred from enforcement, albeit the last category may be distinguishable as being "unlawful," the bar against enforcement being merely procedural (see *L.T.S.S. Print and Supply Ltd.* v. *Hackney B.C.* [1976] Q.B. 663 (below, p. 201). See further (1972) 36 Conv. 421). The cases provided no support for distinguishing between these various categories of existing right. The interference

[31] *Gill* v. *Secretary of State* [1985] J.P.L. 710; *Penrith D.C.* v. *Secretary of State* [1977] J.P.L. 371; *Kingston on Thames B.C.* v. *Secretary of State* [1973] 1 W.L.R. 1549; *City of London Corporation* v. *Secretary of State* (1973) 23 P. & C.R. 169. See (1972) 36 Conv. 421. A grant of planning permission cannot *per se* remove existing rights: *Newbury D.C.* v. *Secretary of State* [1981] A.C. 578. See also below, pp. 173–174.

must of course be justified on the basis that the removal of the existing right is relevant to the proposed development. Thus existing rights cannot be removed purely as a quid pro quo.

PLANNING GAIN AND UNREASONABLENESS

This leads us to the question whether the authority can require a developer to provide "planning gain" either by imposing a condition upon a grant of planning permission or by refusing planning permission until such gain is forthcoming. Planning gain consists of some additional public benefit outside the development applied for, for example, the highway demanded in *Hall*, an open space provided in a shopping precinct or the use of profits to subsidise socially desirable facilities. Infrastructure such as drains is also seen as a kind of planning gain (see further below, Chap. 7).

It is lawful for an authority to impose a condition requiring planning gain or to take the possibility of planning gain into account provided that the gain to be sought is (a) relevant to planning purposes; (b) relevant to the proposed development and (c) not unreasonable. In other words planning gain must be evaluated against ordinary principles and is not a separate concept.

For example, a local authority can require land to be so earmarked as an open space for public recreation in connection with a residential development but not actually to donate the land to the public (*Shanley* v. *Secretary of State* [1982] J.P.L. 380). Similarly, an authority could require that an office development include traffic management provision or a car park or perhaps even a residential element (*Westminster City Council* v. *Secretary of State* [1984] J.P.L. 27) provided that the gain is related to the needs of the development and falls short of requiring the developer to shoulder burdens that properly belong to a public authority. In this context the notion of relevance is particularly important. There seems to be a distinction between duties which exist independently of the particular development and duties which are generated by the development itself, *e.g.* infrastructure. Only in the latter case is gain legitimate (compare *Hall* and *Royco* (above) with *Westminster Renslade, Richmond,* and *Bradford* cases (below)).

Planning gain is sometimes but not necessarily designed to compensate for environmental, social or economic disadvantages inherent in the applicants proposal. An authority cannot refuse planning permission solely because no planning gain is provided and must always consider whether the absence of gain is outweighed by other factors (*Richmond B.C.* v. *Secretary of State* [1984] J.P.L. 24). Thus planning permission cannot be "sold."

It is sometimes said that a planning condition cannot require the payment of money. This view is based upon the constitutional presumption embodied in the Bill of Rights 1688 against taxation without clear statutory authority.[32] It is true that an applicant cannot be required to pay for a publicly controlled facility, such as a car park (*Westminster Renslade* v. *Secretary of State* (1984) P. and C.R. 255 but, providing that the normal principles of relevance and reasonableness are complied with, there seems to be no objection in principle to the requirement of an *earmarked* financial contribution. The amount sought must: (i) be earmarked for the purpose of overcoming a problem created by the development in question; (ii) be no greater in extent than the share of the problem created by that development and (iii) must not subsidise a service which the authority has a statutory duty to provide.

This solution has been accepted in the United States. Subject to tests of relevance and proportionality local authorities can demand "exactions" from developers and can also deal with the problem of rationing development by means of a "points system" giving priority for permissions to developers that are prepared either to provide infrastructure or make a financial contribution to the provision of public services or public amenities.[33] It could be argued that such devices are inevitable in a market based planning system and that, unlike the case in Britain, the bargaining element in American planning is at least open, structured and subject to judicial control.

City of Bradford M.B.C. v. *Secretary of State* [1986] J.P.L. 598 goes some way to supporting the view that proportional contributions can be exacted. Planning permission was granted for residential development subject to a condition requiring the developer to pay towards the widening of an existing road. The developer's contribution was not proportionate to the burden placed on the road by the development and so the condition was invalid. However, the Court of Appeal said that there is no general principle that a condition requiring a developer to bear a proper proportion of the cost of providing a public service is

---

[32] See *R.* v. *Bowman* [1988] 1 Q.B. 663; *Westminster Renslade* v. *Secretary of State* (1984) P. & C.R. 255. The Bill of Rights in fact forbids only *prerogative* taxation.

[33] See *Golden* v. *Town of Ramapo* 285 N.E.2d. 291—points system of contributions. *City of Dunedin* v. *Contractors and Builders Association* 312 So 2d. 763 (1975) "impact fee." *Associated Home Builders* v. *City of Walnut Creek* 484 P.2d.606—charges for parks etc. *Quaere* whether anticipated growth sparked off by the development is relevant.

always unlawful.[34] Their Lordships also thought that the developer's voluntary acquiescence in the condition might be relevant to its reasonableness, thus allowing the judgment of the market to enter the calculations. On the other hand, it was emphasised that consent will not in itself save a condition because of the overriding importance of the public interest.

The main limitation upon the achievement of planning gain is that the gain must be related to the proposed development. We shall consider later whether this limitation can be overcome by seeking gain through agreement rather than by imposing a condition (below pp. 167–168).

UNREASONABLENESS AND "NO EVIDENCE"

A decision that is entirely without relevant factual evidence is invalid (*Coleen Properties* v. *M.o.H.* [1971] 1 W.L.R. 433). This could be regarded as an example of "unreasonableness" in the sense of irrationality. Two distinctions are important. First, the question of *weight* of evidence is normally for the authority. No evidence means that there is no connection at all between the facts relied on and the decision and thus differs from the American "substantial evidence" test. However, the distinction is easily blurred. In an extreme case the weight given to a piece of evidence could be unreasonable (above, n. 3). Once the wall between no evidence at all and "some" evidence is breached there seems to be no logical way of preventing a court from substituting its own view of the merits for that of the authority. Indeed, this seems to be the rationale of the much criticised *Niarchos* v. *Secretary of State* [1978] 35 P. & C.R. 259 (above, p. 134). In general the English courts are reluctant to impose stringent standards of evidence. *c.f. Wyre Forest D.C.* v. *Secretary of State* [1989] J.P.L. 270—inadequate investigation led to unreasonable finding.

Secondly, a distinction must be made between decisions that depend upon a factual basis and those which are essentially value judgments. In the latter case no supporting facts are required.[35]

---

[34] See *Wimpey* v. *Secretary of State* (1978) 250 E.G. 241. There are sometimes statutory arrangements for contributions from developers. Grant, pp. 377 *et seq. e.g.* Water Act 1945, section 37; Water Act 1973, section 16; Highways Act 1980, section 278.

[35] *Winchester City Council* v. *Secretary of State* (1979) 39 P. & C.R. 1 at 6; *Trust House Forte* v. *Secretary of State* [1986] J.P.L. 834; *Banks Horticultural Co.* v. *Secretary of State* [1980] J.P.L. 33; *Wholesale Mail Order Supplies* v. *Secretary of State* [1976] J.P.L. 163; *Kent C.C.* v. *Secretary of State* (1977) 33 P. & C.R. 71.

Value judgments include purely aesthetic judgments, applications of the professional expertise of the Inspector holding the inquiry, and the merits of planning policy.

Conditions—a note

The principles of relevance and reasonableness that we have discussed in this chapter are applicable to all kinds of planning decision. However, planning conditions are often treated separately. It may therefore be appropriate to summarise a few matters relating particularly to conditions.[36]

1. A condition must be "certain" and to this end will be construed generously and in the light of published planning policies with a view to upholding it if possible.[37]

2. The general power to impose conditions applies only to land subject to the application (section 29). There is, however, a specific power to attach conditions to other land *under the control of the applicant* "so far as it appears to the local planning authority to be expedient for the purposes of, or in connection with the development authorised by the permission" (section 30(1)).

Control is not confined to legal ownership but is a question of fact and can be achieved, for example, by agreement (*George Wimpey and Co.* v. *Secretary of State* [1979] J.P.L. 314). Furthermore it seems that a *negative* condition could be attached to the development relating to other land not under the applicants' control. In *Grampian Regional Council* v. *City of Aberdeen D.C.* (1984) 47 P. & C.R. the court upheld a negative condition that no development should begin until a road had been closed on neighbouring land. Such a condition was reasonable in that it placed no burden on the owner of the other land. The "Grampian" device may be useful in other contexts, for example to prevent development until infrastructure is adequate (see *Daws* v. *Secretary of State* [1989] J.P.L. 358).

Where the other land is not under the control of the applicant it must be included in the application (*Atkinson* v. *Secretary of State* [1983] J.P.L. 599) thus ensuring a degree of procedural protection for the owner (above, p. 117).

3. A condition must not be inconsistent with the actual development proposed. For example, a scheme for houses of two storeys cannot be permitted subject to a condition requiring

---

[36] See also the question of "severance" (above, pp. 41–43).
[37] *Fawcett Properties* v. *Bucks C.C.* [1961] A.C. 636 (above, p. 35); *Shanley* v. *Secretary of State* [1982] J.P.L. 380.

152   THE DISCRETION OF THE AUTHORITY

bungalows. However, the question is one of degree. A condition can certainly require incidental modifications to a scheme such as the removal of windows or means of access. The test seems to be the common sense one of whether the application as modified is substantially different from the original application so as to entitle persons affected to make further representations.

4. A condition that is in practice unenforceable is not as such unlawful (*Bromsgrove D.C.* v. *Secretary of State* [1988] J.P.L. 257; compare Circular 1/85).

5. In addition to the general power to impose conditions there are specific powers to deal with special problems. These include:

(i) Conditions requiring the removal of buildings or works or the discontinuance of uses authorised by planning provisions granted for a limited period and also reinstatement of the land (section 30(1)(*b*)).

(ii) Time limit conditions for the commencement of operational development (section 30(2)).

(iii) "Aftercare conditions" relating to planning permission for mining operations subject to a condition requiring restoration of the land after the development has ceased (section 30A. See also section 44A). These allow the authority to regulate the use to which the land is subsequently put which may be agriculture or forestry not itself requiring planning permission. An aftercare condition must be imposed for the purpose of bringing the land up to the standard required for its new use.

(iv) "Outline Provisions." A condition can be imposed under the general law providing for the authority to approve the detailed implementation of the permission, *e.g.* approval of waste deposits (*Bilboe* v. *Secretary of State* [1979] J.P.L. 100).[38] In the case of applications for the erection of a building the matter is regulated by the General Development Order 1988, Arts. 7 and 8. This allows permission to be granted in principle, subject to a condition that it shall not be implemented until the authority has approved specified "reserved matters." These include siting, design, external appearance, means of access and landscaping. The authority can also attach further conditions requiring its approval of other matters. Having granted outline planning permission the authority's only power is to approve or disapprove the reserved

[38] Reversed on a different point on appeal. (1980) 39 P. & C.R. 495.

matters. It cannot refuse consent on any other ground nor alter the permission itself (see *R.* v. *Castle Point D.C.* [1985] J.P.L. 473). It would also be unlawful to impose a condition requiring the consent of a third party, *e.g.* the highway authority, to some action.

(v) In certain circumstances there is a duty to attach conditions requiring the preservation or planting of trees (section 59).

7. Planning Agreements

INTRODUCTION

Local Planning Authorities (the central government has no direct powers in this respect) make frequent use of agreements with applicants for planning permission in order to achieve what is often called "planning gain." This must be distinguished from negotiations which take place as part of the normal application process for the purpose of ironing out problems relating to the physical details of the development. Planning agreements usually involve formal contracts entered into under various statutory powers (see below, p. 159). "Planning gain," although having no accepted legal meaning, has been defined by the Department of Environment as meaning some benefit relevant to planning generally but extrinsic to the particular development (see circular 22/83), e.g. agreeing to provide a by-pass in return for permission to build an out-of-town supermarket (see also above p. 148). Others define planning gain more narrowly and restrict the concept to benefits that would be ultra vires if sought by means of the ordinary statutory powers to refuse planning permission or to attach conditions.[1] One reason for the emergence of planning agreements is a belief (perhaps misplaced) that the courts have unduly restricted the scope of legitimate planning objectives and of the power to impose conditions. However, it is becoming clear that limitations upon the exercise of statutory powers cannot be avoided by means of an agreement.

Some local authorities have "institutionalised" planning gain by imposing gain criteria in their statutory development plans. This

[1] See Loughlin (1980) O.J.L.S. 61. For general discussions of planning gain and its problems, see Suddards [1979] J.P.L. 661; Grant [1978] J.P.L. 8; Grant and Jowell [1983] J.P.L. 427; Grant, *Urban Planning Law* (1983), pp. 359–382; Jowell [1977] J.P.L. 414; Ward [1982] J.P.L. 74; Heap and Ward [1980] J.P.L. 631; PAG Report HMSO (1981) "Development Control—30 Years On" (*J.P.L.*, *Occasional Papers* 1979) pp. 23, 27, 35.

helps to overcome objections based upon secrecy but does not cure any legal objections that might otherwise exist (see above, p. 143).

The use of planning agreements has been justified, narrowly, by claiming that they help to get round problems which would otherwise be a reason for refusing planning permission, and that they speed up the planning process, and justified broadly by invoking the ideal of planners and developers co-operating to achieve social and economic goals. The practice has been seen as a departure from the "adjudicative dispute resolution" view of planning which sees the planner essentially as an extension of the law of nuisance, towards a goal-orientated "corporatist discretion" model. There is also the political argument that planning gain ensures that some of the profit generated by planning permission accrues to the community.[2]

Others have pointed to dangers inherent in planning by agreement; for example unequality of power, secrecy and the absence of any statutory or common law procedural safeguards such as public consultation. At its worst the practice is seen as a form of bribery, and "selling" planning permissions as a modern equivalent of the medieval market in indulgences.

Indeed, the notion that public authorities can exercise powers through bargaining can be seen as an affront to the rule of law. As against this it is argued that a discretionary system of planning makes bargaining inevitable and that economic forces reinforce this.[3] Moreover at a time of restricted public expenditure it is thought desirable to require private developers to shoulder some of the costs—pressure on public services, need for increased road and sewage capacity—generated by their developments.

We have argued earlier that the scope of relevant planning considerations is wide and the courts have not restricted the powers of local planning authorities as much as is sometimes assumed. For example, certain financial contributions to car parking facilities, or road improvements could be secured by a condition. Occupancy conditions are permissible and only extreme limitations on private property rights will justify judicial intervention. Similarly the profits realised by development can be earmarked for improvements to other related land (p. 137).

Does this mean that planning agreements are unnecessary? There are two other advantages of planning agreements as compared with the ordinary statutory powers. First, an agreement

[2] See Loughlin, *op. cit.* above, n. 1; Jowell (1977) 30 C.L.P. 63.
[3] Grant, *Urban Planning Law*, at 374–377; Reade [1982] J.P.L. 8; Loughlin *op. cit.* above, n. 1.

might reinforce the ordinary development control mechanism by overcoming the problems arising out of the clumsy enforcement machinery (below, Chap. 9). For example, an interlocutory injunction based upon breach of contract might be a more effective remedy than an enforcement notice.[4] In particular, an obligation to pay money is inherently more appropriate to enforcement through contract law. The Law Society has condemned the use of agreements in cases where ordinary powers could be used on the ground that they may restrict the developers opportunities to appeal or to apply for planning permission in the future ([1982] J.P.L. 346). However, these can be safeguarded by appropriate terms contained in the agreement. In any event an agreement that attempts to restrict statutory duties is unenforceable (below, p. 164).

Secondly, an agreement is more flexible than a condition. It can be renegotiated without the need to reapply for planning permission or appeal against a condition. (However, this advantage entails one of the main objections to the practice of planning bargaining—that of by-passing statutory procedures and overriding the interests of third parties such as local residents).

There is said to be a third advantage of an agreement. Both conditions and agreements must be for planning purposes but it may be that an agreement need not relate to the development for which permission is sought (below p. 167). If this is correct which, as we shall see, is unlikely, then the scope for negotiated planning is very wide.

The Department of Environment's current guidelines for planning gain are to restrictive (Circular 22/83). They contemplate that gain should only be sought (whether by agreement or condition) in four cases: (i) where the gain is needed to enable the development to go ahead, *e.g.* provision of adequate access, water supply or sewage (infrastructure); (ii) in the case of financial payments, will contribute to meeting the cost of providing such facilities in the future, or (iii) is otherwise so directly related to the proposed development and to the use of the land after its completion that the development ought not to be permitted without it (*e.g.* car parking provision) or (iv) is designed in the case of mixed development to secure an acceptable balance of uses.

[4] See *Beaconsfield D.C.* v. *Gams* (1975) J.P.L. 704; *Avon C.C.* v. *Millard* [1986] J.P.L. 211; *R.* v. *Westminster City Council ex p. Monahan* [1989] J.P.L. 107. As with a condition the agreement must be sufficiently certain. *Quaere* whether a public or private law test is appropriate (see *Shanley* v. *Secretary of State* [1982] J.P.L. 380). The difficulties inherent in obtaining an injunction to reinforce the exercise of statutory enforcement powers may also be avoided (see below, p. 183).

These boil down to saying that gain is acceptable only if the development would be unsatisfactory without it. This arguably is not "gain" at all. The policies in the circular seem to be more limited than would be legally permissible. Even in the case of a condition, let alone an agreement, it has been held that additional benefits can be required[5] and the test of "necessity" embodied in the circular has never been applied by the courts.

Types of planning gain

There have been several attempts to classify the kinds of gain that have been sought by planning authorities throughout the country.[6] A useful approach is provided by Loughlin (1980) O.J.L.S. at 66 who identifies three main kinds of gain with sub-categories of each. Each kind of gain could in principle also be achieved by condition, including a condition which requires subsequent activities to be approved by the local planning authority.[7]

1. Exerting detailed or continuous control over the development.

   (a) Restoring land or rehabilitating property.
   (b) Extinguishing the existing use or demolishing existing buildings (*Beaconsfield D.C.* v. *Gams* (above, n. 4)).
   (c) Occupancy conditions, *e.g.* in favour of local people (*Shanley* v. *Secretary of State* (above, n. 4))—the problem there was that the condition was not sufficiently specific.
   (d) Timing or phasing of development. Provisions preventing implementation of a planning permission can be included (*e.g. Ames* v. *North Bedfordshire D.C.* [1980] J.P.L. 182; *Hope* v. *Secretary of State* (1975) 249 E.G. 627).

2. Provision of infrastructure or contributions to the cost of infrastructure. This is one kind of gain that appears to have the blessing of the Department of Environment (above). It is sometimes thought that this kind of gain cannot be achieved by means of a condition, but as we have seen this is an unacceptably narrow interpretation of the cases (above, p. 149). However, a public authority cannot require a developer to perform its own

---

[5] See, *e.g. R.* v. *St. Edmunsbury B.C.* [1985] 1 W.L.R. 1158; *Brittania (Cheltenham)* v. *Secretary of State* [1979] J.P.L. 534.

[6] See *e.g.* Jowell [1977] J.P.L. 414; Byrne, "Development Control—Thirty Years On" (*loc. cit.* n. 1 above at 43–4).

[7] See *Roberts* v. *Vale Royal D.C.* [1977] J.P.L. 369; *R.* v. *Surrey C.C. ex p. Monk* [1987] 53 P. & C.R. 410. There is provision for a right of appeal. See section 36(1)(*b*).

statutory functions and this applies equally to agreements and conditions. In the case of infrastructure the terms of the particular legislation imposing the function of providing infrastructure are crucial. In cases where there is a power, as opposed to a duty to provide the relevant infrastructure,[8] there would seem to be no objection in principle to requiring a contribution from the developer. The same applies where a duty becomes operative only after planning permission has been granted. In these cases planning permission can be refused because of lack of infrastructure and it would follow that a contribution can be required.[9] In all cases the contribution must be proportionate to the direct costs of the development (above, p. 149).

3. A "taxing" device to enable the local authority to share in the profits of the development, e.g. provision of residential units in office development, provision of community facilities such as open space or improved public transport. This is the most controversial kind of gain because it raises the spectre of "selling" planning permission. Indeed, some local authorities have expressly included provision of this kind in their development plans and justified it on the basis that the public have a claim to share in the increase of land values generated by development (see Loughlin op. cit. above at p. 72). This kind of gain goes beyond gain required to meet problems generated by the development. As many writers have remarked[10] the issue is linked to more general problems about the nature and purposes of planning control. Is planning control limited to environmental matters, i.e. meeting amenity objections to proposals or does it embrace social engineering matters? We have argued that as far as the courts are concerned it does indeed embrace wider social objectives (above, p. 130). There is therefore no legal objection to using agreements to achieve gain in this wide sense provided that the gain required is "reasonable," and broadly related to the particular development (see below, p. 166).

The legal basis of planning agreements

Planning agreements may be authorised under Local Acts of

---

[8] e.g. Highways parking etc. See Bradford M.B.C. v. Secretary of State [1986] J.P.L. 598 (above, pp. 148–150).

[9] e.g. Water Act 1973, section 16. See Wimpey v. Secretary of State [1978] J.P.L. 776; Water Act 1944, section 37.

[10] e.g. Loughlin op. cit. above, n. 1; Reade [1981] J.P.L. 8. See also U.S. law, e.g. Associated Home Builders Inc. v. City of Walnut Creek 484 P2d 606 (1971).

Parliament which create a special regime as regards purpose, formalities and the question of the impact on third parties.[11] Agreements are most commonly made under general statutory powers. There are three main provisions. Under the Local Government Act 1972, section 111 a local authority can "do anything which is calculated to facilitate or is conducive to any of their functions." This authorises agreements made for planning purposes and can include the payment of money.[12] This section is appropriate for "once-and-for-all promises but not for continuing obligations such as restrictions on the use of land, since the section does not contain any mechanism to bind successors in title of the developer. Apart from the landlord and tenant relationship an agreement relating to land is enforceable against successors in title only in equity under the rule in *Tulk* v. *Moxhay* (1848) 18 L.J.Ch. 83). This applies only to negative obligations and requires that the obligation benefit land owned by the person who wishes to enforce it. Unless the agreement benefits land owned by the authority it will thus be enforceable only between the original parties (*L.C.C.* v. *Allen* [1943] 3 K.B. 642, 664).

SECTION 52 AGREEMENTS

The second provision purports to avoid this difficult. Section 52(1) of the 1971 Act authorises local planning authorities "to enter into an agreement with any person interested in land in their area for the purpose of restricting or regulating the development or use of the land." Subsection (2) provides that

> "an agreement made under this section with any person interested in land may be enforced by the local planning authority against persons deriving title under that person in respect of that land as if the local planning authority were possessed of adjacent land and as if the agreement had been expressed to be made for the benefit of such land."

This section, which derives from section 34 of the Town and Country Planning Act 1932, has received little attention from the courts. Its intention is clearly to enable successors in title to be sued. Its method of doing so is to introduce the fiction that the authority

---

[11] See, *e.g. Beaconsfield D.C.* v. *Gams* [1975] J.P.L. 704; Leeds Corporation Act 1966; Loughlin *op. cit.* n. 1, above, p. 67.

[12] See also L.G.A. 1972 section 139—gifts, but see *County and District Properties Ltd.* v. *Horsham U.D.C.* (1970) 215 E. G. 1339—commuted car parking payment not gift. Gift must be gratuitous. However, section 111 seems broad enough to cover cash payments.

owns benefited land and thus to take advantage of the equitable rules governing restrictive covenants.[13] Section 52(2) raises several technical problems and a strict construction of the provision could severely limit its usefulness. It is unfortunate that Parliament should choose to provide for what are essentially public law transactions by incorporating the machinery of private restrictive covenants.[14] Not only is this a notoriously complex and incoherent branch of the law, but the same objectives could have been achieved more directly by making planning agreements binding on successors in title (subject to contrary intention) "as if they were original parties to the agreement" (compare positive covenants below).

First, the formula in subsection (2) does not seem to go far enough in incorporating the *Tulk* v. *Moxhay* doctrine. Equity requires not only the expression of an intention to benefit land owned by the covenantee (which is supplied by section 52(2)), but also the further requirement that the land be *in fact* capable of benefiting from the covenant (see Preston and Newsom, *Restrictive Covenants Affecting Freehold Land* (6th ed.), pp. 70–72), albeit the requirement of benefit is a liberal one (*Wrotham Park Estates* v. *Parkside Homes Ltd.* [1974] 1 W.L.R. 798).

Where the agreement is one that in principle could benefit defined land (*e.g.* an undertaking not to build) the courts may not balk at inferring that benefit accrues to the authority's imaginary land. However, many obligations, although desirable from a planning point of view, are not in their nature capable of benefiting any defined land at all, for example, to allow public access to the developer's land; but to extend the equitable rules to include these may be asking a judge to make a greater imaginative leap than Chancery flesh and blood could stand (see *Gee* v. *National Trust* [1966] 1 W.L.R. 170.)

Secondly, the section makes no mention of enforceability by successors in title *against* the local authority in respect of the authority's obligations under the agreement. However, this does not seem to be a serious problem. At common law the benefit of a covenant will pass to a successor in title against the original covenantor. The covenant must benefit land in which the covenantee holds a legal estate, but the covenantor need not hold any land. There is therefore no difficulty in transmissibility as long

---

[13] The more complex equitable rules relating to *benefit* may, however, be relevant once the burden has passed. But see L.P.A. 1925, section 78; *Federated Homes Ltd.* v. *Mill Lodge Properties Ltd.* [1980] 1 W.L.R. 594.

[14] See particularly *Pioneers Aggregates* v. *Secretary of State* [1985] A.C. 132. It is arguable that the terms of a section 52 agreement are not subject to the application for judicial review procedure.

as the authority's obligation benefits identifiable land owned by the covenantee or and his successors who must possess a legal estate.

Thirdly, section 52 can pass the burden only of negative covenants. The section cannot therefore be used to impose obligations to carry out work, or provide facilities, unless the obligation is to bind only the original covenantor (but see [1976] J.P.L. 216). Section 52 provides that agreements may contain incidental and consequential provisions of a financial character but these presumably will not run with the land. This raises wider questions concerning the relationship between planning agreements and the exercise of statutory powers to grant planning permission or to take enforcement action. We shall examine these later confining ourselves for the moment to basic mechanics.

Fourthly, section 52 uses the term "agreement" which although wider than contract is often used to mean "contract." In the absence of specific statutory provision no agreement is legally enforceable unless it is made under seal or supported by consideration. It is unlikely that a developer would make a gratuitous promise under seal and so the question of consideration is crucial. Section 52 makes no provision for enforcement, but its incorporation of the *Tulk* v. *Moxhay* doctrine suggests that a contractual relationship between the original parties is contemplated. *Ransom and Luck* v. *Surbiton B.D.* [1949] Ch. 180 is the only case where the general nature of section 52 agreements was discussed. The case turned upon the question whether the authority could offer as consideration an undertaking which restricted the future exercise of its statutory powers. The Court of Appeal held that such consideration was unlawful (see below, p. 164), and did not need to answer more general questions. It has been argued that consideration is unnecessary at least where a successor in title is concerned because the obligation runs with the land as a property right vested in the authority (see Grant, p. 385). However, under the *Tulk* v. *Moxhay* doctrine which is embodied in section 52 the *successor* need not provide consideration but the doctrine presupposes the existence of an enforceable contract supported by consideration between the original parties (equity will not assist a volunteer).

It has also been argued that a section 52 agreement should be considered as an independent statutory obligation taking effect in public law and free from private law restrictions (*Loughlin op. cit.* note 1 above at pp. 76–78). This is attractive particularly in the light of the emerging judicial tendency to separate private from public law, but difficult to reconcile with the language of section 52. Earlier cases such as *Ranson and Luck* v. *Surbiton B.C.* [1949] Ch. 180 and

Gee v. *National Trust* [1966] 1 W.L.R. 170 (dealing with an analogous provision) are equivocal and strong language is required to displace what is one of English law's most firmly entrenched shibboleths. Moreover the language of Lord Greene M.R. in the *Surbiton* case is consistent only with the proposition that the obligation arises out of contract, although as he said (at p. 195) "it goes *beyond* mere contract in that it gets the characteristics of a restrictive covenant." He also emphasised (at p. 195) that "[section 52] is of very limited application: it merely allows local authorities to enforce restrictions as if they had been entered into for the benefit of an adjoining land-owner." Moreover his Lordship discussed what forms of consideration could be provided in order to persuade landowners to enter into section 52 agreements, accepting that the section would be nugatory if no consideration was available. It is thus likely that consideration is necessary.

If consideration is required, difficulties arise. A local planning authority cannot promise to exercise its statutory powers in any particular way either to grant planning permission or to refrain from enforcement action since that would amount to an unlawful fettering of its discretion. Nor can the authority merely undertake to take the applicant's undertaking into account since it must do so anyway as a relevant consideration. We shall deal with these matters later.

A final limitation of section 52 is that it applies only to agreements to restrict or regulate "the development or use of the land." Thus outright gifts of land are excluded, as are payments of money unless they are "incidental or consequential" to the development or use of the land (section 52(1)). It is not clear what other positive obligations might fall within section 52, although undertakings to provide facilities or to carry out work on the land itself would certainly do so. But, as we have seen, positive obligations cannot under section 52 pass to successors in title.

POSITIVE COVENANTS

These are governed by the Local Government (Miscellaneous Provisions) Act 1982, section 33. This provides that an instrument under seal made between a person having an interest in the land and a local authority or district council which contains a "covenant...to carry out any works or do any other thing on or in relation to" land shall be enforceable against successors in title to that land.

The instrument must be executed for the purpose of the carrying out of works on land in the council's area, or of facilitating the development or regulating the use of land in or outside the council's area or is otherwise connected with land in or outside the council's area in which the other person has an interest.

The drafting of this shows a marked improvement upon section 52. First, it confers liability directly upon successors in title. Secondly, the term "agreement" is not used and any undertaking under seal will therefore be enforceable. Thirdly, the section provides its own enforcement machinery, including a provision for the authority to enter the land and carry out the work. This is in addition to any other remedies such as injunction or damages.

However, section 33 is limited in scope to covenants involving acts relating to the land itself. It could conceivably include the transfer of land to the authority (which as we have seen is outside section 52, even as regards the original parties). Nor does section 33 authorise the payment of money to the authority even in lieu of works carried out on the land.

Registration

Agreements under both section 52 and section 33 must be registered. The position is affected by the changes in the law relating to registration brought about by the Local Land Charges Act 1975 (see Law Commission, Transfer of Land; Report on Local Land Charges (1974); Law Com. No. 62). This Act is an attempt to distinguish between public and private obligations binding land. Unfortunately it does not achieve this objective where planning agreements are concerned.

Prima facie any prohibition or restriction on the use of land enforceable by a local authority under any covenant or agreement made with them is a local land charge (section 1(1)(b)(ii)). Positive obligations imposed under the Local Government (Miscellaneous Provisions) Act 1982 are also local land charges.

If a local land charge is not registered as such it remains binding upon all persons, but a purchaser is entitled to compensation in respect of any loss suffered by virtue of the failure to register (1975 Act, section 10). By contrast a failure to register an ordinary land charge makes it void against a purchaser.[15] This reflects the public interest in the enforceability of local land charges and it is appropriate therefore that all planning agreements be regarded as local land charges.

However, section 52 agreements seem to be excluded from the company of local land charges. Section 2 of the 1975 Act excludes certain obligations from the definition, one of these being "a prohibition or restriction enforceable by . . . a local authority under any covenant or agreement being . . . binding on successive owners of the land affected by reason of the fact that [it] is made for the benefit of land of the . . . local authority." This presumably is intended to preserve the principle that ordinary restrictive covenants made with an authority *qua* landowner are registerable in the same way as ordinary land charges.

Section 52 agreements seem to fall within the exemption since their enforceability against successors depends upon the fictitious land owned by the authority. It is doubtful whether Parliament intended that positive and negative planning agreements should thus differ as to enforceability. The public element in such agreements, particularly in view of the increased use being made of them suggests that they should no longer be treated merely as restrictive covenants and that their public law character be formally recognised. They could be registered as local land charges and additionally placed in the public register of planning applications and permissions. This may help to overcome the secrecy in which planning agreements are sometimes shrouded.

The relationship between planning agreements and statutory development control powers

After a period of uncertainty it seems to have been settled that a planning authority cannot restrict or fetter the exercise of any of its statutory powers by means of a planning agreement. It cannot promise in return for planning gain either to grant planning permission or to refrain from enforcement action.[16] Nor can

---

[15] L.C.A. 1972 section 4(*b*); L.R.A. 1925, section 50(1).

[16] *Windsor and Maidenhead Royal Borough Council* v. *Brandrose Investments Ltd.* [1983] 1 W.L.R. 509. This is despite section 52(3), which provides that "nothing in this section or any agreement made thereunder shall be construed (a) as restricting the exercise . . . of any powers exercisable . . . under this Act so long as those powers are exercised in accordance with the development plan . . . ." This would seem to permit a fettering of discretion but is ambiguous. Does it mean (i) an agreement cannot fetter a decision that is consistent with the plan or (ii) an agreement consistent with the plan can fetter? The latter seems consistent with section 52(3)(*b*) but the *Brandrose* case seems to make section 52(3) meaningless.

planning permission be refused solely on the ground that no gain is provided unless the "gain" is necessary to overcome some problem that in itself would entitle the authority to refuse planning permission. Nor can the fact that provisions for gain are included in the development plan legitimise the obtaining of gain in any particular case.[17]

A planning agreement could be linked with a planning permission in the following ways, none of which would involve an unlawful fettering of discretion.

(1) A unilateral contract in which the developer promises that if planning permission is granted he will provide the gain. This means that the authority may take his offer into account (provided that it is relevant and reasonable) but does not oblige it in any circumstances to grant planning permission. The formal grant of permission is the acceptance of the offer so that there is provision for negotiation as part of the normal application procedure. Such an agreement should preferably be under seal (see above, p. 162). A seal also avoids any argument about the absence of consideration based on the proposition that planning permission should have been granted even without the undertaking.

(2) A condition could be imposed upon the grant of permission requiring an agreement to be made. It is often thought that such a condition is unlawful, and even if it is not the Department of Environment might strike it out on appeal. However, conditions requiring negotiations and agreements have been upheld in the courts.[18]

Such a condition may create enforcement problems because the range of possibilities open to an enforcement notice is limited (below, p. 192). In particular, a failure to agree could not in itself be the subject of an enforcement notice. A condition that the planning permission cannot be

---

[17] See *Westminster Renslade* v. *Secretary of State* [1984] 48 P. & C.R. 255; *Westminster City Council* v. *Secretary of State* [1984] J.P.L.; *Richmond on Thames B.C.* v. *Secretary of State* [1984] J.P.L. 24. However, such provision may be a valuable way of making the issue of planning gain more open.

[18] *R.* v. *Surrey B.C. ex p. Monk* (1987) 33 P. & C.R. 410; *McLaren* v. *Secretary of State* [1981] J.P.L. 423; *R.* v. *West Oxfordshire D.C. ex p. Pearce Homes* [1986] J.P.L. 523; but see *Shanley* v. *Secretary of State* [1982] J.P.L. 380.

implemented until the agreement is concluded may be appropriate.[19]

(3) The authority could postpone granting planning permission until an agreement was made, or in appeal proceedings the inspector might adjourn to permit negotiations between the parties.[20] These devices enable an agreement to be openly taken into account as part of the process for applying for planning permission and to some extent counter the allegations that planning agreements involve secretive bargaining within the "sub cultures" of developers and officials from which the public and sometimes elected officials are excluded.[21]

Planning agreements that offer planning gain may therefore be taken into account by a local planning authority when exercising its statutory powers and the developer's obligations may be enforced either through the development control powers or through private law remedies including an injunction. However, this is subject to limits as to the scope of a planning agreement.

It is arguable that a planning agreement cannot enlarge the range of matters which could lawfully be taken into account in deciding the application for planning permission. This is because of the basic principle that statutory powers cannot be enlarged by consent. As far as "planning considerations" are concerned the agreement must therefore be related to land use matters (above, p. 130) but could include a money payment earmarked for land use purposes. The agreement must probably also be related to the proposed development (see below). For example, planning permission for industrial use could be subject to an agreement requiring restrictions upon other industrial uses in order to offset the

---

[19] See *Grampian D.C.* v. *Secretary of State* [1984] J.P.L. 590; *Daws* v. *Secretary of State* [1989] J.P.L. 358. A time limit for implementation could be required or phased implementation. There is a right of appeal to the Secretary of State (section 36(1)(*b*)). See also *Hildenborough* v. *Secretary of State* [1978] J.P.L. 708 where it was suggested that a developer might be estopped from implementing a planning permission pending an agreement *Sed quaere*. American law has achieved sophisticated methods of incorporating agreements including phased development on a points system, quotas, and transferrable development rights. See *Golden* v. *Town of Ramapo* 285 N.E.2d 291 (1972); *Construction Industry Association* v. *City of Petaluna* 552 F.2d 897; *Penn Central Transportation Co.* v. *City of New York* 366 N.E.2d 1271. These devices raise constitutional problems relating to equal protection and certainty that would not arise here but benefit from an equally wide notion of the purposes of land use controls. See, *e.g. Lockard* v. *City of Los Angeles* 202 P. 2d 38 (1949); *Berman* v. *Parker* 348 U.S. 26 (1954).

[20] *Solihull D.C.* v. *Secretary of State* [1987] J.P.L. 208; *McLaren* v. *Secretary of State* (above, n. 18).

[21] See Reade [1981] J.P.L. 8; Suddards [1979] J.P.L. 661; Loughlin [1978] J.P.L. 290.

environmental impact of the new development. An agreement to provide community facilities or to lay out an open space may be relevant to a proposed shopping centre or residential development,[22] but not an agreement to provide, say, an old peoples' home or contribute to public car parking facilities generally. An agreement to provide employment on site A to make up for loss of employment because of a change of use on site B would also be relevant but not the provision of compensation to affected employees. Similarly, an undertaking not to use site A as a residence in return for permission to develop site B as a residence would be valid. The condition rejected by the House of Lords in *Newbury D.C.* v. *Secretary of State* (above, p. 136) to demolish a building after the cesser of a use could not be achieved by means of an agreement.

Finally, any charges exacted, *e.g.* for car parking, services or infrastructure must be no larger than a reasonable estimate of the increased burden generated by the particular development upon the fund for which the charge is earmarked (see *Bradford M.B.C.* v. *Secretary of State* [1986] J.P.L. 598, above, p. 149; *Richmond B.C.* v. *Secretary of State* [1984] J.P.L. 24).

It would seem also that an agreement cannot be used for purposes which, although related to the development, are unreasonable under the general law, such as an agreement to dedicate land or to perform a statutory function on behalf of the authority. The Court of Appeal left the point open in *Bradford M.B.C.* v. *Secretary of State* (above)—(unreasonable road widening condition) but Lloyd L.J. expressed doubts as to whether it was permissible to achieve by agreement an objective which cannot be achieved under statutory powers. On the other hand, in *Shanley* v. *Secretary of State* [1982] J.P.L. 380 a condition was held to be unlawful but the court seemed to accept the possibility of a section 52 agreement.

In *R.* v. *Gillingham B.C. exp. F. Parham Ltd.* [1988] J.P.L. 337 Roche J. held that a section 52 agreement need not satisfy the requirements of relevance to the proposed development applicable to planning conditions. The application was for outline permissions to build housing and the agreement required the developer to extend and modify a road. It was held that the agreement was not unreasonable and also that the planning permission was valid even

---

[22] See *Britannia Cheltenham* v. *Secretary of State* [1978] J.P.L. 554; or to provide extra retail space. *R.* v. *St. Edmunsbury D.C.* [1985] 3 All E.R. 234 but not to dedicate the land to the public (below). See *Shanley* v. *Secretary of State* above, n. 18.

if the agreement was unrelated to the proposed development. (It was made for the purpose of facilitating the development of other neighbouring land). Roche J. did not regard that objection as fatal provided that the agreement was made for a planning purpose. However in *R. v. Westminster City Council ex p. Monahan* (above p. 132) Kerr L.J. thought that an agreement could not be used for a purpose that could not have been achieved under the ordinary statutory powers. This crucially restricts the ambit of planning gain. It relegates agreements to auxiliary devices rather than instruments of negotiated planning. Strictly speaking Kerr L.J.'s views were obiter and the issue awaits a decisive resolution.

Roche J. in *Parham* thought that there could be little point in enacting section 52 of the 1971 Act if its scope was the same as that of conditions. To this it might be answered that section 52 agreements are concerned with binding successors in title, that they need not necessarily be concerned with planning permission and that there are advantages relating to enforcement in using the law of contract rather than the statutory enforcement machinery. Furthermore a section 52 agreement, (if planning permission is granted) cannot be the subject of an appeal to the Secretary of State. If the *Parham* case is correct then it opens the way to a range of bargaining devices possibly approaching the American concept of "transferable development rights" by which rights to build on unrelated pieces of land can be sold, or exchanged with the City Council acting as broker. This device has the advantage of providing a form of compensation for planning restrictions by allowing a developer to "buy" development rights elsewhere. It also provides a tool of social engineering.

Conclusion

The law relating to planning agreements is incoherent largely because of a failure to grapple with fundamental questions about the objectives of the planning system, with the result that limitations and safeguards have been examined in a vacuum. Loughlin has said ([1982] J.P.L. at 352) that planning agreements occupy the "conceptual space between legitimate use of conditions and corruption." Within this space it has been settled that statutory power cannot be fettered, and that planning permission cannot be refused solely because gain is not forthcoming. Thus planning gain can be sought only where there are objections to an application. It would appear, however, that gain can be balanced against other advantages and disadvantages of the application and not merely used to overcome problems generated by the proposed development.

Various safeguards have been suggested for the purpose of making the practice of planning agreements more open and structured.[23] It must be remembered, however, that regulation of bargaining by formal rules militates against some of the justifications for using bargaining in the first place, i.e. flexibility. It has often been remarked (see, e.g. Loughlin, above, n. 23) that some reform proposals adopt the false perspective of a rapacious authority and a reluctant developer. In reality neither are likely to object to the practice of planning bargaining and a right of appeal to the Secretary of State is of little relevance where the agreement is in the developer's interests. If ordinary principles of reasonableness apply to planning agreements it may be that the general law of judicial review provides an adequate remedy for third parties. In addition, the Local Commissioners for Administration may have a part to play.[24] Perhaps the *Brandrose* case (above, p. 164) could also be re-examined in order to permit a limited power to fetter the exercise of discretion.

As regards the "relevance" issue which is central to the scope of planning bargaining, it is suggested that "non-controversial" principles cannot provide a solution. The courts should therefore refrain from intervening with the result that planning gains could be lawful whether or not related to the proposed development. On the other hand the court should equally not interfere in cases where particular authorities choose to adopt a more restrictive policy.

[23] These include arbitration, "public participation," appeals, inclusion in statutory plans or in development briefs, increased powers of the Lands Tribunal, increased power of Secretary of State. See Jowell and Grant [1983] J.P.L. 427; Suddards [1979] J.P.L. 661; Loughlin (1980) 1 O.J.L.S. 61; Lichfield [1989] J.P.L. 68.

[24] The L.C.A.'s jurisdiction does not include "action taken in matters relating to contractual transactions" but exempts from this exclusion (a) transactions for or relating to the acquisition or disposal of land and (b) all transactions in the discharge of functions exercisable under any public general Act: L.G.A. 1974, Scheds. 5, 3 (1) (3). Planning agreements linked to planning permission would seem to fall within (b).

8. The Legal Effect of Planning Permission

A proprietory right?

Except where it provides otherwise, a planning permission runs with the land and will bind and benefit all persons from time to time interested in the land (section 33(1)). Applications and permissions must be registered in a public register kept by the local planning authority (section 34).[1] Failure to register an application may result in the court quashing the permission in judicial review proceedings. Apart from this an unregistered permission will still be binding. A condition or limitation attached to a planning permission is registerable as a local land charge.[2]

There are several ways in which planning permission can be brought to an end.

First, it will lapse if the development is not commenced within a statutory limit of five years (section 41). This provision introduced in 1968 was designed to combat land hoarding and includes special rules dealing with outline permissions and with those granted before 1969. A development is "commenced" for this purpose when any of certain prescribed activities take place (section 43(2)). These include most material changes of use (see section 43(3)) and such matters as digging a trench, or laying roads (but not merely demolishing existing buildings). As long as they are broadly related to the proposed development and are lawful they need not conform exactly with the plans which formed the subject of application (*Spackman* v. *Secretary of State for the Environment* [1977] 1 All

---

[1] See Town and Country Planning General Development Order 1988 Art. 28 (S.I. 1988 No. 1813). Details of local authority proposals for development must also be included, this being a mandatory procedural requirement: *Steeples* v. *Derbyshire C.C.* [1981] J.P.L. 582. Section 53 applications are also included. There is also a register of enforcement notices, stop notices and established use certificates (below Chap. 9).

[2] If imposed after the commencement of the Local Land Charges Act 1975, sections 1(*b*), (*c*) and 2(*e*).

E.R. 257; *Clwyd County Council* v. *Secretary of State* [1982] J.P.L. 696).

The courts have construed the lapse rules generously. Thus the commencement of part of a development extending over several plots of land has been held sufficient to stop time running in respect of the entire permission.[3] Moreover, virtually any contribution to an operation will suffice (*Malvern Hills D.C.* v. *Secretary of State* (1983) 46 P. & C.R. 58). The courts will look for good faith, the aim of the lapse rules being to counteract speculation. It must be remembered that once planning permission has been granted the developer has a vested right and questions of deference to administrative discretion are less likely to arise.

The converse case of a development started but not finished within the time limit is dealt with by section 44. Here the authority may serve a "completion notice" which states that the planning permission will cease to have effect within a specified time, which must be at least 12 months. The notice must be confirmed by the Secretary of State. The effect of the notice is that the permission remains valid in respect of development carried out before the time limit but any development thereafter will require a fresh application for permission. The original permission can be renewed if application is made before the time limit expires, and a simplified procedure is available for such applications. The section 44 procedure is not particularly effective and the same result can be achieved by an express condition requiring implementation within a time limit.

The authority may also revoke a planning permission before it is implemented (section 45) and after implementation may prohibit any use or require the alteration or renewal of any building or works (section 51). Both powers require the payment of compensation and are exercised only sparingly. There are provisions for confirmation by the Secretary of State and for an inquiry.[4] There are also special time limits relating to permission for mining operations (section 44A).

Apart from these specific powers a temporary planning permission can be granted by means of a suitable condition and the Act empowers the authority to require that the land be restored to its original state at the end of the prescribed time (section 30(1)(*b*)). An authority can grant permission personal to the applicant for

---

[3] See *Salisbury* v. *Secretary of State* [1982] J.P.L. 702. *obiter* perhaps if the permission is severable. See *Wivenhoe Port* v. *Colchester B.C.* [1985] J.P.L. 396.
[4] In the case of section 45 unopposed orders do not require confirmation: see section 45(2), section 45, section 51(4).

example on humanitarian grounds. Thus a non-conforming business use could be permitted in a residential area on condition that it remain personal to the applicant as being his sole means of livelihood.

These methods of terminating a planning permission are statutory. In *Pioneer Aggregates Ltd.* v. *Secretary of State* [1985] A.C. 132 the House of Lords were unanimous in rejecting the argument that private law notions such as abandonment could be used to supplement clear statutory language in areas such as planning where there is a comprehensive legislative code. Their Lordships agreed that a planning permission cannot on general principle be abandoned. *Pioneer Aggregates* concerned a planning permission for mining operations that had not been completed and which the previous owners of the site expressed an intention to discontinue. The applicants then acquired the site and recommenced the development by a token action of blasting. Their Lordships held that they were entitled to rely on the planning permission.

The limits of this decision are important. It applies only to the abandonment of an uncompleted planning permission. Once a planning permission has been fully implemented it is no longer effective except as proof of whether existing activities on the land were lawfully instituted. Any conditions of course remain as continuing obligations (see *West Oxfordshire D.C.* v. *Secretary of State* [1988] J.P.L. 324 below, n. 5). Planning permission is for *development* and not for buildings, mines or uses as such. Therefore in the case of operations once the operations are completed the question of abandonment of the permission no longer arises. For example a completed building if burned down cannot be rebuilt without a new planning permission (See *Fraser* v. *Secretary of State* [1988] J.P.L. 344). Similarly, once a change is made from a permitted use to another use the earlier permission is spent and in the absence of special statutory provisions cannot be relied upon.[5] It is

---

[5] *Young* v. *Secretary of State* [1983] 2 A.C. 662. See above, p. 79 and below, p. 201; *Cynon Valley D.C.* v. *Secretary of State* [1987] J.P.L. 760 (fast food use—temporary use as antique shop—fast food use, Original permission spent, therefore permission required to revert to fast food use). *Cynon Valley* was doubted by Grahame Eyre Q.C. in *West Oxfordshire D.C.* v. *Secretary of State* [1988] J.P.L. 324 who thought that *Cynon Valley* and *Pioneers Aggregate* were inconsistent and that a planning permission for a change of use is not spent if the use is discontinued. His Lordship was influenced by considerations of certainty in favour of relying on the register of permissions (below). However, the physical state of the land coupled with an inspection of the register would usually suffice to make clear what changes of use are permissible. See also *White* v. *Secretary of State* [1989] T.L.R. 10th February.

irrelevant in this connection whether the change is intended to be permanent or temporary. Similarly, a *use* can be lost by abandonment and it is irrelevant whether or not it has planning permission (above, p. 79).

Lord Scarman in *Pioneer Aggregates* identified three special cases which superficially look like abandonment of a planning permission but involve different principles. First, there is the case of the cessation of a use by abandonment or change. Secondly, there is the "new stage in the planning history" doctrine. We have already discussed both these special cases (above, pp. 78–81). In the case of the "new history" doctrine, Lord Scarman seemed to contemplate only cases where new development is sanctioned by a planning permission. The logic of the doctrine suggests that planning permission is irrelevant, the underlying rationale being that of a major physical change in the condition of the land, so that the local planning authority should have an opportunity to take a fresh look at the whole planning position (see also *Newbury D.C.* v. *Secretary of State* [1981] A.C. 578).

Lord Scarman's third special case concerns mutually inconsistent planning permissions. Once the applicant implements a planning permission other permissions are extinguished to the extent that they are inconsistent. There is nothing in the legislation to prevent any number of simultaneous planning permissions existing in relation to a piece of land. Furthermore a permission can be partly implemented.[6]

Prima facie an applicant can combine the benefits of any planning permissions he holds. In *Lucas* v. *Dorking R.D.C.* (1964) 62 L.G.R. 491 the applicant held two permissions in respect of the same site, one for 28 high-density houses, the other for six larger dwellings. It was held that a planning permission does not in itself *require* a development to be carried out but merely prevents it from being illegal. Thus there was nothing to prevent the developer from building some of each kind of house as long as in either case the stipulated number was not exceeded. The resulting development of course bore little relation to what the authority had in mind. Taken alone *Lucas* represents a sympathetic judicial attitude to vested rights.

It has been argued that *Copeland B.C.* v. *Secretary of State for the Environment*, (above, p. 71), weakens the authority of *Lucas* in that it requires a permission to be implemented as a whole (see Purdue, *Planning Law Cases and Materials*, (1977) p. 185). However *Copeland* held only that the construction of a house

---

[6] Subject to section 44—completion notice (above, p. 171).

constitutes a single indivisible "building operation" so that if the roof were made of the wrong materials the house as such would be without permission. The question is one of law and not of construction of the planning permission. It does not follow that everything within a given planning permission is a single act of development. For example it would be absurd to treat a permission for the construction of 200 dwellings as a permission for one building operation. Indeed, the position of a resident on an uncompleted housing estate would be precarious if the *Copeland* reasoning was thus extended. The questions of what is a "building operation" and what operations are authorised by a given permission are separate, the latter being entirely a question of construction. Furthermore planning permission can be granted for part only of the development specified in the application, but not for a substantially different development.[7]

The *Lucas* principle can be avoided by drafting a planning permission to be exercisable only as a whole or only as an alternative to any other planning rights which may exist in respect of the site. In *Pilkington* v. *Secretary of State for the Environment* [1973] 1 W.L.R. 1527 the developer held three separate permissions each for a single bungalow on different parts of the same site. It was held that he could build only one bungalow, since in each case the permission provided that the bungalow was to be the only one on the site (see also *Ellis* v. *Worcestershire C.C.* (1961) 12 P. & C.R. 178; *Langley* v. *Warwick D.C.* (1974) 29 P. & C.R. 358).

Another application of the "inconsistent permission" doctrine concerns the question whether a condition attached to a planning permission can lawfully forbid the implementation of an earlier permission or indeed the exercise of other existing rights. Such a condition is lawful notwithstanding the traditional presumption against interference with vested rights (above, p. 147). The condition is of course binding only if the later planning permission is implemented.

The limited scope of the concept of abandonment is supported not only by the policy of separating private from public law but also in the interests of certainty. A purchaser of land should be entitled to rely upon his knowledge of what is happening on the land, coupled with an inspection of the planning register to see what planning permissions are in force or in contemplation.

[7] *Wheatcroft* v. *Secretary of State* [1982] J.P.L. 37. The test seems to be one of broad impression. Would the permission granted be "so different as to deprive those who should have been consulted of the opportunity of consultation." (*per* Forbes J.). Only public authorities have to be consulted (above, p. 117), so this seems unhelpful and certainly offers little guidance to an L.P.A.

Planning permissions behave in some respects as proprietory rights. However, English law falls short of the position in the United States where "development rights" are sometimes transferable by agreement from one piece of land to another. On the whole it would be misleading to regard planning permissions as proprietory rights.

Construction of planning permissions

The rules relating to the construction of a planning permission are influenced first by a deliberate judicial policy of eschewing the formal literal approach to the construction of documents that characterises private law, and secondly by a recognition that a planning permission is a public document that must be relied upon for an indeterminate period by all persons concerned with the use of the land. Thus clear limits must be established concerning the use of extrinsic evidence as an aid to interpretation.

The general approach is as follows.

(1) A planning permission must be construed as a whole in the light of planning policy and in particular the development plan in force at the time it was granted. It must be construed with a presumption in favour of its validity. For example, in *Fawcett Properties* v. *Bucks C.C.* [1961] A.C. 636 a condition limiting occupation of a country cottage to persons whose employment or latest employment was in agriculture or an industry dependent on agriculture was challenged for uncertainty. The House of Lords held that any ambiguity could be cured by interpreting the condition in the light of the prevailing planning policy in favour of protecting agriculture and concerning the green belt (see also *Miah* v. *Secretary of State* [1986] J.P.L. 756).[8]

(2) Their Lordships in *Fawcett* took the view that ambiguity *per se* was not sufficient to invalidate a planning permission for uncertainty. A permission would be invalid only if it was so uncertain as to make it impossible to give it any sensible meaning in the light of proper planning policy.

(3) The *contra proferentem* principle familiar in private law does not apply to a planning permission (*Crisp* from the *Fens Ltd.* v. *Rutland C.C.* (1950) 1 P. & C.R. 48).

(4) The courts will give statutory terms such as "use" their normal statutory meaning unless the context requires otherwise. Thus

---

[8] A similar test seems to apply to enforcement notices (below, p. 194). See also *Shanley* v. *Secretary of State* [1982] J.P.L. 380. *R.* v. *Basildon D.C.* [1987] J.P.L. 663.

permission for a use will not automatically include permission for buildings converted in connection with the use (*Wivenhoe Port* v. *Colchester B.C.* [1985] J.P.L. 396).[9]

(5) Extrinsic evidence is not generally available as an aid to construction (*Slough Estates* v. *Slough B.C.* [1971] A.C. 958 at 962). Even though the public have access to council, committee and sub-committee meetings, and to associated documents,[10] evidence of these matters is probably not admissible. The application and any accompanying plans and documents are admissible if, as is usually the case, the are expressly referred to in the planning permission itself (*Manning* v. *Secretary of State* [1976] J.P.L. 635; *Slough Estates* v. *Slough B.C.* (above); *Miller Mead* v. *M.o.H.* [1963] 2 Q.B. 196). It may be that these documents are admissible even if not expressly incorporated. This is because copies of all applications must now be placed in a register and are thus available to the public (G.D.O. 1988, Art. 21). Other documents such as letters are admissible only if expressly referred to in the application, a practice that has been judicially criticised (*Wilson* v. *West Sussex C.C.* [1963] Q.B. 764 at 777). The reasons for imposing conditions can be looked at (*Miller Mead* v. *M.o.H.* [1963] 2 Q.B. 196 at 215).

Extrinsic aids can only be resorted to in two kinds of case, first where the permission is ambiguous, or contains obvious errors and secondly, in order to save the validity of the permission. The surrounding physical circumstances relating to the state of the land can also be looked at, but in general where a planning permission is clear and self-contained in its face the permission must be construed without resort to extrinsic aids or surrounding circumstances.

It is therefore essential to determine what actually constitutes a planning permission. The authority resolves to grant planning permission by means of a resolution taken at a council or committee meeting. The G.D.O. provides that permission must be notified in writing to the applicant but there is no requirement that the permission itself be in writing. However, it was held in *R.* v. *Yeovil B.C. ex p. Trustees of Elim Pentecostal Church Yeovil* (1971) 23 P. & C.R. 39 that the notification document and not the preceding resolution constitutes the actual planning permission. If this is so then the terms of the council's resolution cannot be considered as part of the permission but only as an extrinsic aid for the limited purposes mentioned above. This somewhat artificial rule is out-of-

---

[9] This does not necessarily apply to other technical legal terms. See *Commercial and Residential Property Co.* v. *Secretary of State* (1981) 80 L.G.R. 443.

[10] Local Government (Access to Information) Act 1985. Except for a large category of "exempt" material.

step with general principle as regards local government decision-making and has been subject to considerable criticism (see Albery (1974) 90 L.Q.R. 351; Garner [1972] J.P.L. 194). The point was not necessary to the decision in *Yeovil* itself. The council had resolved to authorise its town clerk to grant permission for a youth centre subject to evidence of an agreement concerning car parking. Before the decision was notified the council changed its mind and resolved to refuse permission. It was held that no planning permission existed until the decision had been notified and thus the council's *volte face* was effective. The decision to the same effect in the *Slough Estates* v. *Slough B.C. (No. 2)* [1969] 2 Ch. 305 was followed but without referring to the fact that *Slough* turned on the pre-1948 law which, unlike the present G.D.O., did not distinguish between the permission and its notification (see *Albery, loc. cit.*, p. 353). Moreover because of the terms of the resolution it was held that the council had not granted any planning permission but had delegated the power to do so to the town clerk. Nevertheless the *Yeovil* principle has consistently been applied (see *R.* v. *West Oxfordshire D.C. ex p. Pearce Homes* [1986] J.P.L. 523).

From the constitutional point of view it is worth preserving the principle that a local government body acts through its resolutions since these take place at public meetings. It is both artificial and undesirable to prevent the resolution from being looked at as part of the permission. It is at least clear from *Co-Operative Retail Services Ltd.* v. *Taff Ely B.C.* (1980) 39 P. & C.R. 428 that a notification is ineffective unless a resolution to grant permission has in fact been made. There the council had made no formal resolution, but a clerk was panicked into sending a notification that permission had been granted. It was held that no planning permission existed. The resolution must therefore be examined at least to this extent. Should the position be any different where, for example, the notification omits a condition? (See also *Norfolk C.C.* [1973] 1 W.L.R. 1400.)

Questions of construction are likely to arise in connection with enforcement proceedings. For example, the developer may raise a defence to a prosecution that his activities fall within the language of an existing planning permission.

The courts are not sympathetic to technical or semantic arguments. For example, in *Kerrier D.C.* v. *Secretary of State* [1981] J.P.L. 193 planning permission was granted for the construction of a bungalow. A condition was attached limiting occupation to agricultural workers. The applicant's bungalow differed from the plans submitted with the application to the extent that an additional basement was included. The applicant argued that his building was

materially different from that specified in the permission
construed in the light of the plans, so that he had not
implemented the permission and was therefore not bound by the
condition. It was held that a broad common-sense approach
should be taken. What he had done was in purported reliance on
the permission, and minor differences could be ignored. Not only
was he bound by the condition but the authority could amend the
permission to include a basement without the need for a fresh
application. Similarly a planning permission is construed as a
whole unless it naturally breaks up into entirely separate acts of
development, for example, where separate planning units are
involved.

Another problem of interpretation concerns the question
whether words in a permission are descriptive or functional. The
problem often arises in the context of section 33(2). This provides
that "where planning permission is granted for the erection of a
building... if no purpose is... specified the permission shall be
construed as including permission to use the building for the
purpose for which it is designed." "Designed" has been
construed as 'intended" (*Wilson* v. *West Sussex C.C.* [1963] Q.B.
764—"agricultural" cottage). On this basis the use of words such
as "agricultural" are likely to be taken as functional in order to
limit the purpose for which the land can be used (*ibid.*). This
creates an express "limitation" (below).

Two separate questions then arise. First, does the description
of the use contained in the planning permission create a
limitation? If so then the permission will not authorise changes to
uses outside the limitation even if such changes are not
development (*Waverley D.C.* v. *Secretary of State* [1982] J.P.L.
105—permission for "cattle transport depot" did not include
general haulage). A description in a planning permission cannot
in itself define a use for the purpose of the general definition of
"material change of use" (*Aberdeen D.C.* v. *Secretary of State*
[1987] J.P.L. 296—"counter service restaurant"). The second
question is therefore whether any proposed change would be
development on general principles (see also *Williamson* v.
Stevens (1977) 34 P. & C.R. 117).

Finally, it is worth remembering that questions of construction of
a planning permission could arise in a range of legal proceedings
including actions for breach of covenant by a landlord. Since vested
legal rights are necessarily involved it is unlikely that public law
judicial review proceedings will be appropriate even in disputes
directly involving planning authorities. A developer may therefore
seek a declaration in ordinary proceedings.

Conditions and limitations

The Act contemplates that "limitations" may be imposed upon a planning permission but does not explain what a limitation is. Breach of a limitation is in theory a breach of planning control in its own right and can therefore be the subject of enforcement proceedings.[11]

The difference between a condition and a limitation seems to be essentially semantic. A limitation seems to be part of the description of the permitted development and specifies the purpose to which the land is to be put (*e.g. West Sussex and Waverley* cases above). The same result could equally be achieved by an express condition, for example, that occupation be limited to agricultural workers (*Fawcett Properties* v. *Bucks. C.C.* [1961] A.C. 636). However, it seems that the effect of a limitation is weaker than that of a condition. In *Carpet Decor* v. *Secretary of State* [1981] J.P.L. 806 it was held that a limitation—premises to be used only for the storage of papers—cannot prevent a change to the storage of carpets which is excluded from being development under the Use Classes Order. By contrast an express condition could have prevented such a change of use. This distinction seems highly questionable.

There is also a distinction between limitations and the description of the development. It has been held that physical limits imposed upon *operational* development, principally in the General Development Order but also in express planning permissions are not limitations or conditions but define the development itself.[12] This means that if the requirements of the permission are disregarded the *entire development* is without permission and can be enforced against as a whole.

By contrast provisions restricting the nature of a *use* have been held to be limitations only.[13]

Another difficulty is that *conditions* cannot be *implied* into a planning permission but must be express. By contrast limitations can apparently be implied. In *Kwik-Save Discount Ltd.* v. *Secretary of State* (1981) 42 P. & C.R. 166 premises were previously used as a garage and motor accessories shop. The premises were then

---

[11] See, *e.g.* sections 23(8), 87(3)(*b*), 88B(1), (6), (2). But see section 243(5).

[12] *Copeland B.C.* v. *Secretary of State* [1976] 31 P. & C.R. 403; *Garland* v. *Secretary of State* (1968) 20 P. & C.R. 93; *Rochdale M.B.C.* v. *Simmonds* (1980) 40 P. and C.R. 432.

[13] *Cynon Valley D.C.* v. *Secretary of State* [1987] J.P.L. 760: use as a shop under the G.D.O. except for certain specific purposes held to be permission subject to a limitation.

subdivided into separate units, one of which was sold with planning permission for retail sales. The Court of Appeal held that in the light of the surrounding circumstances and the history of the site there must be implied into the permission a limitation restricting sales to products concerned with the motor trade.

It appears that the suggestion of Dillon L.J., in *Peacock Homes* v. *Secretary of State* ([1984] J.P.L. 229), that the term "limitation" in the Town and Country Planning Act 1971 is superfluous, is somewhat optimistic. An authoritative rationalisation of this obscure corner of the law is needed. In particular the consequences of a breach of limitation should be clarified. The implication of some of the cases (*e.g. Carpet Decor* (above), *Waverley B.C.* (above, p. 178) is that, although a breach of limitation is in theory a breach of planning control, it may not in practice be enforceable in its own right. Suppose, for example, the use of premises is limited to use as a solicitor's office. The occupier then introduces an additional use as an estate agent, which is not development (Use Classes Order 1987). The limitation would be ineffective.[14]

In general, the concept of a limitation seems unnecessary and artificial and at least one commentator argues that limitations include only time limits (Leach [1987] J.P.L. 584). However, this is difficult to reconcile with the language of the Act (*e.g.* section 23(5), (8)) and is entirely inconsistent with the cases. Indeed, in *Miller-Mead* v. *M.o.H.* [1963] 2 Q.B. 196 the Court of Appeal held that the 28-day limited period permission granted by the G.D.O. did not merely create a limitation but could not apply at all to a development that exceeded the 28 days.

---

[14] The objective could be achieved by an express condition but this would attract an appeal to the Secretary of State. There seems to be no right of appeal against a limitation. See section 36(1).

9. Enforcement

Introduction

The law governing the enforcement of development control is complex and technical. It provoked Harman L.J. to describe planning as "a subject which stinks in the noses of the public and not without reason" (*Britt* v. *Bucks C.C.* [1964] 1 Q.B. 77, 87), and more recently was criticised both by the Divisional Court and the Court of Appeal (*Brooks and Burton* v. *Secretary of State* (1978) 35 P. & C.R. 27, 31 and 47). The principal method of enforcement is by serving an enforcement notice under section 87, but in certain cases an injunction can be granted. The statutory powers may also be reinforced by a planning agreement. This can be enforced independently of the statutory machinery.

The development of the subject since 1947 has been dominated by attempts by Parliament and by the courts to reduce the number of cases in which enforcement notices are struck down for technical defects. It provides many examples to rebut the belief that the English judiciary is excessively sympathetic to private property rights. On the contrary, the cases recognise and make provision for the difficulties faced by local authorities in taking enforcement proceedings and are hostile to technical arguments. For example in *West Oxfordshire D.C.* v. *Secretary of State* [1988] J.P.L. 324. Graham Eyre Q.C. said (at 325) "courts ... willingly bade farewell to the proposition that there had to be ... 'a strict and rigid adherance to formalities'." Nevertheless a large proportion of enforcement notices are challenged, and of these a high proportion (about 35 per cent.) are successful, albeit more frequently on planning than on legal grounds. One reason for challenging an enforcement notice is to buy time, since the operation of an enforcement notice is suspended until appeal proceedings are completed, a process which may run into years.

On the other hand, central government policy is currently to inhibit local authorities from issuing enforcement notices, first by imposing additional procedural requirements designed to benefit the landowner (below) and secondly, through circulars stating that enforcement action should be taken only as a last resort (*e.g.* Circulars 22/80, 2/86). This policy can be enforced through the Secretary of State's appellate powers and in particular the power to award costs against the local planning authority.

The basic structure of the Act is weighted in favour of the landowner. First, breach of planning control is not an offence. The only offence lies in disobedience to an enforcement notice, thus imposing an obligation upon the local authority to comply with the relevant procedural reqirements. Moreover, the citizen has a right of appeal to the Secretary of State (usually acting through an Inspector (below, p. 196)). On appeal there is a power to reconsider the whole matter, including the power to grant planning permission for all or part of the development which is the subject of the notice (section 88(1)(*b*)). The Secretary of State can also correct or vary the notice (below, p. 197). There is a right of appeal from the Secretary of State to the High Court on a point of law (section 246 above, pp. 50–51). Finally there must be a successful prosecution. During these events the developer may repeatedly apply for planning permission on the same facts. The criminal proceedings may even be adjourned while these applications and their appeals are wending their way through the governmental machine (but see *Thrasyvalou* v. *Secretary of State* (below p. 215)). There is therefore plenty of opportunity for a developer to postpone the evil day and relatively few breaches of planning control actually result in convictions.[1]

Until 1963 the courts imposed strict requirements upon enforcement notices and treated a notice as a nullity if it was defective in any way, (*e.g. East Riding C.C.* v. *Park Estate Bridlington* [1957] A.C. 223 at 233). The criminal nature of the procedure coupled with traditional common law presumptions in favour of property rights was said to justify this. In those days there was no right of appeal to the Secretary of State so that the courts provided the only remedy.

In 1960 the present right of appeal to the Secretary of State was introduced. This led to a change in judicial attitudes. In addition the planning system had become well established and it was seen as unrealistic to treat planning law as an undesirable violation of private property rights, particularly in view of the fact that refusal of planning permission generally carries no right to compensation. In *Miller-Mead* v. *M.o.H.* [1963] 2 Q.B. 196 the Court of Appeal

---

[1] See generally Jowell and Millichip [1986] J.P.L. 482; [1983] J.P.L. 644.

rejected a strict approach to the requirements of enforcement notices. Technical defects or mistakes of fact should no longer automatically make a notice void but should be treated as matters for the Minister on appeal. As far as its intrinsic validity is concerned an enforcement notice should be judged by a broad common sense standard "Does the notice fairly tell (its recipient) what he has done wrong and what he must do to remedy it?" (*per* Upjohn L.J. at 232). A notice should be void only if it is incomplete or uncertain. This approach has been adopted in later cases. For example, in *Eldon Garages* v. *Kingston-upon-Hull Borough Council* [1974] 1 W.L.R. 276, Templeman J. (as he was then) rejected "ritual incantations" and took the view that an enforcement notice must be read broadly as a whole to see whether it fulfilled the requirements of *Miller-Mead*. His Lordship thought it "time that the pettifogging stopped." (See also *Pittman* v. *Secretary of State* [1988] J.P.L. 391. *Richmond on Thames L.B.C.* v. *Secretary of State* [1988] J.P.L. 396. *Miller-Mead* illustrates the flexibility inherent in the notions that underpin judicial review.

Important statutory reforms were introduced by the Local Government and Planning (Amendment) Act 1981, which removed several procedural difficulties by way of amending the 1971 Act.

Further reforms in the enforcement and appeal procedures are under review (The Enforcement of Planning Control: Report by Robert Carnuath, Q.C. D.o.E. (1989)) (see below p. 202).

Injunctions

A liberal approach has also been taken in relation to the power to obtain an injunction to enforce a breach of planning control. Development without planning permission, although not an offence, is nevertheless unlawful (below, p. 201). A private individual cannot seek an injunction because breach of planning control does not as such violate any private rights[2] but the Attorney-General can seek an injunction on behalf of the public interest whether the breach has occurred or is merely anticipated.[3] A local

---

[2] Unless it is argued that "special damage" is sufficient to ground an injunction *Boyce* v. *Paddington B.C.* [1903] 1 Ch. 109. However, development control does not exist for the benefit of any particular class of persons. See *Lonrho* v. *Shell Petroleum* [1981] 2 All E.R. 456. It could be argued that public rights are created but something more than a statutory prohibition is required: *ibid.* at 462, *per* Lord Diplock.

[3] *Gouriet* v. *U.P.O.W.* [1977] 3 W.L.R. 300—Att.-Gen.'s discretion unreviewable. *Att.-Gen.* v. *Harris* [1960] 1 Q.B. 31. *Att.-Gen.* v. *Smith* [1958] 2 Q.B. 173.

authority can also seek an injunction on behalf of the "inhabitants of its area" (L.G.A. 1972, section 222).[4] The result of an injunction would be to pre-empt the developer's statutory right of appeal to the Secretary of State and also to permit the court to impose penalties other than those specified by the planning legislation, *i.e.* imprisonment for contempt. An interlocutory injunction can be granted swiftly and *ex parte*.

The court has a wide discretion whether or not to grant an injunction. However, there must be some special reason for not resorting to the statutory enforcement machinery or alternatively the statutory machinery must have been used and found wanting. In *Runnymede B.C.* v. *Ball* [1986] 1 W.L.R. 353 an injunction was issued in respect of development as a gypsy caravan site. Enforcement and stop notices (below) had been issued and ignored and permanent damage was taking place to the land. The Court of Appeal emphasised that the jurisdiction to grant an injunction was not confined to deliberate and flagrant breaches of control (although this was the case here) but allowed the court to consider other factors. By contrast in *Runnymede B.C.* v. *Smith* [1986] J.P.L. 592, which also concerned a gypsy caravan site, an injunction was refused on the ground that there was no evidence of permanent injury to the land, that the developers had an arguable case on appeal and that there is nothing improper *per se* in exploiting the statutory machinery. (See *Waverley B.C.* v. *Hilden* [1988] J.P.L. 175—deliberate breach, injunction granted despite other pending proceedings).

If injunctions are used without an enforcement notice first being issued the court itself may be forced to decide whether or not development has taken place. In *Bedfordshire C.C.* v. *C.E.G.B.* [1985] J.P.L. the Court of Appeal held that the appropriate test for this purpose was whether a reasonable planning authority could take the view that the offending activities were development and that only then would the question of the court's discretion arise.[4a]

An injunction has one disadvantage over an enforcement notice.

---

[4] This does not include an Urban Development Corporation. *London Dockland Development Co.* v. *Rank Hovis p.l.c.* [1986] J.P.L. 826. See also *Stafford B.C.* v. *Elkenford B.C.* [1977] 1 W.L.R. 324, 329; *Thanet D.C.* v. *Ninedrive Ltd.* [1978] 1 All E.R. 703—undesirability of permitting developer to profit from unlawful act. *Stoke on Trent City Council* v. *B. and Q. (Retail) Ltd.* [1984] A.C. 754; "deliberate and flagrant breach."

[4a] The local authority's decision to seek an injunction must be challenged by judicial review if the developer had no defence to the injunction itself. In the judicial review proceedings the standard will be "Wednesbury" unreasonableness: *Waverley B.C.* v. *Hilden* [1988] J.P.L. 175.

It issues only *in personam* and cannot therefore bind subsequent owners of the land.

Stop notices

The problem of delay in the enforcement procedure is partly addressed by means of the "stop notice" machinery in section 90. Once an enforcement notice has been served the local planning authority can also serve a stop notice on any person who appears to them to have an interest in the land or who is contravening the enforcement notice. The stop notice requires the breach of control to cease on a date specified in the notice not earlier than three and not later than 28 days from the day on which it is first served on any person (section 90(3)). Disobedience to the stop notice is an offence. A site notice may be placed prohibiting any person from contravening the stop notice (section 90(5)). There is no right of appeal against a stop notice.

The stop notice procedure does not apply to the use of any building as a dwelling-house nor to the use of land as the site for a caravan occupied by any person as his only or main residence, nor to *any* activity begun more than 12 months earlier unless incidental to operational development or the deposit of refuse or waste materials (section 90(2)). Activities required by an enforcement notice are also excluded. If the stop notice is withdrawn or if the enforcement notice is withdrawn, varied or quashed on appeal except on policy grounds (ground (a) of the appeal grounds below, p. 196), the authority is liable to pay compensation even if there is a breach of planning control (section 177). The compensation provisions do not mention the case where the enforcement notice is a nullity. The stop notice is also a nullity, since its validity depends upon the service of an enforcement notice. Thus the recipient should either ignore it or challenge it by an application for judicial review. If he obeys it then it seems that he cannot be compensated (see *O'Connor* v. *Isaacs* [1956] 2 Q.B. 288). This well illustrates one of the weaknesses of English administrative law in that the logic of the ultra vires doctrine, regarded as a bastion of the rule of law, operates indiscriminately both for and against the citizen. Stop notices are not frequently used and the risk of paying compensation may be a disincentive (see Department of Environment Circular 4/87 and Bracken and Kingsby [1986] J.P.L. 538).

Compensation is payable only in respect of loss *directly* attributable to the stop notice. This raises difficult problems of causation, but specifically includes money paid in respect of a breach of contract caused by obeying the stop notice (*e.g.* cancelling building work (section 177(5)).

Obtaining information

The enforcement procedures presuppose that a planning authority has access to information, about what is happening on the land, about the planning history of the site and as to the identity of owners and occupiers. This may be difficult to obtain. However the onus is on the developer to prove that his activities are not in breach of planning control. (See *Asghar* v. *Secretary of State* [1988] J.P.L. 476). Many authorities have no systematic method of monitoring breaches of planning control and rely upon complaints by the public and information provided by other public authorities or other departments. By virtue of section 284, a local planning authority may require information about the present ownership and use of the site from the occupier or landlord of any premises by serving a notice There is also power to enter with a warrant from the Secretary of State or Local Planning Authority for the purposes of surveying the land. This is confined to "reasonable times" and at least 24 hours' notice must be given (sections 280, 281). These powers are arguably too limited but may serve as a "warning shot" (see preface).

Time limits

There are important provisions regarding the time limit for serving an enforcement notice. In the case of change of use development the change must, subject to one exception, have taken place after 1963 (section 87(1)). Changes of use before 1964 occupy a limbo, since they are immune from enforcement notice procedures but at the same time cannot be admitted to the company of lawful uses (below, p. 201).

It may be difficult, particularly in the case of development by intensification, to discover the exact date upon which the change of use took place. Even where the change took place after 1963 the date is still important, because the notice must specify the steps required to remedy the breach of control. It must therefore, preserve any lawful activities that existed immediately prior to the alleged change of use (*Mansi* v. *Elstree R.D.C.* (1964) 16 P. & C.R. 153, below). The correct date is a question of fact for the authority,

TIME LIMITS 187

with which the court will not interfere in the absence of unreasonableness. For example, in cases of "creeping" intensification, it may suffice to preserve the level of activity as it existed on January 1, 1964 (see *Trevors Warehouses* v. *Secretary of State* (1972) 23 P. & C.R. 215; *de Mulder* v. *Secretary of State* [1974] Q.B. 792, 798–799). A person who seeks the benefit of this time limit can apply for an "established use certificate" (section 94). This records the existence of uses (other than use forbidden by an effective enforcement notice) which (i) have subsisted continuously since before the beginning of 1964, either without permission or in breach of a condition, or which (ii) started after the beginning of 1964 but without there being since 1963 any subsequent change of use requiring planning permission. A certificate cannot be obtained in respect of a use which at any time after 1963 had the benefit of a planning permission. (*Bolivian Tin Trust Co.* v. *Secretary of State* [1972] 1 W.L.R. 1481; *Vaughan* v. *Secretary of State* [1986] J.P.L. 840). The certificate can be issued by the local planning authority upon the application of any person interested in the land. There is a right of appeal to the Secretary of State, which includes a deemed application for planning permission, (section 95). Under section 94(7) the terms of a certificate are conclusive for the purpose of an appeal to the Secretary of State against an enforcement notice served after the date of the application for the certificate (section 94(1)); see *Broxbourne B.C.* v. *Secretary of State* [1979] 2 All E.R. 13. Established use certificates are irrelevant in other proceedings (*Moran* v. *Secretary of State* [1988] J.P.L. 24).

In the case of operational development and also of change of use *to* use as a single dwelling-house, a time limit of four years from the date of the breach applies to the service of an enforcement notice (section 87(3)). The four-year time limit also applies to conditions or limitations relating to operational development (section 87(4)(*b*)).[5]

As in change of use cases the exact moment when the breach takes place may be difficult to establish. In the case of mining operations we have already seen that each "bite with the shovel" is a separate operation (above, p. 71). Thus time will never run in favour of *continuing* mining operations. This analysis does not apply to other kinds of operation, so that, for example, the building of a house constitutes a single operation (above, p. 71), the test

---

[5] See *Peacock Homes* v. *Secretary of State* [1984] J.P.L. 729—4-year rule not confined to conditions requiring or restricting operational development but any condition relating to such development in a broad sense, *e.g.* a condition requiring demolition, or arguably one restricting occupancy of an office.

being whether the operation produces something which is complete in itself. It is necessary to decide whether time runs from the beginning or the completion of the operation. The Secretary of State takes the view that "substantial completion" is the test. However, this appears to be based upon the wording of the 1962 Act, which referred to the "carrying out" of the development (section 45(2)(a)). Under the 1971 Act time runs from "the date of the breach" (section 87(4)). This must surely be the beginning of the operation, since to hold otherwise would mean that no notice could be served at all until a building had been completed, which is not only absurd but opens the way to wholesale evasions of planning control (see *St. Albans D.C.* v. *Norman Harper (Autosales) Ltd.* (1978) 35 P. & C.R. 70). However, the "substantial completion" test has been adopted in some first instance decisions so that the authority seems to have the best of both worlds.[6]

Sometimes operational development can be prohibited even if it took place more than four years ago. This is certainly the case where the operations in question are closely connected with a breach of control, for example, a change of use, which took place within the time limit.[7] In *Perkins* v. *Secretary of State* [1981] J.P.L. 755 it was said, *obiter*, that the same principle might extend to operations that are not necessarily connected with the use if their prohibition is one of the steps required in relation to the discontinuance of a use (see section 87(9)). This seems right since the issues of what count as a breach of planning control and what steps can be required to remedy the breach are distinct. It has also been held that a use which was established before 1963 can be reached by an enforcement notice if it is inextricably interrelated with a post-1963 use (*Denham* v. *Secretary of State* [1984] J.P.L. 347).

Service of an enforcement notice

A copy of the enforcement notice must be served[8] upon the owner, the occupier and upon other persons whose interest in the land the authority considers to be materially affected. The definition of owner is an artificial one. The "owner" for this purpose is not necessarily the same person as the owner who receives notice of an application for planning permission (see above, p. 117). "Owner"

---

[6] *Howes* v. *Secretary of State* [1984] J.P.L. 439; *Ewen Developments* v. *Secretary of State* (1980) J.P.L. 404.
[7] *Murfitt* v. *Secretary of State* [1980] J.P.L. 598; *Ewen Developments* v. *Secretary of State* (above).
[8] See section 283.

means "a person other than a mortgagee not in possession who . . . is entitled to receive the rack rent of the land or where the land is not let at a rack rent would be so entitled if it were so let" (section 290(1)). The meaning of this is obscure, and depends upon the application of the law of landlord and tenant to an actual or hypothetical rent. There can, it seems, be more than one owner. For example, a landlord and tenant are both the "owner" where the tenant has sub-let at a rack rent. If, however, the freeholder lets rent-free or at a low rent the hypothesis of a rack rent does not apply, so that the freeholder is not the owner (see *London Corporation* v. *Cusack-Smith* [1955] A.C. 337). It is difficult to see the relevance of these considerations to the enforcement of planning control.

The definition of "occupier" has been left to the courts. Here private law concepts have been abandoned in favour of treating the question as one of fact. An occupier is a person who is in occupation of the land on a permanent basis, whether or not he has an estate in the land. Thus a dweller on a permanent caravan site is an occupier, even if he is a licensee or squatter (*Stevens* v. *Bromley B.C.* [1972] Ch. 400; *Scarborough B.C.* v. *Adams* [1983] J.P.L. 673).

At one time a notice was void if it was not served on all persons entitled to be served. Moreover, all had to be served on the same date, the theory being that an enforcement notice is one, not several notices, and must take effect a prescribed number of days after service (*Bambury* v. *Hounslow B.C.* [1966] 2 Q.B. 204).

These technicalities have been superseded by section 87(5). A distinction is made between *issuing* and serving a copy of the notice. It suffices that all are served within 28 days of issue and not later than 28 days before the notice takes effect (below).

Failure to serve on any person can be challenged only by way of appeal to the Secretary of State, who has a discretion to disregard the failure if neither the appellant nor that person has suffered substantial prejudice (section 88A(3)). He may also ignore minor defects relating to the time of service (*Porritt* v. *Secretary of State* [1988] J.P.L. 414).[8a]

The decision to enforce

An authority may issue an enforcement notice when "it appears to them" that there has been a breach of planning control after 1963

[8a] For exception see below n. 14.

and where they think it expedient to do so (section 87(1)). A breach of planning control consists either of development without permission or of breach of a condition or limitation. There is no obligation to serve a notice, and the decision whether to do so must be taken in the light of "the provisions of the development plan and other material considerations" (*ibid.*). The decision can therefore be challenged in the courts on the same grounds as a decision upon an application for planning permission. Indeed, a local resident could arguably apply for mandamus against an authority which fails to prosecute its functions with sufficient zeal (*cf. R.* v. *Metropolitan Police Commissioner, ex p. Blackburn* [1968] 2 Q.B. 118 and [1973] Q.B. 241), albeit the width of the authorities' discretion means that chances of success are not high.

A notice is valid even where no breach of planning control has in fact taken place (*Jeary* v. *Chailey R.D.C.* (1973) 26 P. & C.R. 280). This is because it need only "appear to the authority" that there has been a breach and also reflects the general proposition that mistakes of fact do not in themselves invalidate government action. It is therefore no defence to maintain that development did not take place unless the authority's belief is unreasonable or based on an abuse of discretion (see below, n. 14 for an exception). It is important to bear in mind that the offence consists of disobedience to an enforcement notice and not breach of planning control as such. The validity of the notice is therefore the central issue. The onus of proof is on the developer to prove that the notice is invalid or that his activities are not a breach of planning control (above p. 186). The authority is entitled to act on any reasonable information available and does not have to carry out a thorough investigation before issuing a notice (*Ferris* v. *Secretary of State* [1988] J.P.L. 777).

Defects in the notice can be challenged either by alleging that the notice is a nullity or by appealing to the Secretary of State and from him to the High Court (below, p. 195). Once a valid notice has been issued and rights of appeal exhausted, the terms of the notice are conclusive. For example, if a notice is drawn too widely so as to embrace established uses there is no legal remedy (*South Staffordshire D.C.* v. *Secretary of State* [1987] J.P.L. 635, see below, p. 193).

Form and content of a notice

There is no compulsory standard form of notice, and authorities have drafted their own documents, sometimes with disastrous results, judging by the large amount of litigation which enforcement notices attract (see Department of Environment circular 36/81 for model notices).

The Act merely requires that the notice contain certain information. It need not use any particular form of words or technical language. In *Eldon Garages* v. *Kingston-upon-Hull B.C.* [1974] 1 W.L.R. 276, Templeman J. emphasised that rigid statutory recitals were unnecessary and deprecated the use of what he described as "magic words" or "ritual incantations." The notice is valid if, read as a whole, and in the light of the recipients' knowledge of the land—but not of other documents (*Miller-Mead* v. *Minister of Housing* [1963] 2 Q.B. 196, 224)—it conveys the required information. If the information is incorrect, as opposed to missing, the Secretary of State may, and sometimes must, quash the notice on appeal (below, p. 197). This relaxed approach, though superficially attractive is arguably too crude. Technical language is designed to achieve certainty and, because enforcement notices bind all subsequent owners of the land, certainty is particularly important.

NATURE OF BREACH

The Act first requires that the notice state the nature of the breach of control that is alleged. This must include a description of the essential facts. Furthermore, according to the weight of authority, the notice must also state which of the two kinds of breach of planning control is involved, *i.e.* development without permission or breach of condition.[9] Failure to provide this information makes the notice a nullity—so much waste paper. However, no specific form of words is required and the notice can be read as a whole to see if the nature of the breach is identified (*Eldon Garages* above.) There are cases, notably those involving failure to comply with height or density requirements, or disregard of time limits where the correct classification is problematic. An incorrect statement, as opposed to a missing one, will not apparently nullify the notice but must be dealt with on appeal by the Secretary of State (below). It is arguable that this should apply even where the kind of breach is not specified at all. After all the distinction between a failure to specify and an incorrect specification may be a highly technical one suitable for the discretionary powers of the Secretary of State (below, p. 197).

[9] *Eldon Garages* v. *Kingston-upon-Hull Corporation* [1974] 276 at 281; *Miller-Mead* v. *M.o.H.* [1963] 2 Q.B. 196 at 225, 226; *cf. Rochdale M.B.C.* v. *Simmonds* [1981] J.P.L. 191. Other dicta concern the different case of an *incorrect* classification (see below, n. 20). This distinction is often overlooked.

An enforcement notice is not void because it fails to state whether the breach consists of operational or change of use development nor, *a fortiori*, the kind of operation involved since these are not express statutory requirements.[10] On the other hand, these distinctions are often important and if the notice fails to state them or states them wrongly the Secretary of State may quash or correct it on appeal (section 88A(2) below). Similarly the notice need not expressly recite that the breach took place within the relevant time limit. Thus it need not alert the recipient to possible escape routes.[11]

Words in an enforcement notice need not be given a strict legal meaning and errors of terminology can be corrected on appeal. Thus an enforcement notice was upheld which described a number of derelict lorries as "vehicles," the court refusing to apply the subtleties of road traffic law to the question.[12] In general it is sufficient to describe the breach in factual terms without giving a full legal analysis nor attempting in a change of use case to describe the previous use. The onus is on the developer to show that his activities are not development. (See *Westminster City Council* v. *Secretary of State* [1983] J.P.L. 602; *Richmond Borough Council* v. *Secretary of State* [1988] J.P.L. 396).

STEPS TO BE TAKEN

Secondly, the notice must specify any steps required to be taken in order to remedy the breach (section 87(7)). This means steps (a) for restoring the land to its condition before the development took place or (b) for securing compliance with conditions or limitations attached to a planning permission. It has been doubted whether these provisions entitle an authority to "under enforce," *i.e.* to require anything less than full

---

[10] *Scott* v. *Secretary of State* [1983] J.P.L. 108; *Wealdon D.C.* v. *Secretary of State* [1983] J.P.L. 234; *Harrogate D.C.* v. *Secretary of State* [1987] J.P.L. 288. Model notices for each kind of development are provided. (See Circular 38/8).
[11] *Eldon Garages* v. *Kingston-upon-Hull Corporation*, above n. 9. Compare *Hughes* v. *Secretary of State* (below, n. 20).
[12] *Backer* v. *Uckfield R.D.C.* (1970) 21 P. & C.R. 526. See also *Hammersmith L.B.C.* v. *Secretary of State* (1975) 30 P. & C.R. 19; "guest house" or lodging; *Westminster City Council* v. *Secretary of State* [1983] J.P.L. 602; *Mayflower Hotels* v. *Secretary of State* (1975) 30 P. & C.R. 280; (compare *Duffy* v. *Pilling* (1977) 33 P. & C.R. 85—prosecution, notice strictly construed, arguably wrongly decided). *Ferris* v. *Secretary of State* [1988] J.P.L. 777. "Base" use need not be specified.

restoration.[13] However, the discretionary language of section 87 suggests that under enforcement should be permissible. In any event subsection 10 permits a degree of flexibility. An authority can require either that an unlawful development comply with the terms of any planning permission, thus covering the "Copeland" problem (above, p. 71) or that any injury to amenity caused by the offending development be removed or alleviated. In addition section 87(11) empowers the authority to require that an unlawful deposit of refuse or waste materials be modified by altering its contours.

As we have seen (above, p. 186) the notice must preserve the right to carry out activities that are immune from enforcement or which can lawfully be exercised independently of the development prohibited by the notice. These include for example "established uses," ancillary uses, and uses that have expanded beyond their permissible level (above, pp. 77–78). This is known as the "Mansi" rule (after *Mansi* v. *Elstree R.R.D.* (1964) 16 P. & C.R. 153). The Mansi rule raises considerable difficulty. For example, where the offending development consists of "creeping" intensification or an ancillary use that has become independent of its parent, it may be impossible to specify the precise level of activity that is permissible. The Mansi rule is particularly important where the notice on its face prohibits an entire class of activity, *e.g.* "storage" even though there was previously an element of lawful storage on the site. It has even been suggested that hypothetical future uses such as ancillary uses might have to be specified in the notice at least where inconsistent with the language of the notice.

It seems that general phrases will suffice even though they may require magistrates in criminal proceedings to make planning judgments. For example, in *Runnymede B.C.* v. *Singh* [1987] J.P.L. 283 an enforcement notice was upheld that prohibited religious practices in a dwelling-house except as ancillary to domestic premises. Indeed, in *Swinbank* v. *Secretary of State* [1987] J.P.L. 781, David Widdicombe Q.C. suggested that an enforcement notice need not expressly refer to activities within the Mansi rule at all. A notice would be "pro tanto ultra vires" if it was construed as extending to ancillary or established uses.

This approach raises difficulties. The question whether the matters specified in the notice constitute a breach of planning control or fall outside the time limits for enforcement is a matter for the Secretary of State on appeal (below, p. 196). Such matters cannot

---

[13] Compare *Copeland B.C.* v. *Secretary of State* (above, p. 71) with *Iddenden* v. *M.o.H.* [1972] 1 W.L.R. 1433. A notice can apply to part of a planning unit or to an ancilliary use. (*Richmond Borough Council* v. *Secretary of State* [1988] J.P.L. 396).

usually be raised elsewhere.[14] Once the appeal machinery is exhausted the terms of the notice are conclusive even in proceedings relating to other enforcement notices. Thus established uses cannot be relied upon unless expressly preserved by the notice (see *South Staffs D.C.* v. *Secretary of State* [1987] J.P.L. 635). Established uses should therefore expressly be mentioned in the notice even if only in general terms and the Secretary of State should amend the notice on appeal.[15] However the position with ancilliary uses is different. An ancilliary use has the same legal nature as its parent (above p. 81). Therefore suppose, for example, an enforcement notice prohibited the use of part of shop premises as "an office" this would automatically exclude any office use which was ancilliary to the shop without any need to openly mention this on the notice (see *Richmond B.C.* v. *Secretary of State* [1988] J.P.L. 396).

UNCERTAINTY

The Mansi rule raises the question of uncertainty in the terms of an enforcement notice. A notice that fails to satisfy the "Miller-Mead" test (above, p. 183) is a nullity. A notice will only be "uncertain" in this sense if it fails to provide a definite criterion for determining what steps it requires. The fact that the terms of a notice may require Justices to make value judgments or decide vague questions of degree does not appear to be fatal. Conceptual uncertainty on the other hand *is* fatal.[16] Moreover, the notice can leave the particular

[14] There are exceptions:
   It does not follow that *all* the appeal grounds can be raised elsewhere in these exceptional cases. Some of them are matters of policy and do not concern the validity of the notice (below p. 196).
   (i) Section 93(2) resumption of prohibited use after discontinuance is an offence only if *in fact* in breach of planning control.
   (ii) Proceedings against persons not served with copy of notice and without actual or constructive notice of it: section 243(2) (see also section 110(2)).

[15] See *Cleaver* v. *Secretary of State* [1981] J.P.L. 38; *Card* v. *Secretary of State* [1981] J.P.L. 40; *Trevors Warehouses* v. *Secretary of State* (1972) 23 P. & C.R. 215; *Monomart Warehouses* v. *Secretary of State* [1977] 34 P. & C.R. 305; *North Sea Land Equipment* v. *Secretary of State* [1982] J.P.L. 384.

[16] *Metallic Protectives* v. *Secretary of State* [1976] J.P.L. 166—all possible action to minimise effect of acrylic paint—notice void (*sed quaere*). Compare *Runnymede B.C.* v. *Singh* [1987] J.P.L. 283; religious practices ancillary to domestic premises —valid. See also *Dudley Bowers* v. *Secretary of State* [1986] J.P.L. 689; "summertime"—notice void. *Sykes* v. *Secretary of State* [1981] 1 W.L.R. 1092 "paddock" not descriptive of use—void. *Hounslow L.B.C.* v. *Secretary of State* [1981] J.P.L. 510 "comply or seek compliance" with condition—void. *Choudry* v. *Secretary of State* [1983] 265 E.G. 384—"part of ground floor" void. *Meach* v. *Secretary of State, The Times,* November 4, 1985: "open to the public" after 12 midnight—valid. *Pittman* v. *Secretary of State* [1988] J.P.L. 391; "leisure plot"—valid *c.f. Warrington B.C.* v. *Garrey* [1988] J.P.L. 752—stricter approach in criminal cases —sed quaere?

steps to be taken to be determined by agreement between the developer and the authority, provided that provision is made for resolving deadlocks, *e.g.* by a reference to the Secretary of State.[17] Finally, the notice must be interpreted with a view to upholding its validity and recognising that it is issued by a representative body in the public interest (*Ivory* v. *Secretary of State* [1985] J.P.L. 796). There is no evidence of a judicial bias in favour of the landowner.

DATES

The notice must specify two dates. The first is the date on which it takes effect. This must be at least 28 days after all copies of the notice are served. However, on appeal the Secretary of State can condone a failure to comply with this time requirement. (*Porritt* v. *Secretary of State* [1988] J.P.L. 414). During this period the authority may withdraw the notice (section 87(14)) and an appeal may be made to the Secretary of State (below). The second date is the time limit for compliance with the notice. This is a matter for the authority's discretion and as with other requirements can be altered by the Secretary of State on appeal if no injustice is caused to the appellant or the authority.

FURTHER REQUIREMENTS

The Act empowers the Secretary of State to specify additional requirements to be included in an enforcement notice (section 87(12)). Under the Town and Country Planning (Enforcement Notices and Appeal) Regulations 1981 (S.I. 1981 No. 1742) a notice must specify (i) the reasons why the authority deem it expedient to issue the notice and (ii) the precise boundaries of the land to which it relates. In addition they must attach an explanatory note to every notice providing information about the right of appeal to the Secretary of State including relevant time limits. This is not part of the notice.

In this way the central government has tipped the balance a little in favour of the developer.

Challenging enforcement notices

There are three methods of challenging an enforcement notice:
    1. By appeal to the Secretary of State under section 88. This can

---

[17] See *Perkins* v. *Secretary of State* [1981] J.P.L. 755: notice amended on appeal.

be exercised by any person with an interest in the land whether or not served with a copy of the enforcement notice. Thus an occupier who is served may not be able to appeal (*e.g.* a licence).

2. By means of an application for judicial review.

3. By means of a defence to a prosecution for disobedience to the notice.[18]

An appeal to the Secretary of State can be brought upon eight grounds. If a complaint falls within these grounds no other means of challenge is normally possible (section 243(1)).[19] The grounds of appeal are as follows (section 88(1)):

(a) that planning permission ought to be granted for the development to which the notice relates or that a condition or limitation ought to be discharged. This is a policy matter and is the ground which most often succeeds.

(b) that matters alleged in the notice do not constitute a breach of planning control.

(c) that the breach of planning control alleged in the notice has not taken place. This includes an incorrect description of the breach.

Grounds (a) and (b) can be pleaded together. Indeed, every appeal is deemed to be an application for planning permission for the development to which the notice relates (section 88B(3)). The Secretary of State can grant permission for that development or for part of it (section 88B(1)). Conversely an appellant accused of violating the terms of a planning permission is not estopped from arguing that no planning permission is required (*Newbury D.C.* v. *Secretary of State* above, p. 113).

Grounds (d) and (e) concern the time limit for the issue of the notice.

Ground (f) involves defects in the service of the notice (p. 188).

Ground (g) is that the requirements of the notice are excessive, and ground (h) that the period for compliance is unreasonably short.

These appeal arrangements demarcate the spheres of the Court and of the Secretary of State. We shall discuss the appeal procedure itself in the next chapter.

---

[18] In theory a landowner could also sue an official who enters his land in reliance upon an ultra vires notice (see *Stroud* v. *Bradbury* [1952] 2 All E.R. 76 at 77).

[19] s. 243(1). For exceptions, see n. 14 above. The right of appeal need not be available. See *Scarborough B.C.* v. *Adams and Adams* (above p. 189). *c.f. R.* v. *Greenwich L.B.C. ex p. Patel* [1985] J.P.L. 851—s. 91 power of entry might be challengable because "validity" of notice not in issue. See also *R.* v. *Keeys* [1988] J.P.L. 28.

There is a right of appeal from the Secretary of State to the High Court on a point of law (section 246). This must be exercised within 28 days (see further above, pp. 50–51).

The other methods of challenge presuppose that the enforcement notice is ultra vires and void (*Miller-Mead* v. *M.o.H.* [1963] 2 Q.B. 196, 226), except of course that a defence can be raised to a prosecution that the notice was in fact obeyed or does not as a matter of construction apply to the defendant's activities. None of the matters specified as grounds of appeal can make the notice void. As we have seen, a notice is void only if (i) it is defective on its face, *i.e.* an essential requirement is missing as opposed to being incorrectly stated (*Miller-Mead* above) (ii) if it is uncertain (above), (iii) it is issued in abuse of discretion (iv) if it is issued by a person not properly authorised to issue it.

Challenging a void enforcement notice is a public law matter and therefore appropriate for judicial review. Nevertheless it seems clear that a defence to a criminal prosecution is still available and that the courts will not always require the developer to institute proceedings for judicial review (above, pp. 45–46).

The alternative methods of challenge are sometimes explained by distinguishing between a void notice and an "invalid" notice. A void notice can be challenged only in the courts. An invalid notice can be challenged only by way of appeal to the Secretary of State and it was once believed that he must quash the notice if the defect was "material". However since 1981 the Secretary of State has been empowered to correct *any* defect or error or vary the notice provided that no injustice results either to the appellant or the local planning authority (section 88A2). This power has been interpreted broadly and seems to apply to any defect short of those which make the notice void including any case where the breach of planning control is wrongly described.[20] Quashing an enforcement notice now depends on all the circumstances and not upon the kind of defect as such. The courts have moved away from a technical approach. However, whether they are willing to take the further step of confining review of the Secretary of State's power to cases of "Wednesbury" unreasonableness remains to be seen.

In the case of an appeal to the Secretary of State the enforcement notice is suspended pending the determination of the appeal

---

[20] See cases cited above, nn. 9 and 10 and *R.* v. *Secretary of State ex p. Ahern* (T.L.R. March 29, 1989). See also *Copeland D.C.* v. *Secretary of State* (1976) 31 P. & C.R. 403 at 410; *Garland* v. *M.o.H.* (1969) 20 P. & C.R. 93 at 101; *Pilkington* v. *Secretary of State* [1973] 1 W.L.R. 1527 at 1535 for conflicting pre-1981 views. See also *West Oxfordshire D.C.* v. *Secretary of State* [1988] J.P.L. 324.

(section 88(10)). This suspension applies while an appeal is taken through the courts under section 246. (*R.* v. *Kuxhaus* [1988] J.P.L. 545. Previous decisions at first instance had confined the suspension to the proceedings before the Secretary of State himself with obvious difficulties if the matter was later remitted by the Court to the Secretary of State (above p. 50).[21] If *Kuxhaus* is correct then once a notice is appealed it remains suspended at least until the time limit for an appeal to the High Court has expired. However, the courts have insisted that the time limit for launching an appeal is strictly observed.[22]

The Court of Appeal in *Kuxhaus* reached its decision reluctantly, being aware of the opportunities it was offering for delaying tactics (see 551–552). In that case the original enforcement notices were over eight years old. Unlike the judicial review procedure leave to appeal is not required under section 246 so that unworthy cases cannot be filtered out.

In theory the spheres of appeal and judicial review are separate and self-contained. However, due to the statutory arrangements for appeal on a point of law to the High Court this area of the law is beset by muddle and technical confusion. First, section 246 is not expressly made the exclusive means of challenging the decision of the Secretary of State. In theory judicial review is an alternative. However, the court will usually not give leave to apply for judicial review if an equally appropriate statutory remedy is available. In many cases the section 246 appeal will be equally appropriate, but there are important differences between the two procedures (see also above, pp. 50–51).

(i) The courts' powers are wider in judicial review cases and include a power to quash the enforcement notice. There is also a wider power to consider factual issues (above, p. 43). Procedural matters such as breach of natural justice are probably more appropriate for judicial review.

(ii) The section 246 appeal is as of right and leave to appeal is not required.

---

[21] *Dover D.C.* v. *McKeen* (1985) 50 P. & C.R. 250; *London Parachuting Ltd.* v. *Secretary of State* [1986] 52 P. & C.R. 250. These cases turned essentially on a literal reading of section 88(10). The justices could adjourn proceedings pending an appeal; *R.* v. *Polly Newland* [1987] J.P.L. 85; *R.* v. *Cardiff JJ.* (1987) *The Times*, February 24; *R.* v. *Smith* (1987) *The Times*, July 6.
[22] See *Howard* v. *Secretary of State* [1975] Q.B. 235 (below, p. 205); *Lenlyn D.C.* v. *Secretary of State* [1985] J.P.L. 82—notice must *reach* the department the day before the 28th day. Loss in the post seems to be irrelevant: *R.* v. *Secretary of State ex p. Jackson* [1987] J.P.L. 740.

(iii) The time limit for seeking leave to apply for judicial review is three months compared with 28 days for launching a section 246 appeal.

(iv) The enforcement notice is not suspended during judicial review proceedings but the court has a discretion to stay its implementation (R.S.C. Ord. 53. R. 3(10)).

(v) Only matters actually raised before the Secretary of State can be raised under section 246 and the court has no power to examine questions of fact (above p. 50).

It has also been argued that the section 246 appeal (and also the section 88 appeal to the Secretary of State) cannot apply where the enforcement notice is a nullity (see *Miller-Mead* v. *M.O.H.* [1963] 2 Q.B. 196). This is based upon the logical if artificial proposition that there is nothing upon which to found the appellate jurisdiction either of the Secretary of State or the Court. However, the notion of nullity is not applied strictly in public law.[23] The constitutional argument that an ultra vires government act should have no legal consequences is often outweighted by considerations of practical convenience. Indeed, there seems to be no reason in principle why "a point of law" should not include a decision or notice that is alleged to be ultra vires. In *Dudley Bowers* v. *Secretary of State* (1988) 52 P. & C.R. 365 the court accepted jurisdiction under section 246 in respect of an enforcement notice that was claimed to be void for uncertainty, albeit this was with the consent of the parties.[24] If a notice is a nullity it can also be challenged in judicial review proceedings or its nullity raised as a defence to a prosecution.

It has also been held that the section 246 appeal does not apply to a case where the Secretary of State is alleged to have improperly refused to determine the appeal (*Lenlyn Ltd.* v. *Secretary of State* [1985] J.P.L. 482). In this case, as in the converse case where the Secretary of State improperly accepts jurisdiction, judicial review is the only remedy.[25]

---

[23] See Aldous and Alder, *Applications for Judicial Review*, (1985) Chap. 2; Craig, *Administrative Law*, (1983) Chap. 11.

[24] See also *Rhymney Valley D.C.* v. *Secretary of State* [1985] J.P.L. 27 appeal; *R.* v. *Greenwich L.B.C. ex p. Patel* [1985] J.P.L. 581.

[25] The notice would remain suspended. But see *Button* v. *Jenkins* [1975] 3 All E.R. 585—decision by Secretary of State that appeal lapsed held to be decision on appeal and therefore section 246 appropriate and notice suspended only until time limit for section 246 expired. See further [1985] J.P.L. 485. On a prosecution the court could adjourn pending judicial review proceedings or even pending another application for planning permission. See *R.* v. *Polly Newland* [1987] J.P.L. 85; *R.* v. *Cardiff J.J.* (1987), *The Times*, February 24; *R.* v. *Smith* (1987), *The Times*, July 6.

There is much to be said for simplifying this dual system of challenge in the courts perhaps by abolishing the section 246 right of appeal. Challengers would then have to use the judicial review procedure with its safeguards in favour of the government and pointless demarcation disputes would be minimised. Suspending the enforcement notice would be a matter for the courts' discretion.

The legal effect of an enforcement notice

Once a valid enforcement notice has been issued and the appeal mechanism is exhausted the notice becomes binding. An enforcement notice is not discharged by obedience and remains permanently in force (section 93). It cannot be withdrawn and is discharged only by the grant of planning permission for the activities to which it relates (section 92). Reinstatement of or restoration of buildings or works is deemed to be a breach of the original notice (section 93(3)). However, if a use forbidden by the notice has been discontinued its resumption is unlawful only if it is *in fact* a breach of planning control (section 93(2)). Thus it is open to the accused to argue that the resumption in question is not a material change of use either because of the Mansi rule (above) or in the light of changed circumstances.

Except in respect of the discontinuance of a use or compliance with conditions or limitations the owner who was actually served is liable to prosecution (section 89(1)). If before the period specified for compliance there has been a change of ownership, he may require the subsequent owner to be brought before the court. The subsequent owner may be convicted and the original owner must be acquitted if he can show that he took all reasonable steps to secure compliance (section 89(3)). In use or condition cases any person actually using the land or causing or permitting the breach is liable (section 89(5)). The offence does not arguably, require mens rea (see *R.* v. *Wells Street Magistrates' Court* [1986] 3 All E.R. 4).

Finally, the authority can enter the land and take steps to restore the land to its condition before the breach took place other than requiring discontinuance of a use (section 91).[25a] The owner at the time of entry is liable for their costs but he can recover these as a civil debt from those who actually committed the breach of control. He is deemed to be an agent for

---

[25a] Removal of a caravan does not apparantly count as the discontinuance of a use (see *Midlothian Regional Council* v. *Stevenson* [1986] J.P.L. 913).

such persons both for these and any other expenses incurred in complying with an enforcement notice (section 91(2)). The power of entry applies only to steps required to remedy the breach and not to the alternative measures provided for by section 87(7)(b) above.

As we have seen remedial steps can include requiring operational development associated with a use to be undone even if this took place more than four years ago (above, p. 188).

OBEYING AN ENFORCEMENT NOTICE

As well as prohibiting the unlawful development itself the notice can require the undoing of operations or the discontinuance of uses that would not in themselves be unlawful provided that they are sufficiently related to the development to be enforced to count as steps required for the restoration of the land (see *Somak Travel Ltd.* v. *Secretary of State* [1987] J.P.L. 630).

Subject to the Mansi rule (above) a developer who has made an unlawful change of use has no lawful use rights at all since all previous planning permissions are extinguished. Section 23(9) deals with this by permitting a developer who has discontinued a use in obedience to an enforcement notice to use the land "for the purpose for which (in accordance with the provisions of this part of this Act) it could lawfully have been used if the development" (the subject of the enforcement notice) "had not been carried out."

The courts have interpreted section 23(9) strictly against the landowner. First, a "lawful" use does not include a use that would have been exempt from enforcement only by virtue of the statutory time limits (*L.T.S.S. Print and Supplies Ltd.* v. *Hackney B.C.* [1976] 2 W.L.R. 253) and therefore includes only uses the change to which had planning permission or which did not require planning permission. Secondly, the subsection does not allow the developer to travel notionally back in time until reaching a safe haven in a lawful use. It permits the developer only to revert to a lawful use which existed *immediately* before the use which is the subject of the enforcement notice.[26] In *Young* v. *Secretary of State* ([1983] 2 A.C. 662) land had been used from 1912 to 1969 as a laundry (this use being lawful). From 1969 to 1970 there was a change of use to food processing. This was permitted development under the G.D.O. and therefore lawful. In 1970 the laundry use was restored (unlawful,

---

[26] In *Fairchild* v. *Secretary of State* [1988] J.P.L. 472 it was held that s.23(9) entitled the developer to revert to a previous use that had been abandoned. No reasons were given for this which seems contrary to the language of s.23(9) as well as the reasoning in *Young*.

see below) and finally in 1977 the land was used for light industrial purposes (unlawful). An enforcement notice was issued in respect of this. It was held that all previous use rights including the original laundry use were extinguished by the subsequent changes of uses and that section 23(9) was not available. The laundry use was the only possible use within the subsection and this was unlawful. As we have seen, (above, pp. 172–173) planning permission is granted for a *change of use* and not for the use itself. It was therefore irrelevant that the 1970 laundry use was the same kind of use as the laundry use commenced in 1912. This earlier laundry use was lost as a result of the change to food processing in 1969, and what happened in 1970 was a different change.

Conclusion

The enforcement cases show the courts at their most sensitive to the problems of government and that they have consistently refused to give the benefit of the doubt to the landowner. The most notable pro landowner rule is the rule about the suspension of the notice pending an appeal but responsibility for this lies squarely within the legislation itself. Perhaps the two outstanding weaknesses in enforcement law are firstly the possibility of repeated bites at the cherry (although the *Thrasyvalou* case (below p. 215) has mitigated this a little, and secondly the confusion that pervades the dual remedies of judicial review and the section 246 appeal.

10. Planning Appeals

The legal framework

There is a right of appeal to the Secretary of State against most development control decisions adverse to the developer, but not against favourable decisions. Only the applicant can appeal against a refusal or conditional grant of planning permission and third parties cannot appeal at all (section 36). In the case of enforcement appeals any person having an interest in the land to which the notice relates may appeal (section 88(1)). We are concerned primarily with appeals against a refusal or conditional grant of planning permission and against an enforcement notice. The procedure in each case is broadly similar, although there are important differences of detail. New inquiry procedure rules apply to planning permission appeals and "called in" cases.[1]

The central feature of the appeal procedure is that the appellant and the authority are entitled to a hearing before a person appointed by the Secretary of State (sections 36(4) and 88(7). This may take the form of a public local inquiry and arguments about the

---

[1] See Town and Country Planning (Inquiries Procedure) Rules 1988 (S.I. 1988 No. 944), and Town and Country Planning Appeals (Determinations by Inspectors) (Inquiries Procedure) Rules 1988 (S.I. No. 945). Circular 10/88. Welsh Office 15/88. Enforcement appeals and written representation appeals are governed by older rules with less provision for discovery and time limits. (See S.I. 1981 No. 1743; S.I. 1987 No. 701). References in text are to the new rules unless otherwise stated. Where the Inspectors Rules differ they are cited second. There is also a right of appeal against: (i) refusal of consent, agreement or approval of the authority required under a condition or a development order (section 36(a); (ii) a section 53 determination (section 53(2)); (iii) a certificate of established use (section 95). The Secretary of State has "called in" powers in relation to the latter (section 95). "Call in" decisions follow a similar inquiry procedure (see below, n. 24), but are always decided by the Department of Environment. See Barker and Couper (1984) 6 *Urban Law and Policy* 363 at 428–430. Several decisions require confirmation by the Secretary of State. See section 44(3): Completion Notice; section 45(2): Revocation of planning permission; section 51(4): Discontinuance orders.

nature and purpose of such inquiries form the focus for discussion of the appeals procedure.[2] The decision may be made by the Secretary of State personally, or by officials in his department or under statutory powers of delegation by the inspector who holds the inquiry. In practice all but the most important or unusual appeals are decided by the inspector, whose decision is in law the decision of the Secretary of State.[3] The inspector may be assisted by assessors[4] and a council for the inquiry may be appointed. Other forms of hearing are also available (below, p. 216).

The powers of the appellate decision maker are very wide, going well beyond the traditional supervisory role of the central government. In the case of planning permission appeals, the Secretary of State or the inspector can consider the whole matter again as if he were the first instance decision maker (section 36(3)). This reinforces the dominant role of central government in the planning process and encourages appeals. In the case of enforcement appeals (section 88) specific grounds of appeal are prescribed (above, p. 196). However, every enforcement appeal is deemed to be an application to the Secretary of State for planning permission (section 88B(3)) and the Secretary of State or inspector has an unfettered discretion to grant planning permission for all or part of the development prohibited by the notice, discharge conditions or limitations or determine the lawful use of the land (section 88B(1)). Arguably such wide powers are not appropriate for enforcement appeals, given that the developer could previously have applied for planning permission. The Secretary of State or inspector may also quash a defective enforcement notice (section 88A) but can correct or vary it only if this can be done without injustice to the appellant or the local planning authority (section 88A(2)). It would seem to follow that the notice must be quashed where injustice has been caused.

The appeal procedure has a strong judicial flavour modelled on

---

[2] See generally Barker and Couper (1984) 6 *Urban Law and Policy* 363–476; Grant Chap. 13; Kemp, O'Rearden and Purdue (1984) 15 Geoforum 677; Rowan Robinson (1981) 4 *Urban Law and Policy* 373; "Planning Inquiries: The New Dimension" (1983) J.P.L. *Occasional Papers*; Drapkin [1974] P.L. 220.

[3] See Sched. 9; Town and Country Planning (Determination of Appeals by Appointed Persons (Prescribed Classes) Regulations (S.I. 1981 No. 804). The power can be revoked (Sched. 9, para. 3A.) The transferred procedure does not apply to appeals by statutory undertakers concerning operational land or to "called-in" applications. The Secretary of State recovers jurisdiction in cases which are either large scale or which raise issues of general importance (Encyclopaedia 2–921. Barker and Couper *op cit.* above n. 2 at 439–449.

[4] See Housing and Planning Act 1986, Sched. 11, para. 12. R.9 and 14(3); R.9 and 17(1).

the procedure of a court. There is considerable emphasis on time limits. In the case of an enforcement appeal the appeal must be lodged *before* the date on which the notice takes effect (*Howard* v. *Secretary of State* [1975] Q.B. 235). The Secretary of State may prescribe a time limit within which the appellant must submit his grounds of appeal and other information and the local authority its submissions. If these requirements are not followed he may dismiss the appeal or quash the notice as the case may be (section 88(4)–(6)). He may also decide the appeal without a hearing and without considering grounds of appeal that have not been submitted in time (section 88(8)). A planning permission appeal must be lodged within six months (G.D.O. 1988 Art. 26).

In addition, the time limit for appealing has been strictly, if not ferociously, applied (*R.* v. *Secretary of State ex p. Jackson* [1987] J.P.L. 790: appeal documents lost in the post—appeal barred; see section 283 and [1985] J.P.L. 461 *c.f. R.* v. *Secretary of State ex p. J.B.I. Financial Consultants* [1989] J.P.L. 365—service by hand on Sunday is valid).

The new inquiry procedure rules have introduced further timetable requirements. Pre-inquiry information must be exchanged within six weeks for the authority, nine weeks for the appelant of the "relevant date" (R.6 R.10). This is the date on which the Secretary of State gives notice of the decision to hold an enquiry (R.1). A timetable may also be imposed on the inquiry itself (R.8) and the Secretary of State can unilaterally fix the date of the inquiry (R.10).

The problems of the appeal process

The appeal process is beset by fundamental problems and has generated much litigation. The problems include first, the practical problem of the length of time occupied by the appeals procedure. The inquiry itself usually lasts only one or two days but depending on the kind of inquiry held (see below) the *median* times for the first quarter of 1987 ranged from 55 to 28 weeks [1987] J.P.L. 684, but some appeals take much longer.[5] There is also a high success rate averaging about 30 per cent. The time taken by the appeal process is of course an element in the cost of land and housing. The time taken to decide first instance decisions has also caused anxiety (see [1988] J.P.L. 148).

---

[5] The Sizewell appeal took over 3 years the inquiry lasting 340 days at a cost of over £25 million. See generally O'Riordan, Kemp, Purdue. "Sizewell B, An Anatomy of the Inquiry" (1988).

There have been many attempts to shorten and simplify the appeals process. These include the Secretary of State's powers in relation to time limits (above, p. 205); the introduction of written representation and informal hearing procedures (below, p. 216) and administrative practices including timetables for the various procedural stages and in some cases provision for "instant" decisions by inspectors.[6] The modern practice of delegating almost all appeals to inspectors has shortened the median time taken by about one third. The latest inquiry procedure rules were introduced primarily or the purpose of reducing delay and have greatly increased the powers of the inspector and the Secretary of State to control the procedure.

There is also a power to award costs but this applies only against a party guilty of unreasonable conduct and is sparingly exercised against developers.[7]

Other problems are more fundamental. They centre upon questions as to what is the proper function of a planning appeal and in particular of a public local inquiry.

The Department of Environment has traditionally adopted a quasi-judicial role as arbitrator between the conflicting interests involved, including those of local authorities. This is illustrated by the frequent use of public inquiries presided over by semi-independent inspectors. On the other hand the appeals procedure is a method of implementing central government policy. The development control system is the only major area of government activity where appeal always lies to a Minister and not to an independent tribunal (see Barker and Couper, (1984) 6 *Urban Law and Policy* 363).

Development control appeal decisions embrace a wide variety of issues ranging from the purely factual and local, e.g. what is the established use of the premises to major issues of regional or national concern—the building of a nuclear power station, or the opening of a mine.

---

[6] See Encyclopaedia 2–931 and Circulars 38/81, 201/85, 18/86, 11/87.

[7] L.G.A. 1972, section 250(5); 1971 Act, section 282(2); Housing and Planning Act 1986, Sched. 11(9). The power to award costs applies equally to inspectors' decisions and transferred decisions, and applies even where no inquiry is held (*e.g.* written representation cases). See also 1971 Act, section 110(1) (enforcement appeals). However, costs are increasingly being awarded against local authorities, *e.g.* Circular 2/87 emphasises the possibility of "unreasonable" refusals of planning permission with strong presumptions in favour of granting planning permission and against planning gain. See *R.* v. *Secretary of State ex p. Havering L.B.C.* [1987] J.P.L. 840. See also [1988] J.P.L. 145. Costs decisions must be challenged by judicial review.

Enforcement appeals can be broadly distinguished from planning permission appeals partly because factual and technical issues are more likely to predominate and partly because delay is often in the appellant's interest. It will be recalled that the operation of an enforcement notice is suspended during the appeal process."

At the heart of the appeal system is the ambiguous role of the Secretary of State. In one sense he is required to act in a judicial capacity, as arbitrator between developer and local planning authority, but at the same time he has an inbuilt bias in favour of the government policy of the day. This is particularly the case where the developer is a public corporation required to implement governmental policies relating, for example, to nuclear energy.

A broad distinction has been made between ordinary planning inquiries and "big inquiries." Ordinary inquiries centre on local issues, questions of fact, and usually the application of established policies. The rules relating to fettering discretion and the interpretation of circulars are particularly important in this context (above, p. 140). Big inquiries raise issues beyond those relating to the particular locality and parties and usually involve major political and economic controversies. They involve the formulation of policy and challenges to policy as well as applications of policy. The most well-known recent examples are the inquiry into the Windscale nuclear reprocessing plant in 1977 and the Sizewell nuclear power station inquiry in 1985.[8] Apart from the scope and sophistication of the issues the time taken to hear and process evidence is a serious cause of concern.

Broadly speaking planning inquiries are modelled on the adversarial procedures of a court of law with opposing parties, speeches, evidence, cross-examination and discovery of documents. This is generally regarded as satisfactory in the case of ordinary appeals but less so for big inquiries. This is because adversarial procedures are arguably not suited to large political and economic issues which transcend the interests of the particular parties and the chance matter of location. In particular the inspector's role is largely negative—to process what self-selected parties choose to place before him—alternative proposals cannot easily be canvassed and the resources of the parties may be grossly unequal, private individuals and voluntary pressure groups being ranged against large and sometimes government backed corporations. Inspectors have some leeway within the procedure to depart from strict adversarial forms and the final decision can include matters not taken into account at the inquiry. Such initiatives run

[8] See [1983] J.P.L. 508; [1984] J.P.L. 549; [1985] J.P.L. 686.

the risk of legal challenge so that caution may be administratively expedient. Use of a counsel for the inquiry helps to focus the issues and to modify the extremes of the adversarial procedure.

Proposals for the reform of "big inquiries" favour splitting the procedure up into stages with an initial investigation of general policy issues, adversarial inquiries to deal with purely local aspects and perhaps a Parliamentary input.[9] Under the existing procedure preliminary meetings are sometimes held for the purpose of defining the issues but the inspector has no general power or resources to carry out his own research. Under section 48 certain kinds of planning permission appeal can be referred to a Planning Inquiry Commission. These include cases involving considerations of "national or regional" importance, or "unfamiliar" technical or scientific matters. The Commission which consists of a chairman and between two and four others (section 47) is empowered to carry out its own investigations and research and the responsible Minister can refer it to the question of alternative sites. The Commission may also hold an ordinary local inquiry (section 49).

The Planning Inquiry Commission has never been used. Objections to procedures of this kind centre upon the advantages of the formal adversarial procedure in terms of thoroughness and fairness to the main protagonists. These objections have been countered by attacks on the "conflict model" and the allegation that public inquiries are largely cosmetic. Adversarial procedures are not designed to elicit what is best in the public interest or even to discover the truth.[10] There are also constitutional objections to placing decision-making in the hands of bodies who have sufficient status and power to be independent of the central government. The traditional inquiry is designed to legitimate existing government policies and to discuss purely local issues but not to provide a mechanism for democratic participation (see *Bushell* v. *Secretary of State*, (below)). The British system of government into which the

---

[9] See "The Big Public Inquiry" Outer Circle Policy Unit (1979). "J.P.L. Planning Inquiries—The New Dimension" (above, n. 2); R.T.P.I. Final Report of the Public Participation Working Party (1982). See [1974] J.P.L. 3; [1980] J.P.L. 216, 306, 711; [1982] J.P.L. 6; [1987] J.P.L. 208. O'Riorden etc. (above n. 5) pp. 343–347; Harlow and Rawlings, *Law and Administration*, (1984), pp. 464–473. A government employed "devil's expert" has also been suggested (see Tristam Eve in "Planning Inquiries—the New Dimension" (above) at 33. See also Rowen-Robinson, *loc cit.* n. 2 above. The 1988 procedural rules provide for pre-inquiry meetings at which the inspector has a wide discretion to set the agenda (R.5; R.7).

[10] See *Air Canada* v. *Secretary of State* No. 2 [1983] 2 A.C. 394 at 438, 441. The inquiry procedure is, however, partly inquisitorial (below, p. 213).

public inquiry fits awkwardly, recognises democracy only in its representative form.

Another mechanism that is sometimes used within the traditional inquiry system is that of separate but linked inquiries or joint inquiries. These take place, for example, in connection with applications concerning out-of-town retail developments where there may be several competing applications. Each appeal must be decided separately but the circumstances of related appeals can be taken into account. The same inspector may preside over separate inquiries or there may be one "joint" inquiry (see Couper and Barker [1981] J.P.L. 631). The Secretary of State then decides the appeals together. Variations might include different inspectors but with a common assessor. Barker and Couper's research (above) indicates that linked procedures do not provide any significant time saving. Furthermore joint inquiries may be less thorough and more heavily dominated by professional interests than smaller individual inquiries and therefore less effective as a means of public participation. There are also problems relating to natural justice arising out of any failing of co-ordination.

Barker and Couper (above) propose a two-stage procedure within the existing framework; first, an initial inquiry into policy issues, e.g. the impact of a superstore on the local community, followed by separate inquiries into the details of individual proposals. In other words there should be a closer connection between the "planning" and development control aspects of the planning system than is provided by the tenuous system of structure plans.

The problems we have outlined produce conflicting beliefs about the nature and purpose of the inquiry procedure. The law itself is an uneasy compromise between these different beliefs and perhaps satisfies no-one. The competing beliefs can be expressed as three "models": (i) the "administrative" model; (ii) the "judicial" model; and (iii) the "participatory" model. This is an area of law where Professor McAuslan's analysis of the ideologies of planning is of considerable relevance (above, Chap. 1).

The administrative model

The administrative model is the model originally recognised by the common law. It regards the inquiry as a procedure for providing the decision maker with information. As long as the parties are given a fair hearing at the inquiry itself the law will not intervene (*Franklin* v. *Minister of Town and Country Planning* [1948] A.C. 87). The decision maker is not bound by any findings or recommendations made at the inquiry and can freely take additional matters raised by third parties into account. The inspector's report is a confidential document between the inspector and the Minister and the parties are not entitled to see it (*Local Government Board* v. *Arlidge* [1915] A.C. 120). The Secretary of State can of course obtain information from his officials without disclosing it at the inquiry (*Bushell* v. *Secretary of State* [1980] 2 W.L.R. 22).

This model has been superseded by statute but retains residual importance.

The judicial model

The "judicial" model regards the inquiry as an independent decision-making technique for deciding between arguments and evidence raised by the parties. This model has never been applied in its pure form although in practice many simple local appeals may conform to it, particularly now that most planning appeals are decided by the Inspector who holds the inquiry. The judicial model is important because judicial procedures, aping those of courts of law, have been superimposed upon the basic administrative model, largely due to the report of the Franks Committee in 1957. Franks recognised that planning appeals were neither purely administrative nor purely judicial and thought that the procedure must strike a balance between the two. The emphasis of Franks was on the inquiry as a means of hearing people closely affected by planning proposals. The resulting legislation and the procedural rules made under it have arguably tipped the balance too far in favour of the judicial model. This has several implications:

(i) **A rigid procedural straitjacket** has been created that may cause delay and is inherently unsuitable for "big" inquiries (above). Wider issues such as the need for the development and alternative sites cannot be accommodated within the judicial model.

(ii) **Judicial trappings** may lead the participants to believe, erroneously, that the "result" of the inquiry should be decisive and therefore to reject the inquiry procedure as cosmetic. This is accentuated by the fact that the inquiries procedure rules are made by the Lord Chancellor.

(iii) **Burden of proof** problems arise which are arguably irrelevant to the planning process there being no legal "right" to develop land.

In relation to enforcement appeals the burden of proof is on the appellant in relation to questions of fact (*Nelsovil* v. *M.o.H.* [1962] 1 W.L.R. 404). In the case of planning permission appeals the language of section 36 suggests that the ordinary presumption in favour of granting planning permission should apply (see *Winchester City Council* v. *Secretary of State* (1979) 39 P. & C.R. 1). However, this is a matter of policy for the Secretary of State or inspector. Clear cut reasons mut be given for refusal of permission but there is no formal burden of proof analogous to the practice of the courts. See *Federated Estates Ltd.* v. *Secretary of State* [1983] J.P.L. 812.

(iv) **Distinctions** must be made between issues suitable for judicial procedure, *i.e.* those which can be handled at the inquiry and those which are for the political discretion of the decision-maker. In order to express this a line is drawn between matters of "fact" on the one hand and matters of "policy" or opinion on the other.

The Secretary of State can freely override the inspector's decision on policy matters and can consult with anyone he wishes after the inquiry. It appears that "policy" must be disclosed at the inquiry for information and to permit the parties to argue that a special exception to the policy should be made in particular local circumstances. However, there is no right to cross-examine government representatives on the merits of policy.[11]

As regards questions of fact these must be disclosed and can be cross-examined and the inspector's findings must be supported by factual evidence. The court is not concerned with whether the factual evidence is of sufficient weight. New facts and new evidence can be taken into account but if they are likely to prejudice the parties they must be disclosed as must new arguments raised by a party and communicated to the Secretary of State.[12]

Strict rules of evidence do not apply and the inspector can draw professional or policy conclusions from the evidence but

---

[11] See *Bushell* v. *Secretary of State* (above); *R.* v. *Minister of Transport* [1984] 48 P. and C.R. 239; *Kent C.C.* v. *Secretary of State* [1977] 33 P. & C.R. 70 at 78; *Lavender* v. *M.o.H.* [1970] 1 W.L.R. 1231, 1241; *Re Trunk Roads Act 1936* [1939] 2 K.B. 515; *Denton* v. *Auckland City Council* [1969] N.Z.L.R. 263. *Fourth Investments* v. *Secretary of State* [1988] J.P.L. 620.

[12] *French Kier Developments* v. *Secretary of State* [1977] 1 All E.R. 296; *Performance Cars* v. *Secretary of State* [1977] J.P.L. 585; *Powis* v. *Secretary of State* [1981] 1 All E.R. 748 at 796–797; *Reading B.C.* v. *Secretary of State* [1986] J.P.L. 115; *Coleen Properties* v. *M.o.H.* [1971] 1 W.L.R. 433. The test is whether substantial injustice is likely. See *R.* v. *Bickenhall Parish Council* [1987] J.P.L. 772.

must disclose any new facts s/he discovers, for example in the site visit.[13]

These distinctions are reflected in the present statutory procedural rules.

"If the Secretary of State disagrees with the inspector's findings of material fact and is for that reason disposed to disagree with an inspector's recommendation he must invite the parties who were entitled to appear and who did appear to make representations within 21 days. In cases where new evidence or facts have been taken into account he must reopen the inquiry if requested to do so by the appellant or the local planning authority (R.16(4); R.17).

In other cases he has a discretion to reopen the inquiry which must be exercised in the light of the common law rules of natural justice.

These rules lead to difficult distinctions between questions of fact on the one hand and questions of policy and opinion on the other. The courts have defined questions of fact narrowly. Value judgments—good, bad, ugly, serious impact, etc., are all matters of opinion as are predictions about the future unless possibly based entirely on expert evidence and also such matters as need and economic viability.[14] A rule of thumb appears to be that if reasonable disagreement is possible on the same evidence then the matter is one of opinion. Hence the question of the proper statistical methods to use as a basis for policy judgments has itself been treated as a question of policy (*Bushell* v. *Secretary of State* (above)).

(v) **The inspector.** The position of the inspector is ambivalent. Appointed by the Secretary of State he is essentially an instrument of central government policy but also has a judicial role. However, unlike a judge the inspector is not confined to matters arising at the

---

[13] *Fairmount Investments* v. *Secretary of State* [1976] 1 W.L.R. 1255; *Hibernian Properties* v. *Secretary of State* [1973] 27 P. & C.R. 197; *Sabey* v. *Secretary of State* [1978] 1 All E.R. 586; *Wass* v. *Secretary of State* [1980] J.P.L. 170.

[14] *Winchester City Council* v. *Secretary of State* [1978] J.P.L. 467—prediction as to future need to subdivide house; *Luke* v. *M.o.H.* [1968] 1 Q.B. 172—local impact; *J. Sainsbury and Co. Ltd.* v. *Secretary of State* [1978] J.P.L. 661; *Camden L.B.C.* v. *Secretary of State* [1975] J.P.L. 661—economic viability; *Vale Estates (Acton)* v. *Secretary of State* (1970) 69 L.G.R. 453—aesthetic judgment; *Calfane* v. *Secretary of State* [1981] J.P.L. 879—economic viability. Compare *Pryford Properties* v. *Secretary of State* [1977] J.P.L. 724 "local firm" (fact); *Thanet D.C.* v. *Secretary of State* [1978] J.P.L. 251—practicability of restoration (fact); *Pollock* v. *Secretary of State* [1981] J.P.L. 420—character of use (fact); *R.* v. *Bickenhall Parish Council* (above, n. 12)—existence of change in policy—fact (*sed quaere*).

inquiry itself but is free to take into account other relevant considerations unless given the administrative costs involved it would be unreasonable to expect him to do so. His role has been described as investigatory rather than judicial but it has also been held that he is not bound to carry out an investigatory function and can normally confine himself to the matters raised before him. The same standards apply to the Secretary of State and the L.P.A.[14a] Unlike their counterparts in the U.S.A., English judges have not been concerned to lay down standards of evidence and stringency of investigation and have confined themselves to minimal notions of relevance and reasonableness. This shows itself not only in this context but also in relation to factual evidence (above p. 150) and the duty to give reasons (above p. 55). The inspector has neither the power nor the resources to carry out research or to require others to do so except for a power to summon witnesses and call for documents (L.G.A. 1972 section 250). He can apply his own expert judgment to issues of fact and policy. (see *Southwark B.C.* v. *Secretary of State* [1987] J.P.L. 36).

In cases decided by the inspector, the inspector has the same powers as the Secretary of State (Sched. 9, para. 2). This presumably includes a power to depart from established policies in exceptional cases (but see *Sears Blok* v. *Secretary of State* [1982] J.P.L. 248). In practice, however, an inspector is unlikely to depart from government policies (see *R.* v. *Secretary of State ex p. Guest* [1987] J.P.L. 645).

It may be that the inspector has the worst of both worlds. His quasi-judicial role encourages him to distance himself from the departmental administration while at the same time he may not be familiar enough with the details of government policy and the all-important departmental culture to do justice to the arguments. The bias rule of natural justice applies to inspectors but reflects the community of interest between the inspector and the Department contrasted with the need for the inspector to distance himself from

---

[14a] *R.* v. *Vincent* [1987] J.P.L. 597; *Prest* v. *Secretary of State* [1984] J.P.L. 112; *Federated Estates* v. *Secretary of State* [1983] J.P.L. 812—in exceptional cases involving impact a more positive approach may be required; *Bradwell* v. *Secretary of State* [1981] J.P.L. 276—A change in facts arising after the inquiry must be taken into account. See also *Newham B.C.* v. *Secretary of State* [1980] J.P.L. 606; *Sir Brandon Rhys Williams* v. *Secretary of State* [1983] J.P.L. 113; *Wilson* v. *Secretary of State* [1988] J.P.L. 540 at 543–4; *Rhodes* v. *Minister of Housing* [1963] 1 All E.R. 300; *R.* v. *Westminster City Council ex p. Monahan* [1988] J.P.L. 561–2—same principle applicable to L.P.A.; *cf. Chris Fashionware (West Wales)* v. *Secretary of State* [1980] J.P.L. 678.

the local planning authority.[15] The ambiguous relationship between the inspector and Department is particularly important now that most planning appeals are decided by an inspector and a positive decision must be made to recall jurisdiction within the Department.

Most inquiries are held before members of a full-time inspectorate attached to the Department of Environment and with a tradition of independence. Some inquiries are heard before land management professionals either practicing or retired or by eminent lawyers (above). There is also a "Lord Chancellor's" panel composed mainly of retired professionals, often with military antecedents, who conduct inquiries on an ad hoc basis. This panel is nominated by the Lord Chancellor. The choice of an inspector for a particular inquiry depends upon the importance of the matter and the degree of government involvement. Staff inspectors are used for routine matters, and "panel" inspectors for more controversial ones, since they are regarded as independent of the government. Lawyer inspectors are appointed only exceptionally.[16]

The Franks recommendation that all inspectors be appointed by the Lord Chancellor has not been implemented (paras. 291–303). The reason usually given for this is that it would give a false impression that an inquiry is a judicial proceeding. Franks also recommended that inspector's reports be published. The decision maker must give written reasons for the decision (above, pp. 54–58) and the inspector's report usually accompanies it. The statement of reasons must include a summary of the inspector's conclusions and recommendations and any party who appeared at the inquiry and who wished to be notified of the decision can require a copy of the report (R.17; R. 18).

(vi) **Issue estoppel.** There is no doctrine of precedent in the planning appeal context (*Trustees of the Castell-y-Mynach Estate* v. *Secretary of State for Wales* [1985] J.P.L. 440). Inspectors are not bound by their previous decisions. Indeed, a developer may raise the same issues over and over again, for example, by repeatedly applying for planning permission or by appealing against first, a refusal of planning permission and secondly, against an

---

[15] *R.* v. *Vincent* (above)—Inspector and Department of Environment made joint application to courts—no bias; *Simmons* v. *Secretary of State* [1985] J.P.L. 253—conversation in empty room between inspector and chairman of council—bias; *Furmston* v. *Secretary of State* [1983] J.P.L. 49—discussion with local authority reps.; *Halifax B.S.* v. *Secretary of State* [1983] J.P.L. 816—hostility shown by inspector.

[16] See Barker and Couper *loc. cit.* n. 2 above.

enforcement notice on the same facts. This is one cause of delay within the planning system.

The local planning authority may do the same, for example, by serving an enforcement notice in identical terms to a previous notice which was quashed on appeal and hoping to persuade the inspector that the previous decision was wrong. The power to award costs may operate as a limited sanction here as in other cases of unreasonable behaviour.

The question whether issue estoppel applies to planning and other non-judicial decisions is controversial.[17-18] The better view is that issue estoppel applies to questions of law and fact but not to the exercise of discretion. This was confirmed by the Court of Appeal in *Thrasyvalou* v. *Secretary of State* [1988] 2 All E.R. 78. It was held that an inspector in an appeal against an enforcement notice is bound by the decision of another inspector in a previous appeal between the same parties to hold that use of the appellant's premises was a permitted use as a hotel. By contrast, in *Rockhold Ltd.* v. *Secretary of State* [1986] J.P.L. 130, the previous decision concerned matters of planning judgment and Forbes J. held that issue estoppel was not applicable.

The doctrine of issue estoppel has no connection with estoppel in the general sense, which has little or no application in public law (above, p. 109). Issue estoppel is not a true estoppel, *i.e.* the perpetuation of admitted error, but is a reflection of the principle that a valid decision is binding on all to whom it is addressed. Provided that there is no relevant difference in the facts or change in circumstances, a finding of fact or law is binding between the parties in later proceedings of the same kind. The actual decision in *Thrasyvalou* (above) was confined to decisions establishing the appellant's existing legal rights, but this is arguably too narrow.

(vii) **Natural justice.** As we have seen, the common law rules of natural justice or fair procedure are not confined to judicial decisions proper. They apply to the entire planning appeal process but centre upon issues of fact as opposed to matters of policy (above). It is sometimes argued that where statutory procedural rules apply they must be presumed to be sufficiently fair in themselves. There are conflicting dicta but the better view seems to be that procedural regulations made by the Lord Chancellor which now apply to all planning appeals do not raise any presumption of fairness but can be supplemented by the common law (see *Reading*

[17-18] See Wade, *Administrative Law* (5th ed.) pp. 234 *et seq.* Craig, *Administrative Law* 583 *et seq.* See *Cafoor* v. *Commissioner of Income Tax* [1961] A.C. 581.

B.C. v. *Secretary of State* [1986] J.P.L. 115). There is considerable overlap since in many cases the procedural rules reflect the common law. Moreover, neither breach of a statutory procedural rule nor breach of natural justice require the court automatically to set aside the decision. The court will examine whether there was actual prejudice or at least a risk of prejudice to the complainant (see *R.* v. *Bickenhall Parish Council* (above, n. 12); *Performance Cars* v. *Secretary of State* (1977) 34 P. & C.R. 92; *George* v. *Secretary of State* (1979) 38 P. & C.R. 609 at 607). Again, the role of judicial review is seen as limited—to protect individuals rather than to secure legality. The court will examine the whole process, not just the inquiry, to see whether its broad tests of fairness and prejudice have been met (*R.* v. *Transport Secretary ex p. Gwent C.C.* [1987] 2 W.L.R. 961).

Current governmental policy imposes a strong presumption in favour of granting planning permission. This conditions the form of appeal procedure (see Circulars 2/87, 22/80). Subject to the statutory procedural rules the inspector has a discretion as to procedure. However, when an inquiry is held the statutory rules impose a traditional adversarial model. The parties must give advance notice of their submissions and make available any supporting documents. Third parties can be required to do so by the Secretary of State (R6(4)). There are provisions for speeches, witnesses cross-examination and a site inspection and the inspector can *subpoena* witnesses and call for documents (L.G.A. 1972, section 256).[19]

The appellant can require a representative of a public authority to attend where the authority has expressed views or given directions adverse to the appellant, but a government witness cannot be cross-examined on policy matters. Furthermore there seems to be no means of requiring the attendance of government agencies who have expressed support for the development, thus placing third party objectors at a disadvantage (see below n. 25).

The full inquiry procedure is regarded by government as a cause of delay, and simplified procedures have been introduced (see Circulars 38/81, 18/86). There is a written representation procedure which is used in about 75 per cent. of planning permission cases (see S.I. 1987 No. 701; Town & County Planning Act 1971, section 282B). Written representations are sometimes used in enforcement appeals but usually only where the issue is one of planning merits as opposed to legal or factual disputes. There are no statutory regula-

---

[19] There are provisions for simplifying the procedure where witnesses intend to read out written statements (R.13; R.14).

tions governing written representation enforcement appeals as such. Parties must consent to waive their statutory right to an oral hearing (below). The written representation procedure involves a questionnaire, a strict timetable, and usually a site visit. If possible there is only a single exchange of documents (Circular 11/87; see *Wiseman* v. *Borneman* [1971] A.C. 297).

There is also an "informal inquiry" or "hearing' procedure which again depends on the parties' consent. This is extra-statutory and designed for relatively simple cases. Its main purpose is to save time and money and to permit the inspector to take a more active and therefore less "judicial" role in conducting the inquiry. The parties waive their rights to ask for costs, there are stricter time limits for the various stages of the inquiry and there is no right to cross-examine witnesses (see Circular 10/88). The inspector normally writes to the parties within 24 hours of the hearing indicating what his decision will be. This is followed by a formal reasoned decision letter. These procedures may be satisfactory only in very simple cases. They preclude all but the most superficial analysis and may exclude third parties (see *Ricketts and Fletcher* v. *Secretary of State* [1988] J.P.L. 768).

It is arguable that the parties can at any stage revoke their consent to written representation or informal procedures and fall back on their statutory right to an oral hearing (sections 36(4) and 88(7), but see Sched. 9, para. 2(2)(*a*) and section 282B). It is unlikely that private law notions of promissory estoppel have any application in this context. Not only does estoppel have limited application in public law (above, p. 111) but a pre-existing contractual relationship is required (although see *Augier* v. *Secretary of State* (1979) 38 P. & C.R. 219). The power to award costs may be a partial sanction. However Circular 2/87, para. 24 emphasises that costs should not depend on whether the appellant exercises his right to a hearing.

The participatory model

The third model of the appeal process is that of "participation." It is often argued that inquiries should be a forum by which ordinary people can have a say in the process of government.[20] Here we

[20] See Harlow and Rawlings, *Law and Administration* (1984) pp. 438–456. Participation issues also arose in connection with applications for planning permission
(above, pp. 118–120), estoppel (above, pp. 110) and planning agreements, above,
p. 155. See also Harlow and Rawlings *op. cit.* Chap. 14. R.T.P.I. (1982). The
Public and Planning. Means to better Participation. Current government policy
attaches little if any weight to local public opinion as such (see Circular 2/87).

move from the realm of law to that of wishful thinking. The
statutory procedures embody a certain element of third party
involvement, but are not designed as vehicles for public
participation as such. As we have seen, the courts have defined
matters of policy and opinion widely with the effect of excluding
them from effective challenge at the inquiry (above, n. 14). In
Bushell v. *Secretary of State* [1980] 2 W.L.R. 22 Lord Diplock
rationalised this by stating that the purpose of an inquiry is to
inform the Secretary of State about local matters, and not to discuss
the merits of government policy. In practice, particularly in the
case of highway inquiries, general policy issues are often discussed and participation is a value that can be legitimately advanced
within the framework of planning law. However, the notion
of public participation is ambiguous. It can mean either that
policy is formulated by public discussion and implemented by
officials or that policy is formulated by officials and commented
on by the public—the latter is essentially a legitimising device.[21]
Neither version fits easily within the basic framework of law
and conventions that constitute the British Constitution. Our
tradition, if it is democratic at all, is of authoritarian discretionary
government subject to selection and dismissal by a representative
assembly but not subject to popular involvement in its day-to-day
decisions.

The intellectual basis for participatory values depends not upon
constitutional principle or practice, nor upon public opinion, but
upon: (i) *a priori* theories about the nature of society; (ii) the
political views of "single issue" pressure groups such as the
environmental lobby and (iii) arguments taken from the different
political and cultural framework of the United States.[22] As
Professor McAuslan has pointed out, "participation" is essentially
a radical ideology of opposition to the status quo (*The Ideologies of
Planning Law* (1981)). In practice, participation allows wealthy and
articulate vested interests to dominate. Indeed, "environmental"
values can easily become expressions of vested interests in

---

[21] See Skeffington Committee, *People and Planning* (1968). Participation was
envisaged as a means of legitimising professional decisions rather than as a method
of creating policy. See also Dobry Report (1975) para. 1.30.

[22] See, *e.g.* Prosser (1982) *Journal of Law and Society* 1; McAuslan [1971] P.L. 247;
McAuslan (1974) 37 M.L.R. 134; Sewell and Coppock (eds.) *Public Participation
in Planning* (1977); Damar and Hague 42 *Town Planning Review* 217; Habermas,
Communication and The Evolution of Society (1979); Pateman, *Participation and
Democratic Theory* (1970); Richardson, *Participation* (1983); Reich, *The
Greening of America* (1970). "Participation" has many shades of meaning. See
Arnstein (1974) 35 J.Am.Inst. Planners 216.

preserving local amenities and protecting property values (see
Harlow and Rawlings, *op. cit.* pp. 449–456).
The law and practice relating to planning appeals offers little
encouragement to participatory values. For example:
1. Third parties have no right of appeal but are entirely
dependent upon a developer objecting to a refusal of permission,
condition, or enforcement notice. Thus a grant of planning
permission is unchallengeable except on strictly legal grounds by
way of judicial review.
2. Third party participants must bear their own expenses.
3. Inquiries are rarely held outside working hours.
4. The question whether there is to be any sort of hearing
depends on the appellant and the local planning authority. As we
have seen they can waive their right to an oral hearing (above,
p. 217).
Furthermore the Secretary of State is not bound to hold a public
local inquiry. He could hold a private hearing subject only to the
common law rules of natural justice, which would permit the parties
to call evidence and cross-examine and to see each other's evidence
but little more.[23]
In practice the Secretary of State usually hears the parties by
means of a public local inquiry unless the parties opt for the written
representation procedure (above, p. 217). In *R. v. Hammersmith
and Fulham B. ex p. People Before Profit Limited* [1982] J.P.L. 869
Comyn J. referred to the inadequacy of the public inquiry
procedure in safeguarding the rights of third parties such as local
pressure groups. He said that "one consequence of this unhappy
case" was to lead him to believe that "public inquiries very often
have no useful purpose at all" (at p. 870). In that case the authority
altered its local plan and granted planning permission after the
public inquiry in which the evidence had been almost entirely in
favour of the objectors.
If the written representation procedure is used third parties have
certain statutory rights. The local planning authority must notify
all persons who are entitled to be notified or consulted about the
application and also all persons who in fact made representations
about the application (S.I. 1987 No. 701, r. 5). Such persons are
entitled to send in written representations to the Secretary of State.
Any "interested party" may also submit representations. All
representations must be submitted within 28 days of the date the

---

[23] See above p. 203. The inspector has a discretion to exclude "unnecessary"
witnesses and cross-examination. See *Miller* v. *M.o.H.* [1968] 1 W.L.R. 992;
Nicholson v. *Secretary of State* [1978] J.P.L. 39.

appeal is received by the Secretary of State (the starting date, *ibid.* r. 7(*b*)).

Where an inquiry is held, members of the public must be permitted to attend and inspect documents but may not speak without the consent of the inspector (Planning Inquiries (Attendance of Public) Act 1982).

One category of third party—a "section 29(3) party"—has certain privileges in relation to planning permission appeals. Section 29(3) parties are entitled to some of the same procedural rights as the applicant and the local planning authority. Section 29(3) parties can call evidence but they cannot cross-examine (R.11). They can make post inquiry representations but cannot require the inquiry to be reopened except on common law principles of "fairness". For most purposes, section 29(3) parties are those owners and agricultural tenants who were entitled to be notified of the application (see above, p. 117) and who in fact made representations (section 29(3)). This has nothing to do with public participation since section 29(3) parties have proprietary interests in the land. People who made representations in cases where the application for planning permission had to be advertised (above, p. 118) are not section 29(3) parties.[24]

Other third parties have no right to appear unless invited to do so by the Secretary of State or the inspector (R.11). The Secretary of State can require a party who wishes to appear in a planning permission appeal to serve a written "statement of case" in advance. The Secretary of State may also require the L.P.A. to give public notice of the inquiry and to give individual notice to persons specified by him (R.10(6); R.10(5)). Any other rights available to a third party such as cross-examination depend upon common law notions of fairness and legitimate expectation. In this connection it has been held that a resident who previously made representations is entitled to be informed of the appeal.[25]

In the case of enforcement appeals no member of the public other than the appellant and the local planning authority has any right to appear. Publicity arrangements are a matter for the Secretary of State (S.I. 1981 No. 1743, r. 4).

---

[24] Previously people who made representations in "bad neighbour" cases were entitled to appear at "called in" inquiries.

[25] *Wilson* v. *Secretary of State* [1988] J.P.L. 540. Government departments and other public bodies who have expressed views are entitled to appear but their procedural rights after the inquiry are limited to the common law of natural justice (see *R.* v. *Bickenhall Parish Council* [1987] J.P.L. 772).

A third party who in fact appeared has sufficient *locus standi* to challenge the appeal decision in the courts. Indeed in the *locus standi* context the courts have championed the participatory ideology (see p. 52 above). Anyone who appeared at the inquiry is entitled to be notified on request of the decision and its reasons (S.I. 1981 No. 1743, R.16, R.17, R.18).

In general, therefore, the participatory element in the appeal process is dominated by central government, is set in motion only by anti-development local authority decisions and is largely passive and dependent upon administrative discretion. This reflects the primary characteristics of the development central system as a whole and is a convenient note on which to conclude.

Index